# Ubiquitous Music Ecologies

Ubiquitous music is an interdisciplinary area of research that lies at the intersection of music and computer science. Initially evolving from the related concept of ubiquitous computing, today ubiquitous music offers a paradigm for understanding how the everyday presence of computers has led to highly diverse music practices. As we move from desktop computers to mobile and internet-based multi-platform systems, new ways to participate in creative musical activities have radically changed the cultural and social landscape of music composition and performance. This volume explores how these new systems interact and how they may transform our musical experiences.

Emerging out of the work of the Ubiquitous Music Group, an international research network established in 2007, this volume provides a snapshot of the ecologically grounded perspectives on ubiquitous music that share the concept of ecosystem as a central theme. Covering theory, software and hardware design, and applications in educational and artistic settings, each chapter features in-depth descriptions of exploratory and cutting-edge creative practices that expand our understanding of music making by means of digital and analogue technologies.

**Victor Lazzarini** is Professor of Music, Music Department, Maynooth University, Ireland.

**Damián Keller** is Associate Professor at the Federal University of Acre, Brazil, where he coordinates the Amazon Center for Music Research.

**Nuno Otero** is Associate Professor in the Department of Computer Science and Media Technology at Linnaeus University, Sweden.

**Luca Turchet** is an Assistant Professor at the Department of Information Engineering and Computer Science of University of Trento, Italy.

# Ubiquitous Music Ecologies

**Edited by
Victor Lazzarini, Damián Keller,
Nuno Otero, and Luca Turchet**

Routledge
Taylor & Francis Group

LONDON AND NEW YORK

First published 2021
by Routledge
2 Park Square, Milton Park, Abingdon, Oxon OX14 4RN

and by Routledge
52 Vanderbilt Avenue, New York, NY 10017

*Routledge is an imprint of the Taylor & Francis Group, an informa business*

*British Library Cataloguing-in-Publication Data*
A catalogue record for this book is available from the British Library

*Library of Congress Cataloging-in-Publication Data*
A catalog record has been requested for this book

ISBN: 978-0-367-24265-7 (hbk)
ISBN: 978-0-429-28144-0 (ebk)

Typeset in Times New Roman
by codeMantra

# Contents

*Foreword*                                                                          xi
BARRY TRUAX

*Preface*                                                                           xv

*Acknowledgements*                                                                  xvii

*List of contributors*                                                             xviii

**1 The ecologies of ubiquitous music**                                              1
VICTOR LAZZARINI, DAMIÁN KELLER, NUNO OTERO,
AND LUCA TURCHET

   1.1   *Revisiting the ubimus manifesto 2*
       1.1.1   *Other approaches 3*
   1.2   *Ubimus ecologies 4*
       1.2.1   *Ubimus in composition and performance 7*
       1.2.2   *The technologies of ubimus 11*
       1.2.3   *Ubimus in the educational context 13*
       1.2.4   *Creativity in everyday settings 15*
   1.3   *Conclusions 16*

**2 Everyday musical creativity**                                                   23
DAMIÁN KELLER

   2.1   *Introduction 23*
       2.1.1   *Resource qualities 24*
       2.1.2   *Knowledge heterogeneity 25*
       2.1.3   *Fast knowledge transfer 26*
   2.2   *Ground zero: situating little-c music within the field of
       creativity studies 27*
   2.3   *Milestone 1: resource qualities 30*
       2.3.1   *Temporality 31*
       2.3.2   *Rivalry 31*
   2.4   *Milestone 2: knowledge heterogeneity 33*
       2.4.1   *Dialogics 35*

2.5     *Milestone 3: fast knowledge transfer 37*
        2.5.1    *Temporality 38*
        2.5.2    *Semantics 40*
2.6     *Conclusions and glimpses of future developments 42*
        2.6.1    *Temporality 44*
        2.6.2    *Rivalry 44*
        2.6.3    *Knowledge heterogeneity 44*
        2.6.4    *Dialogics 45*
        2.6.5    *Fast knowledge transfer 45*

**3   DIY electronics for ubiquitous music ecosystems**                    **52**
JOSEPH TIMONEY, VICTOR LAZZARINI, AND DAMIÁN KELLER

3.1     *DIY musical hardware: an abridged history 53*
        3.1.1    *The post-second world war beginnings 54*
        3.1.2    *The eighties and decline 55*
        3.1.3    *FLOSS software 56*
        3.1.4    *Rebirth of DIY hardware 57*
3.2     *Analogue and digital hardware 58*
3.3     *Microcontroller technologies 59*
        3.3.1    *The Arduino development board 60*
3.4     *Low-cost general-purpose computing devices 61*
        3.4.1    *Raspberry PI 61*
        3.4.2    *BeagleBone black 62*
        3.4.3    *Intel Galileo and Edison 62*
        3.4.4    *Hard-realtime platforms 63*
3.5     *DIY electronics in the ubimus context 64*
        3.5.1    *DIY as a creativity exploration platform 65*
        3.5.2    *An Internet of Musical Things 65*
        3.5.3    *The ubimus ecosystem 66*
3.6     *Conclusions 67*

**4   A brief report from the land of DIY**                                 **71**
KOKA NIKOLADZE

4.1     *Following the trails vs off the beaten track 72*
        4.1.1    *Beat Machine No. 1 73*
        4.1.2    *Beat Machine No. 2 74*
        4.1.3    *Beat Machine No. 5 75*
4.2     *Solenoid Orchestra 76*
4.3     *KOI 77*
4.4     *Conclusions 78*

5 **Interactive systems and their documentation: a perspective on multimedia installation art** 80

FEDERICA BRESSAN

5.1 *Preservation 86*
5.2 *Immersive and multi-sensory installations 88*
5.3 *Conclusions 91*

6 **Questions and challenges in ubiquitous creativity** 94

JØRAN RUDI

6.1 *Characteristics of ubimus 94*
6.2 *Consequences of ubiquity in music 96*
6.3 *Ubimus in schools and music education 99*
    6.3.1 *Incorporation of ICT in schools 99*
    6.3.2 *Examples of software and workflow design 101*
    6.3.3 *Learning and creativity 103*
6.4 *Summary and conclusions 104*

7 **Ubiquitous music research in basic-education contexts** 109

MARIA HELENA DE LIMA, LUCIANO VARGAS FLORES, AND
JEAN CARLOS FIGUEIREDO DE SOUZA

7.1 *Ubimus and its applications in basic education 110*
7.2 *Musical creativity: cognitive-ecological creative practices 110*
7.3 *Interdisciplinarity and transdisciplinarity in ubimus research 112*
7.4 *Experiencing scientific induction in ubimus with high-school students from CAp 114*
    7.4.1 *Creative experiments in ubimus research 115*
    7.4.2 *G-ubimus partnerships 118*
7.5 *Ubimus research with high-school student-researchers: the student perspective 119*
7.6 *Conclusions 124*

8 **Computational thinking in ubiquitous music ecologies** 129

NUNO OTERO, MARC JANSEN, VICTOR LAZZARINI, AND DAMIÁN KELLER

8.1 *Computational thinking 130*
    8.1.1 *Conditions 131*
    8.1.2 *Loops 132*
    8.1.3 *Goto / functions / methods / subroutines 133*
    8.1.4 *Recursion 133*
8.2 *Computational thinking in music: general concepts 135*
    8.2.1 *Manipulating pitch 135*
    8.2.2 *Manipulating time 141*
    8.2.3 *Delays as computational thinking devices 142*

8.3   *Computational thinking and music composition: challenges related to knowledge transfer  144*
    8.3.1   *Knowledge transfer in CT and ubimus ecologies  145*
    8.3.2   *Ubimus and CT: some ideas on teaching and design of supporting tools  146*
8.4   *Computational thinking and the fostering of learning of music-making practices  147*
    8.4.1   *Abstractions  147*
    8.4.2   *Design patterns  149*
    8.4.3   *Distributed resources  149*
    8.4.4   *Frameworks for creativity  150*
8.5   *Conclusions  150*

**9  Ubiquitous music and the internet of musical things**　　　**154**
LUCA TURCHET, GEORG ESSL, AND CARLO FISICHIONE

9.1   *Musical things for ubiquitous musical activities  155*
    9.1.1   *Smart musical instruments  155*
    9.1.2   *Mobile devices and musical applications  157*
    9.1.3   *Wearables  159*
9.2   *Connectivity for networked ubiquitous musical activities  160*
9.3   *Discussion and conclusions  162*

**10  The browser as a platform for ubiquitous music**　　　**170**
STEVEN YI AND STÉPHANE LETZ

10.1   *Introduction  170*
10.2   *The technologies of the browser platform  170*
10.3   *Design approaches to the browser platform  171*
    10.3.1   *Distribution and installation  173*
    10.3.2   *Sound and music computing with the Web Audio API  175*
    10.3.3   *Platform independence  179*
10.4   *Case studies  180*
    10.4.1   *Browser-based systems  180*
    10.4.2   *Cross-platform systems  181*
10.5   *Conclusions  187*

**11  Adaptive and crossadaptive strategies for composition and performance**　　　**190**
ØYVIND BRANDTSEGG

11.1   *Crossadaptive processing for live use  191*
11.2   *System and signal flow  192*
11.3   *Analyzer and Mediator  194*
11.4   *Perceptual transparence of mappings  196*
11.5   *Perceptual transparence of analysis  197*

11.6    *Accommodation of analysis techniques 198*
11.7    *Normalisation of analysis outputs 201*
11.8    *Intuitive relation to feature extraction 202*
11.9    *Selection of effects as modulation targets 203*
    11.9.1    *Reverb 203*
    11.9.2    *Delay 204*
    11.9.3    *Filters 205*
    11.9.4    *Spectral processing 205*
    11.9.5    *Granular processing 205*
    11.9.6    *Freeze 206*
    11.9.7    *Pitch and frequency shift 206*
    11.9.8    *Balancing tools 206*
11.10   *Effects with direct signal interaction and cross-synthesis 207*
    11.10.1   *Convolution 208*
    11.10.2   *Live convolution 208*
11.11   *Performative habits 209*
11.12   *The role of the interaction scene designer 209*
11.13   *Different types of sessions 210*
11.14   *Conclusions and future work 210*

**12   The analogue computer as a musical instrument**　　　**214**
VICTOR LAZZARINI AND JOSEPH TIMONEY

12.1    *Analogue computing 215*
    12.1.1    *Components 216*
12.2    *Modular synthesisers 219*
    12.2.1    *Modules 220*
    12.2.2    *Programmability 223*
12.3    *Analogue programming examples 224*
    12.3.1    *Linear functions 224*
    12.3.2    *Differential equations 225*
    12.3.3    *Analogue computers as musical instruments 226*
12.4    *New technologies for analogue computing 227*
    12.4.1    *Field-programmable analogue arrays 227*
    12.4.2    *Programmability revisited 228*
    12.4.3    *Hybrid digital-analogue systems 229*
12.5    *Analogue computing in ubimus 229*
    12.5.1    *Access to analogue audio 230*
    12.5.2    *The DIY perspective 230*
    12.5.3    *A ubimus research platform 231*
12.6    Conclusions 232

*Index*　　　235

# Foreword

*Barry Truax*

The ideas (and ideals) of *ubiquitous musical creativity* – here referred to by the authors as *ubimus* – describe an exciting contemporary range of sonic activities and situations, largely facilitated by both digital and analog technology. As they strongly point out, ubimus involves an inherently interdisciplinary range of approaches, as does any information-based communicational approach, particularly if the social and environmental context is being taken into consideration. This type of more holistic thinking is reflected in their use of *ecosystem* and *ecologies* – as distinct from tools and techniques – to describe the interrelatedness of the systems they strive to develop.

As challenging as such notions already are, particularly within today's volatile digital industries, the authors emphasise an even more idealistic goal, which is to extend such systems into the realm of *everyday* practice by members of the non-professional public – referred to as *little-c music*. Here they inevitably have to confront the issue that such members are already being trained as consumers of digital products where agency and control by the *user* are mere selling points. The ubiquitous smartphone equipped with earbuds exemplifies music consumption today, despite the widespread availability of apps for audio production. However, a closely related issue is that professional cultural and commercial forms of musical production set the standard by which users value their own work, and influence their aspirations to produce it.

In his excellent chapter, Jøran Rudi provides a good overview of the characteristics, challenges and consequences of the current ubiquity of music production and consumption, along with some thoughtful caveats about its dysfunctions. I would like to provide some additional background to the topic by re-visiting some basic conceptual and historical issues that may assist readers in finding their way through the maze created by the current situation.

The first involves putting the emphasis on sound and soundmaking, with music in the traditional sense, as a subset of activities regarded as such. Although the ubimus authors clearly wish to be inclusive and egalitarian with respect to style, I have always found it to be most inclusive by regarding sound and listening as fundamental to all manifestations of both everyday and specifically creative activity, and the more we know about all of their aspects the better. For this reason, in a related anthology for which I was a co-editor, *The*

*Routledge Companion to Sounding Art* (Cobussen, Meelberg and Truax 2017), we chose the term *sounding art* as our subject, and included sections on acoustic epistemology, listening and memory, acoustic space, sonic histories, as well as sound technologies and media, in order to deal with some of the contextual aspects which are relevant to contemporary creativity in sound. As an example of this approach, I often introduce the field of soundscape composition as listening to the sonic environment *as if* it were music, that is, with the same kind of aural attention that we traditionally expect in music – as well as its contemporary opposite, not listening to music-as-environment.

In my own attempt at greater inclusivity, I have also suggested that any real-world context can be invoked in creating sounding art where the work is clearly *about* that context, in such an integral way that it is inseparable from it, and is informed at every level by knowledge of that context (Truax, 2018). Of course, the design of such works can be, and most likely will be, guided by aesthetic as well as functional communicational considerations such that the work will be engaging not only at a sensory level, but a semantic one as well. It remains to be seen how an ubimus approach involving *smart* technology will facilitate this approach to creative expression, but the general direction can be seen in the case study summaries indicated in Chapter 1. In my Introduction to the technology section of the *Sounding Art* anthology (Truax, 2018, 398), I concluded that "technology, its organization and uses, are not deterministic or gender neutral, as is often assumed, and that alternative voices can emerge when its design is open-ended and flexible." In addition to the foundation of sound and listening, including the interdisciplinary knowledge that is required to understand them fully, I would also like to discuss emergent sonic complexity in relation to software development. In the early decades of computer music research, the 1950s through to the 1970s, software for sound synthesis and composition relied on testing existing models that were specific enough to allow them to be programmed. With sound synthesis, the software tested acoustic and other mathematical models, and the researchers evaluated the output with aural judgments as to how well the model worked in practice; not surprisingly, deficiencies in the traditional models were quickly discovered. Today, most research tends to assume that sound synthesis issues have somehow been solved (usually phrased as "any sound can be created"), to which I beg to differ. Although simulations of the voice and musical instruments may be regarded as adequate and functional, the complexity of most environmental sounds still evades such veracity.

Similarly, traditional compositional models were tested but typically failed to reproduce the complexity of highly original compositional practice. The relevant point here is that a conservative model of software emerged that favoured instrumental timbres and compositional techniques, mainly because these seemed to be the most amenable to programming. In other words, existing and new ideas may lead to new technology, but can new technology ever lead to new ideas? I have discussed these issues in more detail in the Introduction referred to earlier, but the general answer is that *complex* systems need to be involved. And, to echo the terminology in this volume, that means that new *ecologies* of actors will need to emerge, examples of which can be found in the various chapters here.

Also, as a result, the artist, designer or user of such software will have new roles, usually characterised by an integration of the traditional roles of the composer and performer, and often blurring the usually more passive role the audience. The role of human activity in these processes will be less that of an omniscient and virtuosic controller, and more that of a guiding influence over a complex dynamic process of a seemingly *intelligent* instrument, possibly similar to improvisation. The role of the instrument builder (or DIY) is included in various chapters here, as well as other emerging practices referred to as the *maker movement*. Public and audience interaction may also be involved, and the portability of the technology will open its application to unconventional sites, such as site-specific installations in public spaces, or even simultaneous multiple sites.

Franziska Schroeder and Pedro Rebelo, among others, have created a taxonomy of new forms of sounding art practice that exhibit *distributed* characteristics, such as being de-centralised, ubiquitous and shared. They argue that such systems allow us "to consider relationships of site and sound in the context of the social rather than a particular technology of media… These practices operate in the network but are ultimately concerned with how distributive topologies can promote new collaborative creative environments" (Schroeder and Rebelo, 2017, 449). Teresa Connors and Andrew Denton's audio-visual projects are good examples of sound artists working with specific sonic environments within an ecological framework (Connors and Denton, 2017).

The *dark cloud* that hovers over all of this potential is its dependency on the global industry that controls the development and economics of the technology being used, and hence its consumers. Some may understandably view the situation as a "pact with the devil" given the current social and ethical concerns over its corporate power and practices. More seriously in terms of this book's subject, many of those practices seem incompatible with creative activity. Industries over the last century, for instance, have widely used formats and standards to control the market and protect (or enhance) their share. Today, the pace of enforced obsolescence through near mandatory upgrades has quickened to the point that no system can remain stable for more than a year or so (unless some "guerilla" activity is taken to retain control). Hardware and operating system upgrades often involve making one's existing software unusable. The tradition of developing production skills over some period of time is endangered through this lack of stability in the systems we use.

The concept of *owning* both software and content, and thereby being in control of it, is also being eroded as some form of *renting*, subscriptions or pay-per-use are the only options available. One chapter in this volume outlines the use of contemporary browsers as a resource, and yet we are also seeing proprietary wars on this front as companies vie for market share. One such example is how Google Chrome has invaded the Mac market but refuses to recognise the Mac soundfile format (.aiff), this coming after over a decade of sound-file formats being generally interchangeable. Many people are also becoming very concerned about the increasing problem of e-waste on a worldwide scale generated by constant obsolescence.

Given all of these obstacles, as well as related concerns, we can admire the persistence (and cleverness) of ubimus practitioners in finding solutions and developing new ideas and practices for creative work. Many of these operate at the grass-roots level but have international networks of user experience to rely on. One of the most promising contexts for such work is the educational sphere where skills may be fostered, and (hopefully) alternatives can be explored, despite the wide differences in pedagogical contexts, as described in the chapters based on experiences in Brazil and Norway included here. Sound art installations, as referred to earlier, can also be designed to complement and enhance existing soundscapes, or create entirely virtual ones. Social, political and environmental issues, among others, can be emphasised and gain access to a broader public, including those related to climate change that are of worldwide concern today. Many galleries and museums are starting to become the sites of such work, even though less official spaces may be preferable in some instances.

This volume is designed to provide an overview of some guiding principles that have been gleaned from previous research into ubiquitous musical creativity, as well as technical presentations of relevant issues in its implementation. It is also a multi-faceted *snapshot* of a rapidly evolving field of interdisciplinary work that will likely develop for years to come.

## References

Cobussen, M., V. Meelberg and B. Truax (Eds.) (2017). *Routledge Companion to Sounding Art*. New York: Routledge.

Connors, T. and A. Denton (2017). In environments: The convergence and divergence of practice. *Organised Sound 23*(1), 29–38.

Schroeder, F. and P. Rebelo (2017). Distributed sounding art – practices in distributing sound. In M. Cobussen, V. Meelberg and B. Truax (eds.), *Routledge Companion to Sounding Art*. New York: Routledge.

Truax, B. (2018). Editorial. *Organised Sound 22*(1), pp. 1–3.

# Preface

This book provides a survey of a number of recent topics of research in ubiquitous music (ubimus), a research area that represents an intersection of several disciplines from music to computer science, engineering, education, psychology, and beyond. The contributions in this volume show a glimpse of the state of investigation in four thematic areas: high-end and professional practice, technologies for ubimus, the educational dimension, and musical creativity.

Some of the contributions to this book stem from the Ubiquitous Music Group (g-ubimus), a research network encompassing information technology and music practitioners from several Brazilian universities (UFAC, IFAC, UFRGS, IFRS, UFES, UFSJ, USP), as well as from Maynooth University (IE), Linnaeus University (SE), Griffith University (AU), and Queen Mary University of London (UK). The g-ubimus, active since 2007, fostering the initial activities in ubimus research, first in Brazil and then internationally, by establishing a yearly conference: the Ubiquitous Music Workshops . This scientific gathering has been held in Florianópolis (2010), Vitoria (2011, 2014), São Paulo (2012), Porto Alegre (2013), Växjo, Sweden (2015), Foz do Iguaçu (2016), São João del Rey (2018), and Marseille, France (2019). Its proceedings are available online and extended versions of selected papers have been featured in indexed publications and as edited volumes (*Sonic Ideas* 2013; *Cadernos de Informática* 2014; *Journal of Cases of Information Technology* 2015; *Journal of New Music Research* 2019). Given the collaborative nature of the ubimus project, this volume features scientific research allied with innovative artistic applications, in a tightly-knit interdisciplinary perspective.

The four thematic areas are present at different levels of focus in all of the chapters in this volume, although each contribution presents a clear research core. The opening chapter provides an overview of the current topics in ubimus and discusses these four themes in some detail. Chapters 4, 5, and 11 concentrate on different aspects of high-end and professional ubimus, providing, respectively, a look into multimedia installations, interactive performance, and the composer's perspective. In Chapters 3, 9, 10, and 12 the aim is to discuss cutting-edge technologies that have key applications in ubimus. Elements of the educational context of ubimus are explored in Chapters 7 and 8, while

Chapter 6 discusses creativity within ubimus and education, and Chapter 2 focuses on little-c music.

We expect this volume to be a useful resource for all areas that are touched by ubimus, in particular music, creativity, technological applications, and education. It is our hope that with this book we will be able to extend a debate that began on socially grounded views of creative practice and their technological support to many other areas of scientific and artistic endeavour.

Maynooth, Ireland,                                  *Victor Lazzarini*
Rio Branco, Brazil,                                  *Damián Keller*
Växjo, Sweden,                                            *Nuno Otero*
and Trento, Italy                                       *Luca Turchet*
                                                        December, 2019

# Acknowledgements

At the outset, we would like to acknowledge the love and support from our families, without which projects such as this one would not be possible.

We should also thank Brazilian Research Council (CNPq) for the partial support of this project (through the Research Productivity Grant 300996/2018-7 awarded to Damián Keller). We would like to acknowledge the help from Science Foundation Ireland's International Strategic Cooperation Award, through the Research Brazil Ireland project, which provided funds for travel and meetings, which eventually led to the edition of this volume. Prof. Lazzarini would like to thank Maynooth University, whose sabbatical scheme provided support for the completion of this project, and its Arts and Humanities Institute, for providing a home during this period.

We are deeply indebted to our colleagues and collaborators in the g-ubimus and beyond, some of whom are authors in this volume, for the invaluable discussions and ideas shared throughout the last five years. In particular, our thanks go to Antonio Goulart, Evandro Miletto, Leandro Costalonga, Marcello Messina, Marcelo Pimenta, Mathieu Barthet, Ariana Stolfi, Daniel Barreiro, Fabiano Costa Frederick van Amstel, João Svidzinski, Marcella Mandanici, and Nelson Zagalo, who, although not directly involved in this project, have helped and collaborated with us in the past years. Their insight and knowledge have helped shape much of the ideas contained within the pages of this book.

We would also like to express our gratitude to Barry Truax, who kindly agreed to provide a foreword for this volume. Special thanks should go to an editor at Routledge, Genevieve Aoki for all the help, advice, and support throughout the project. Finally, we would like to acknowledge our contributors, without whom we would not have been able to provide a wide-ranging picture of the state-of-the-art in ubimus research and practice.

# Contributors

**Øyvind Brandtsegg**, NTNU, Trondheim, Norway, oeyvind.brandtsegg@ntnu.no

**Federica Bressan**, Stonybrook University, USA Federica.Bressan@stonybrook.edu

**Georg Essl**, University of Wisconsin, Milwaukee, USA, georg.essl@uwm.edu

**Jean Carlos Figueiredo de Souza**, Federal University of Rio Grande do Sul, Porto Alegre, Brazil, jcfigueiredo@ufrgs.br

**Carlo Fisichione**, KTH Institute of Technology, Stockholm, Sweden, carlo.fisichione@kth.se

**Luciano Vargas Flores**, Federal University of Rio Grande do Sul, Porto Alegre, Brazil, lvflores@inf.ufrgs.br

**Marc Jansen**, Hochschule Ruhr-West, Germany, Marc.Jansen@hs-ruhrwest.de

**Damián Keller**, Federal University of Acre, Rio Branco, Brazil, dkeller@ccrma.stanford.edu

**Victor Lazzarini**, Maynooth University, Ireland, victor.lazzarini@mu.ie

**Stéphane Letz**, GRAME, Lyon, France, letz@grame.fr

**Maria Helena de Lima**, Federal University of Rio Grande do Sul, Porto Alegre, Brazil, helena.lima@ufrgs.br

**Koka Nikoladze**, University of Oslo, Norway, k.nikoladze@gmail.com

**Nuno Otero**, Linnaeus University, Växjo, Sweden, nuno.otero@lnu.se

**Jøran Rudi**, NOTAM, Oslo, Norway, joran.rudi@getmail.no

**Joseph Timoney**, Maynooth University, Ireland, joseph.timoney@mu.ie

**Barry Truax**, Simon Fraser University, Burnaby, Canada truax@sfu.ca

**Luca Turchet**, University of Trento, Italy luca.turchet@unitn.it

**Steven Yi**, Rochester Institute of Technology, Rochester, USA, stevenyi@gmail.com

# 1 The ecologies of ubiquitous music

*Victor Lazzarini, Damián Keller, Nuno Otero, and Luca Turchet*

Ubiquitous music (ubimus) is an interdisciplinary area of research that lies at the intersection of music, computer science, education, creativity studies, and engineering. This paradigm has evolved initially from the concept of ubiquitous computing (ubicomp), attributed to Weiser (1991), which embodies the idea of all-pervasive and invisible computing present in our everyday lives. Extending these ideas, we can think of a parallel concept, propelled by current technologies, specifically directed at music making (in all of its different manifestations, including its intersections with other practices and forms of knowledge). The emergence of ubimus is disruptive in the sense that it has enabled a variety of new ways in which a person can participate in creative musical activities. Traditionally, music composition and performance have been the domain of the specialist (formally or informally trained), typically through the use of instruments from well-defined organological traditions. The conditions for music making and sharing have been expanded in the course of the 20th century by a number of technological developments, including the appearances of the recording studio and broadcasting. It can be argued that such changes, although significant in some ways, have not intrinsically shifted the centuries-old modes of music making centred around the figures of the active musician and the passive audience.

In contrast, the ubimus paradigm that emerges at the onset of the 21st century shatters this hierarchical relationship by reducing the dependency on specialist training. Also, the organic integration of diverse media art practices fosters a change of attitude towards the artistic settings, providing alternative vehicles for the exercise of creativity, first in professional and formal venues and more recently in everyday contexts. Furthermore, the commercial monopoly of music production and transmission is challenged by the internet as a means of resource distribution and sharing. These changes are not limited to the application of technology or to the sonic results. They affect the whole chain of social and material relationships that permeate the musical endeavours. Therefore, these emerging cultural practices demand flexible frameworks that support rapid technical reconfigurations, while enforcing a cautious and responsible attitude towards the potential environmental and social consequences of these changes.

## 1.1 Revisiting the ubimus manifesto

As a field of study shared by a number of practitioners around the world, ubimus has recently reached its first decade of existence and has included several overlapping areas of interest (Figure 1.1). While trying to define the core attributes of its research programme, it is worth taking a step back to look at key stages of its development. A first marker was laid by the prologue to *Ubiquitous Music*, entitled *A Manifesto* Keller et al. (2014a). An initial research goal was to evaluate how, in parallel to the field of ubicomp, portable devices, the internet, and new modes of interaction were shaping music making. The adopted approach embraced all forms of creative practice. Consequently, it traced a distinct route from the fields of research based on previously established musical repertoires, such as electroacoustic composition and musicology (see also Section 1.2.1).

The manifesto made a very simple demarcation of ubimus:

> In practice, Ubiquitous Music is music (or musical activities) supported by ubiquitous computing (or ubicomp) concepts and technology.
>
> (Keller et al., 2014a, xiii)

In some sense, this has not changed. However, it is hard to encounter examples of *what is not* ubicomp in current musical practices, as we are surrounded by and frequently dependent on technology.[1] Therefore, from a research perspective it becomes artificial to distinguish the music or the musical activities involving some form of computation from the musical practices that are not

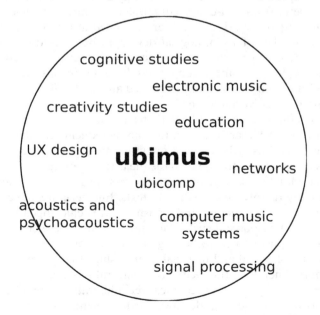

*Figure 1.1* Some areas of ubimus research, as represented in its initial proposals.

based on information technology but that still rely on its tools. This type of reasoning may induce us to think that ubimus has been dissolved into the musical practices that target music made with electronic devices (including computational musicology, electroacoustic music theory, cultural studies in the digital arts, locative media, etc.). We take the view that it is not the case, and that as an interdisciplinary field of study, ubimus has a focus (or a route as noted above) that is distinct from other approaches to information-technology based research.

### 1.1.1 Other approaches

We should note, at the outset, that the term ubiquitous music might comprehend, in its totality, views and research not contemplated by ubimus practice (as represented by this book and all its associated literature). One of the common uses of the term is related to the *ubiquitousness* of music, that is, how music and music consumption are permanently present in daily life. This research direction is, quite naturally, dominated by studies in popular music and culture. An interesting take on this issue comes from the field of marketing theory, where many aspects of how music is shared and consumed have been explored from the angle of a ubiquitous (presence of) music (Oakes et al., 2014). Another perspective, stemming from ethnomusicology and sound studies, investigates how the ubiquity of musical products affects listening and sharing (Quiñones et al., 2013). Although this proposal is directed to the study of popular music, a number of intersections can be established between the current research in ubimus and the ethnomusicological approach, especially when considering the impact of the choice of resources on music education (Lima et al., 2012).

Beyond identifying other lines of research that share terminology with ubimus, it may be necessary to delineate what ubimus is about. We do not deny that the phenomenon of *music all around us* is interesting and important. But an engaged and participative approach to music making demands theories and techniques that take into account the current practices that shape creativity. And these practices cannot be fully grasped by focusing solely on the usage of musical products. It is significant that today we have music anytime, anywhere, by anyone (Pimenta et al., 2014), at the touch of a button. But to fully understand how these phenomena affect us as listeners and consumers, we may need to study how subjects and communities engage creatively with sound making. Therefore a feature of the contents of this volume (and of previous ubimus publications) is a distinction between the passive elements of the musical ubiquitousness and the active counterparts engaged during the creative activities. Furthermore, this active engagement cannot be based on preconceptions on musical genres, subcultures, styles, or formats; all forms of music making are equally valid as targets of ubimus research.

Thus, the term ubiquitous music may take several acceptances depending on the target, the context of usage, and the community involved. Of course, we do not claim ownership of the term. We see this widespread adoption as an opportunity to establish bridges among practitioners of diversified fields – bringing together studies in marketing (Abolhasani et al., 2017, Oakes et al., 2014), education (Thorgersen, 2014), tangible computing (Palaigeorgiou and Pouloulis, 2018), virtual reality (Bernardo et al., 2015), sonification (Barrass, 2015), or robotics (Camporez et al., 2018). The proposal championed by Quiñones et al. (2013) emphasises the aspects related to the usage of ready-made musical products. But at the same time, it points to an interesting potential for intersections with the research centred on *little-c music* phenomena discussed in this book (Chapter 2). What if the sonic layouts of everyday settings were open to creative interventions by casual participants? What if rather than imposing a musical product onto those present in transitional settings, the ubimus ecosystems were tailored for collaborative music making? These new scenarios present difficult challenges regarding the social impact of shared musical practices. But part of these issues are already under scrutiny in the ethnomusicologically oriented proposals.

The permanent expansion of the ubimus research fronts attests to the dangers of prematurely adopting corsets in targets, methods, or theoretical frameworks. The early ubimus projects and publications – grown out of the activities of the Ubiquitous Music Group (g-ubimus) and spanning what has been described as a first wave of exploratory research (2007–2014) – highlight the need for wide approaches to musical interaction and artistic practices (Keller et al., 2011). Despite setting *sound* as a central object of study, ubimus methods have always included elements of other sensorial modalities, they support music making in a wide diversity of formats and encourage the application of the expertise gained in other fields (Lima et al., 2012). Furthermore, the objects of study of music are not limited to the sonic products, usually constrained to *the musical piece*. As demonstrated in the projects described in this book, the targets of ubimus studies are *activities* – designerly, creative, artistic, educational, curatorial, or multidisciplinary – that demand technical knowledge from multiple fields. Therefore, the expanded notions of the musical phenomena suggested by Varese (Wen-Chung, 1966), Schafer (1977), and Small (1986) can be included as valid ubimus research targets.

## 1.2   Ubimus ecologies

The present publication stems from lines of research that predate ubimus and at the same time encounter a rich context to grow through the expanded affordances provided by current technology. The concept of ecology – entailing the integration of social and material factors that interact to shape socio-technological networks – can be traced back to the end of the 20th century. Ecologically inspired frameworks fostered diverse artistic proposals Burtner (2005), Keller (1998), Keller and Capasso (2006), Keller (2000). While some of these initiatives were heavily based on computational resources (Di Scipio, 2008, Keller, 2000, Opie and Brown, 2006), others made an imaginative use of instrumental and electroacoustic sonic means yielding artworks that are difficult to classify using 20th-century musicological molds (Aliel et al., 2018, Basanta, 2010, Connors, 2015, Gomes et al., 2014, Nance, 2018).

The previously mentioned breakthroughs in media computing embody a tendency of convergence and integration of diverse technologies. They serve as a transformational force behind the current practices in music and the digital arts, underpinning the emergence of ubimus. These new functionalities demand broader conceptual approaches which motivate a significant diversification in the roles and skills of the practitioners. In line with these demands, a recent community-constructed definition of ubimus proposes the study of systems of human agents and material resources that afford musical activities through creative support tools. Taking this definition as a starting point, Keller and Lazzarini (2017a) propose a substitution of the generic term *tools* by the concept of *ubimus ecologies*. They argue that the concept of tool – as adopted by the second-wave of human-computer interaction (Harrison et al., 2007) and inherited as a device-centric view on music making by the works targeting NIME[2] – may relegate to an ad hoc function some of the central issues of 21st century music practices.

It is important to note that the choice of *ecologies* to describe our approach in this volume is also partially based, as other aspects of ubimus, on the methods adopted by the computing and interaction design communities. Since the beginning of the century, the word *ecosystem* has been used to describe a set of applications, or software components, that were, either by design or by deployment, associated together in different configurations (Jung et al., 2008). From a music-making point of view, the operating system of a modern computer can be seen as an example of a software ecosystem Lazzarini (2017a). Another instance of such an ecosystem has arisen around the browser platform (its implications for ubimus are discussed in Chapter 10). We borrow from these ideas and extend the term into a wider view of ecologies: the interrelated components of ubimus, which may address musical, educational, technological, or creative concerns, or any intersection among these. In addition, we approach such ecologies as dynamic systems, where the changes and the rate of change of the system variables are as important as their instantaneous states.

Thus, using ecologies as a main thread, we look at a number of facets of ubimus research. The thematic areas we chose for this volume are *professional music and multimedia design, creation and performance, the technologies of ubimus, the educational context,* and *everyday creativity*. These choices are based on their significance and contribution to the ecologically grounded methods on music making and the digital arts. Furthermore, the diversity of areas of application indicates an increased level of convergence and mutual influences among several fields of knowledge that previously were treated as separate and unrelated fields.

In Chapter 3, we see the concept of ecosystems as introduced above, fleshed out in the form of co-operating DIY technologies. This is also mirrored in the development of communities with shared creative interests, whose members provide mutual support and appreciation, a key factor to their sustainability and strength. Thus, ecosystems and communities become elements of a wider ecology, which may also include products, ideas, and knowledge shared among the different players. A good example is given by Nikoladze (Chapter 4) in his description of the Bitraf maker community, which is part of a wider *maker movement*, discussed in Chapter 3. It is particularly striking to see how knowledge and enthusiasm are shared, instilling a collective creative spirit among members. Equally, technologies such as the ones underpinning Internet of Musical Things (IoMusT) (Chapter 9), crossadaptive performance (Chapter 11), and audio on the web (Chapter 10) feature significant potential for the emergence of similar knowledge ecologies.

The cultural groundwork provided by the musical and multimedia artworks of the turn of the century fostered the theoretical elaborations later developed by authors such as Ingold (2013), Manning and Massumi (2014). The implications of these perspectives for ubimus practices are still to be explored, though we can already observe interesting developments. In Chapter 5, Bressan discusses the curatorial demands of artworks that are built through relationships among multimodal elements, highlighting projects based on biosensing technology that yield large amounts of data. These initiatives present challenges to both preservation and scholarly work because they target aesthetic experiences that are generated on-the-fly rather than through the construction of fixed sonic objects. Furthermore, some of these works are built with custom technology, involving devices that quickly become outdated. These factors highlight two aspects of ubimus ecosystems designs: the interactions with systems that involve a large amount of resources and the short life-cycle of the underlying technology. In line with the ubimus design approaches (Stolfi et al., 2019), Bressan proposes the adoption of semantic strategies to deal with biosensing data.

Bressan also stresses the importance of preserving the artistic social capital through a careful documentation of the creative processes. As we move from desktop personal computers to a multi-platform and distributed internet, and to mobile and multiuser computing environments, there is a need to assess the cultural and social significance of these changes. With the enhanced capabilities of portable devices, more sophisticated and possibly more intuitive, support strategies may become available, allowing users to participate in music creation, performance, and experimentation. However, the integration of these strategies, with special care to the local resources, is an area that needs further scrutiny (Keller, 2018). This aspect is underlined by the ecological approach to creativity support, through strategies that encompass interaction, audio processing, and audio synthesis techniques as integrated aspects of music making (Lazzarini et al., 2015). Both the feasibility of creative music making by means of heterogenous and volatile resources and the sustainability of cultural practices beyond the short life of electronic-gadget fashions are issues that demand active multidisciplinary and evidence-grounded methods furnished by the ecological perspectives.

As a recent spin-off of the ubimus initiatives, Keller and Lazzarini (2017b) explore the impact of ubimus practices on musical creativity models. They centre their discussion on two questions: Do the extant musical creativity models consider the creative factors beyond their domain-specific aspects? What variables can be observed through the deployment of these models? Until now, music theory and analysis have dealt with professional mani-festations of creative practice, giving emphasis to eminent creativity. These manifestations rely heavily on domain-specific knowledge. Consequently, the literature on music theory has mostly been concerned with describing, explain-ing, and supporting activities done by professional musicians. As a new field of study, ubimus encompasses recent technological advances that push the boundaries of what is understood as creative music making – for instance, we can mention little-c music (Chapter 2) and the use of the internet of musical things (Chapter 8) as examples. Nevertheless, ubimus methods present several ethical challenges, as discussed in Chapters 4 and 12. After analysing four theo-retical approaches to creativity, Keller and Lazzarini (2017b) conclude that in contrast with the acoustic-instrumental paradigm, the proposed frameworks do not depend on simplified representations of musical materials. Conse-quently, they are applicable to instrumental practices, to concert-oriented elec-troacoustic formats, and to other forms of music making – encompassing performance art, multimedia installations, and the emergent use of everyday technological devices.

The concepts and the range of applications explored in ubimus research highlight the need of renewed music theories and educational practices. Lazzarini (2017b) calls for the development of a curriculum based on computer-music expertise, which would replace the notation-oriented appro-aches to music theory and education. On a similar vein, Brown (2015) lays out a concept of *musicianship* that embraces current practices based on an intense usage of technology but without diminishing the social appeal of music making for community-building and for fostering *meaningful engage-ments*. In line with these proposals, ubimus practitioners push for flexible and comprehensive techniques to support musical knowledge-transfer as an ongo-ing process that could take place at home, on the bus, or at a store (Lima et al., 2017). The technologies introduced in Section 1.2.2 are relevant to the educational approaches that target creativity – see discussions in Chapters 11, 12, and 13. But as previously discussed, these technological advanced need to be placed within the context of human-centric, environmentally friendly, and community-oriented views that encourage the preservation of cultural diversity.

### 1.2.1   Ubimus in composition and performance

An aspect of ubimus that perhaps has had less attention, due to the focus of the ubimus research community in more inclusive practices, is that of the high-end and professional composition and performance of electronic and computer music. Traditionally elected it as a main focus of electroacoustic musicology, this of course is an area that has been treated extensively. Thus, from Schaeffer onwards,[3] there has been a steady stream of theories and analytical methods that have helped to establish the venerable tradition of electroacoustic concert music. More recently, part of the musicological literature has ventured into the genres of pop electronic music, such as for instance electronic dance music (EDM), ambient, techno, acid, and electronica. One of the motivations has been the tentative cross-over between the *learned* variety of electronic and computer music and these commercially friendly practices.

From an ubimus perspective, as a starting point, there is no reason for a classification of genres and sub-genres. Subtle aspects of each musical practice may escape these categories, therefore they are not only irrelevant, they may become intrusive when considering music as a pervasive human endeavour (Blacking, 1973). One of these aspects emerges from the affordances of music-making technologies and how these help us shaping behaviours, out of the interactions with sound-making resources. The conditions for such interactions are not limited by the musical stylistic features and they are possibly shared across multiple cultures.[4] Hence, musical concepts that rely on idiomatic aspects of music making, such as the technique of *reduced listening* (Schaeffer, 2017) and its derivations such as *the loop*; or the concepts of *note*, *chord*, and *harmony* – heavily grounded on the use of acoustic instruments that employ harmonic, pitch-based sounds; or the adoption of the *orchestra* as the ideal model for all forms of social organisation of group music-making (Trueman, 2007) reinforce the separation of audiences from musicians and of artistic venues from everyday settings.

This book provides two examples of what could be described as professional music making, which share many characteristics. In Chapter 4, Nikoladze takes us through a very personal approach in music creation via a kind of creativity-driven luthiery, where instrument-making is the starting point of the creative process. The affordances built into his music machines get revealed to provide the directions from which the musical products emerge. In this particular case, the concepts of do-it-yourself (DIY) and physical computing play a significant role in constraining the available musical outcomes while they trigger ideas grounded on the materiality of the designs.

From another direction but sharing several traits, the crossadaptive performances described by Brandtsegg in Chapter 11 exemplify how sonic interactions can be built into the music creative processes. In this case, the affordances of a complex system of modulation and communication via audio signals foster a new set of musical relationships. Take, for instance, the idea of *playing through* someone else's sound (Section 11.10.2) and how a sonic hybrid is shaped through the exchanges between two performers. By bringing together interaction and sonic processing through ubimus-integrated designs, a new type of musician is born: *the interaction scene designer*. Thus, Brandtsegg's practice of crossadaptive performance brings together two key features of ubimus ecologies: a strong dependency on community-based interaction – highlighting the distributed and socially embedded profile of ecologically grounded creative practices – and a multimodal design process that engages with musical events as units of action and sound (see also the examples of digital delay lines in Chapter 12 and the concept of *time tagging* in (Keller et al., 2010) for related approaches).

A common thread of the examples featured in Chapters 4 and 11, and an essential part of the ubimus approach, is the role of the musician as a creator-designer. In Nikoladze's case, it is the physical-instrument builder and firmware coder. In the case of Brandtsegg, it is the computer-instrument developer and network-system architect. In both cases, these roles are completely merged with the traditional notion of *the musician* (both performer and composer). These roles cannot be separated. This contrasts very much with the composer-technician split of roles, typical in electroacoustic concert-music practices. When Boulez set off to compose his most celebrated piece of live-electronic music, *Répons*, he worked solely on his score.[5] To this a technician provided the realtime signal-processing routines, which may just as well be considered a glorified set of digital audio effects. The composer is, in this case, a mere selector of presets.[6]

The two chapters focused on the cutting-edge advances of composition and performance (which encompass part of the professional side of ubimus) provide an interesting direction for future ubimus work. As previously noted, given that the focus of ubimus is distinct to that of electroacoustic or instrumentally oriented composition and musicology, a range of research avenues could be explored. Particularly, with the emergence of artists who transit easily from the concert hall to the nightclub, there is a host of interesting musical and multimedia practices worth of study – such as rave parties, flashmobs, net art, crowdsourced sound design, and the alternative scenes of performance art that defy the boundaries between the sensorial modalities. The methods employed by the ubimus initiatives appear to be well suited for research that demands rigorous, data-based analytical techniques targeting stringent deployment conditions. An interesting example is provided by Bressan (Chapter 5). The usage of physiological computing for artistic purposes – ranging from the use of biosensors to the capture of body movements – presents a conundrum for documenting and retrieving information within the context of curatorial, design, and ethnological endeavours. As a parallel to the issues raised by the design for little-c music making (see Chapter 2), Bressan proposes rethinking the documentation and preservation strategies of multimedia artworks. She stresses the fact that for artistic proposals centred on processes, it is not enough to have a surrogate or an isolated product as a representation of the artistic experience. The process of documenting the art-making experience becomes very similar to the process of interaction design. It demands a conceptual model – which may involve structured data representations – that is both easily accessible and not dependent on a particular technology, while supporting the capture of the specifics of each artistic iteration.

While many of the advantages of the ecological approaches to ubimus practices have been addressed in each of the chapters, it is also important to identify some of the caveats. The first one relates to sustainability, an aspect which we have already mentioned in relation to the life cycle of technology. This issue is addressed in Chapters 2, 5, and 11. The transitory conditions for the works of art developed for everyday scenarios or based on volatile resources pose a significant problem for their sustainability. In terms of the technologies for crossadaptive performance (Chapter 11), there are however mitigating factors related to the re-use of highly-portable, partly open-source resources. Furthermore, this project adopts a community-grounded approach to system development (much of what is described is based on work sustained by the Csound community). A similar perspective has been adopted in the development of technologies for little-c music making reported in Chapter 2 and Keller and Lima (2016). In this case, there is a strong reliance on ubimus-oriented initiatives (such as the Mobile Csound Platform (Lazzarini et al., 2012)) and the long-standing trend of ubimus designs based on browser technologies – as reported in (Keller et al., 2011, Miletto et al., 2011).

Another issue that may be raised in relation to the type of multimedia artwork discussed in Chapter 5 is the lack of metaphors to interact with massive data, which poses difficulties for artists, curators, and public. There are also reasons to be concerned about the musical quality of the resources available for ubimus systems based on the internet (Truax, 2015). Take, for instance, the observations gathered by Stolfi et al. (2019). While the creative potential provided by the synchronous access to online sonic databases was acknowledged by several participants, the quality of the materials and the inherent delays caused by remote access were negatively evaluated by some of the musicians taking part in the activities. How to enable strategies for fast selection of resources for improvisatory and for other time-sensitive creative activities and how to deal with data or musical products that may exceed a lifetime of listening are the two aspects that require intense research investments to yield viable solutions.

Finally, from a broad ubimus-oriented perspective, we should note that the ideas developed within the highly specialised crossadaptive-performance contexts impose significant demands for casual usage, raising the question of what applications may eventually become accessible outside of the professional music-making milieu. Proposals such as the smart musical instruments (Chapter 9), given their device-centric approach, are geared towards instrumentally oriented forms of music making that present challenges for their integration with 21st century music practices (see the critical analyses proposed by Emmerson (2001), Keller (2000), Lewis (2000) and more recently by (Bhagwati, 2013)). Similarly to live-coding practices (Messina and Aliel, 2019), the technical and domain-specific demands of technologies that target idiomatic live performances may eventually become novice-friendly through a long investment on the design of metaphors for creative action that take into account the ubimus approaches to creative support. For now, they provide an interesting niche for explorations by highly trained stakeholders.

### 1.2.2 The technologies of ubimus

One of the aims of the ubimus field is to study how social interaction with mobile and distributed technologies can lead to novel support tools capable of enabling, sustaining, and fostering creativity in musical practices Keller et al. (2011). The technological aspect plays a central role in the shaping of the ubimus field and its supporting ecologies. Consequently, an increasing variety of hardware and software has been leveraged by ubimus researchers and practitioners. These technologies can be grouped in three broad categories: DIY electronics, browser-based platforms, and interconnected distributed resources.

Many practitioners in the ubimus community have heavily recurred to low-cost hardware (Keller et al., 2014) as well as open source software platforms (Lazzarini, Timoney, and Byrne, 2015, Lazzarini, Keller, Kuhn, Pimenta, and Timoney, 2015) and languages (such as Csound (Lazzarini et al., 2014, 2016)) to create ubimus systems and foster ubimus ecologies around them. Chapter 3 provides a comprehensive overview of the history of DIY electronics applied to musical contexts, in particular considering DIY electronics as a platform within the scope of ubimus. The surveyed technologies include microcontroller units (such as Arduino), single board computers (such as the Raspberry Pi), and dedicated realtime operating systems (such as that of the Bela board (McPherson and Zappi, 2015) or Elk Audio OS by Elk[7]).

In a different vein, a significant strand of ubimus research has focused on the music creation possibilities offered by mobile and internet-based technologies (Wyse and Subramanian, 2013, Miletto et al., 2011). Section 9.1.2 of Chapter 9 aims at surveying the endeavours within this context. In a complementary way, Chapter 10 provides a comprehensive overview of the various browser-based technologies available today to ubimus developers. The discussion reported therein, along with several use cases of systems, provides informative guidelines to developers interested in leveraging the browser as a platform for ubiquitous musical activities.

The latest wave of developments in DIY electronics has focused on how devices can take advantage of the Internet infrastructure and be connected over local and wide-area networks. This is a crucial aspect for the ubimus ecologies that target remote and distributed resources. With respect to this, Chapter 9 explores the intersection between ubimus and the emerging infrastructure of the Internet of Musical Things (IoMusT) (Turchet et al., 2018). The IoMusT refers to ecosystems of interconnected embedded computers (*musical things*), which enable users to produce, interact with, or experience musical content. The IoMusT draws on many lines of existing research including the Internet of Things, new interfaces for musical expression, networked music performance systems, music information retrieval, musical interaction, and participatory art.

Musical things include smart devices dedicated to musical purposes, which embed electronics, sensors, data communication, and processing software. An emerging class of musical things is represented by the so-called smart musical instruments (SMIs) (Turchet, 2019), which feature capabilities of capturing and receiving data supporting instrumental musical practice. Thanks to their portability and self-containedness, SMIs enable novel ubiquitous interactions between performers of digital musical instruments. An example is the ecology reported in Turchet and Barthet (2019c) where a smart guitar is used as a hub for collaborative music making involving mobile devices. Another example is the study reported in Turchet et al. (2019), where a smart guitar player is supported in its creative practices using online music repositories due to the instrument's link to the Internet, interfacing with cloud-based services.

While, on the whole, ubimus tends to leverage the power of digital technologies, there are material possibilities that are worth exploring beyond the digital world. One of these, tackled in this book, is *analogue computing*. For some, this technology was destined to become a footnote in the history of electronics, as the advances in digital hardware should have rendered it obsolescent. However, as argued in Chapter 12, analogue techniques not only embody a different approach to data processing, in opposition to digitally stored-program computing, they also feature unique possibilities for musical applications, especially when considering their creative and educational potential. If placed within the context of the current ubimus DIY initiatives, the field of analogue computing may witness a technological renaissance that inscribes it as a legitimate area for current and future ubimus endeavours.

Overall, the broad variety of technologies at the basis of ubiquitous musical activities parallels the variety of the available computational ecologies. Today, the hardware and software systems for ubiquitous computing that can be exploited for musical purposes represent a burgeoning and rapidly expanding infrastructure. Naturally, the evolution of the ubimus field will continue to be nourished by this technological expansion. But rather than sing the corporate praises to a world of *business opportunities*, ubimus researchers take a stand to analyse critically and without prejudices the social and environmental impact of the development and adoption of information technology in music making and in its surrounding cultural practices. Two venues seem to be particularly sensitive to this impact: the school, or more generally the educational context; and the street, or the urban places where day-to-day interactions are most pervasive.

Some notes of caution should be made with regards to the pitfalls that might be encountered when navigating the DIY hardware and software ecologies. One difficulty arises from their heterogeneity; while there are shared elements, by and large, each platform has specificities with regards to design and application. As noted by Nikoladze in Chapter 4, this specialised knowledge may pose barriers to adoption, particularly for potential practitioners encountering the area for the first time. One strategy to minimise this problem is the maintenance of communities of practice. Although we might envisage the development of strong ties and increased levels of sharing (as it has been the case in the ubimus community), access and exchange of resources by DIY music makers are not yet universal. Another associated issue, which also impacts the technologies discussed in Chapter 12 is their financial cost, which is an ever-present hurdle for the viability of ubimus initiatives in peripheral countries.[8] We should also note by way of caveats that, while the discussion of the IoMusT infrastructure makes clear its potential development for ubimus applications, the area is still in its infancy; many claims are not backed by empirical data and there are multiple cultural and social implications that have not been addressed or analised through actual deployments. Likewise, the web-audio technologies discussed in Chapter 10, while at a later stage of development, still present shortcomings that need to be addressed to enable deployments in areas where the internet access or a stable electrical supply are compromised (see for instance (Yi et al., 2018, Keller, 2004)).

### 1.2.3 Ubimus in the educational context

The educational aspects of ubimus have been central to the research carried out during the first decade in this field. In this volume, we look at concrete experiences in two countries, Brazil and Norway, which, despite their many differences, share some key elements, especially with regards to the central role of creativity in educational contexts. Chapter 7 presents ubimus research targeting formal education, specifically in a basic-education context. One of the main directions taken by the authors is the application of the cognitive-ecological approach in teaching and learning (as targets of research) through the practice of eco-composition. The core of this approach entails enabling creation, composition, collaboration, and sharing experiences through the use of available technological infrastructure, in environments and contexts not originally designed for artistic activity. The text reports on a number of actions at the basic-education level developed at a public school in Brazil, highlighting the multidisciplinary nature of this work, which is supported by the transdisciplinary nature of ubimus.

We observe that, closely related to the ecological perspectives, an educational approach emerges, which is multidisciplinary and fundamentally interwoven with several issues raised by ubimus. In their chapter, Lima and coauthors report the ongoing educational initiatives developed at a research-oriented basic educational facility located in Porto Alegre, Brazil (School of Application). According to the authors, "the mission of the application schools is precisely to produce knowledge and to share experiences centred on basic education, so that these can be reflected upon and replicated. The Ubimus Research in Basic Education Project represents one of such efforts." These initiatives include the first curricular implementation of a course dedicated to ubimus. They also highlight the relevance of the ecologically grounded creative-practice methods with children and adolescents in formal educational settings. An interesting aspect of these proposals is the articulation of a new perspective on social interaction in music, based on the ideas put forth by Paulo Freire. This ubimus field is defined as *dialogics* and involves the active participation of stakeholders with diverse profiles, targeting a community-centred construction of knowledge.

The various academic distinctions received by Lima and her group attest to the impact and the potential for expansion of this perspective. The results discussed in this chapter prompt us to question whether it would be possible to apply the dialogical strategies to deal with lay-musician interactions (see Chapter 2). The heterogenous knowledge-profile that characterises the casual participations in musical activities has traditionally been approached through hierarchical social structures (the orchestra being the most widely adopted model) and through a strict separation of doers from emulators. Dialogics proposes an equal standing for all forms of knowledge, hence decision-making is necessarily approached through negotiations. In a sense, this modus operandi resembles the concept of emergent properties widely employed in eco-grounded creative practice (Keller, 2000). Aesthetic decisions are not originated by a single agent. They result from multiple contributions traceable throughout the creative process. How to enable computational support and data-gathering methods to move forward in this research direction remains to be addressed by future projects.

As a complement to the proposals laid out in Chapter 7, Rudi discusses the educational aspects of ubimus through the lens of ubiquitous creativity in Chapter 6. In Norway, digital technologies have been part of music education in schools for over 20 years. This scenario features a significant potential for the discussion and application of ubimus ideas. The Norwegian educational policies provide ample support for the use of information and computing technology (ICT) for music making. The author notes several well-known mutual benefits: ICT entails engagement and enthusiasm, the teaching of creative disciplines has a direct impact on the teaching of subjects such as mathematics and languages. Given this context, Rudi carries out an analysis of the workflow design of some of the software packages used in schools, discussing aspects of learning and creativity that are relevant to music education. Such aspects are also relevant to the topic of computational thinking (CT) in ubimus, developed in one of the chapters of this volume.

The affinities between music and CT are deeply grounded, particularly within the practice of ubimus. This is comprehensively demonstrated in Chapter 8. The authors propose a detailed exposition of the concepts built into CT with examples of their realisation in musical structures and creative practice. The competences developed through the application of CT reach beyond the traditional areas of computer science, engineering, or mathematics. New insights into musical practice may be promoted and developed through this approach, such as the exploration of design patterns to support ubimus activities. Likewise, by harnessing the potential for musical metaphors and the creative use of computational and mathematical concepts, we can, as noted in Chapter 6, bring about positive results in the teaching and learning of the technically oriented disciplines.

To navigate through the maze of demands of ubimus ecosystems, a certain level of technical expertise is necessary. Until recently, music teachers treated the use of computational resources with suspicion (see (Lima et al., 2012) for an example in ubimus), sometimes judging the tool usage of the students as second-class and superfluous. This 19th century approach to musical education, centred around instrumental performance, places the *artist* against the *technician*. These remnants of a post-romantic worldview – populated by musical geniuses that live their musical lives in concert halls, completely removed from the mundane noises of the streets, the schools, or the homes of the lowly audiences – are hopelessly out of touch with the demands of the 21st century. From the perspective of music composition, the two chapters on professional practice (Chapters 4 and 11) highlight the need for educational approaches that reach beyond the traditional instrument-centred musical training. While this is not particularly new, the requirements of the current technologically savvy musical practices – from the DIY maker culture to the techniques used in audio signal processing, acoustics, and programming – impose a split between the technical and the artistic skills. This separation between the artistic and the technical knowledge is hardly justifiable.

### 1.2.4 Creativity in everyday settings

Everyday musical creativity (little-c music) constitutes a new area of research that targets music making beyond traditional venues. Ubiquitous musical initiatives are enabling new forms of musical interaction, grounded on both local and remote resources, entailing the participation of non-musicians as creative partners, and involving creative strategies that impact both musical products and processes. This section of the book deals with concepts, technologies, and practices tailored for everyday settings. It analyses experimental evidence gathered through several ubimus studies as an attempt to identify key qualities of design that may help future developments of everyday music making. The discussion is organised as a journey through what may constitute the milestones of this area of research: ground zero encompasses the push and pull between domain-specific and general creative factors in everyday contexts, milestone one features two resource qualities that may play a central role in ubimus designs – temporality and rivalry, milestone two proposes dialogics as a strategy to deal with heterogeneous knowledge, and the third milestone discusses two design qualities that have been targeted in ubimus systems to achieve fast knowledge transfer – temporality and semantics.

According to Keller (Chapter 2), the differences between everyday and professional creativity are less related to the temporal investment in the activity than to the access to knowledge during the process of aesthetic decision-making. By reducing the amount of domain-specific knowledge required to achieve an artistic result, the artistic practices resemble the characteristics of a daily chore. This process does not reduce the value or the social importance of music making. Quite on the contrary, it expands the opportunities for participation of untrained stakeholders and pushes the artistic initiatives beyond the walls of the concert hall or the studio. Consequently, despite demanding special cognitive and social conditions, little-c music does not lie beyond the grasp of newcomers.

Professional music making is built upon domain-specific explicit knowledge that depends on a large reservoir of tacit knowledge. Tapping into this reservoir demands long periods of training that involve the use of resources such as scores or electroacoustic soundtracks, forcing the design into the straightjacket of instrumental and studio-centric techniques. These procedures are best exploited in venues especially prepared for artistic performances. When musical activities take place in transitional, leisure-oriented, work-oriented, or domestic spaces, the creative factors at play are not consistent with the contexts used for virtuosistic performances – despite the claims put forth by a currently hegemonic perspective on musical interaction (Wessel and Wright, 2002). Contrastingly, creative music making in everyday contexts involves the active engagement of participants with little or no previous mutual contact or preparation, together with the active pursuit of scaffolds for aesthetic decision-making based on local resources. The analysis laid out by Keller in Chapter 2 suggests that these differences of technical background among little-c music stakeholders may fall under the rubric of *heterogeneous knowledge or knowledge heterogeneity*. The characteristics of the material resources may involve at least two factors: *temporality* (described by the volatile-persistent quality of the material resources) and *rivalry* (entailing the qualities of rival, non-rival, and anti-rival resources). Examples of ubimus strategies applicable to everyday contexts include: dialogics (see Chapter 7), time tagging (Farias et al., 2015, Keller et al., 2010), and semantics-based interaction (Stolfi et al., 2019).

The research on little-c music is still in first stages. It is not yet clear how the different expectations and backgrounds of musicians and casual participants can be accommodated. While solutions that apply a sharp distinction between the role of the audience and the role of the artists are fairly straightforward, when all stakeholders contribute actively to the creative process the mechanisms for negotiation start to show shortcomings. Furthermore, the stringent demands of musical interaction in transitory settings – involving both a tacit pressure for social acceptability and a very limited time for preparation – present serious challenges to creativity-centred design.

## 1.3  Conclusions

In this chapter, we provided a survey of a growing area of artistic research, defining the meaning of the term ecologies in relation to four fields of application (Figure 1.2). The authors of this volume have looked at ubiquitous

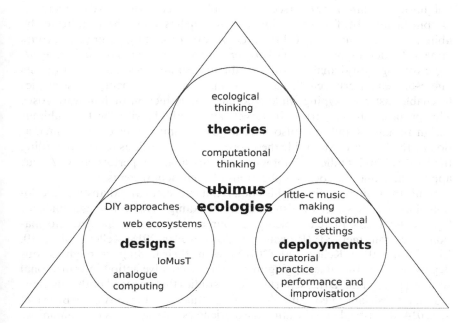

*Figure 1.2* Ubimus ecologies as represented in this book.

music from diverse but consistent perspectives, highlighting aspects of professional music making and multimedia design, creation and performance, infrastructure for ubimus practice, formal and informal educational initiatives, and everyday musical creativity. While these areas do not represent everything there is in ubimus, we feel that each of the contributions and the partial overlaps are significant enough to merit their coexistence in this volume. As a quickly growing field, ubimus features forces that seem contradictory at first sight. How can you expand the frontier of musical knowledge while demanding the inclusion of a larger diversity of participants in musical creative practices? How can you achieve effective support for music creation when the musical activities are removed from the safety of the traditional artistic venues? How can you reduce the financial toll of the musical activities while dealing with a massive amount of distributed resources? These questions have only been partially addressed by the research reported in this volume and they are open to new and exciting initiatives within a field that our community calls *ubimus*.

This volume also sets new markers that aid to delineate ubimus in relation to other fields of research, while helping to unveil a number of common threads for future development. This exercise is not just useful for us to refine a community-constructed definition of ubimus, it also serves to identify promising areas for collaboration and new research avenues that incorporate other fields. We have noted, for instance, that an ecological perspective on ubiquitous listening may intersect with the phenomenon of everyday creativity. Despite being ready for exploration, this overlap has not yet been addressed by ubimus or ethnomusicological research. Another trend for future endeavours targets the development of *systems for ubiquitous sound and music computing* involving hybrid analogue-digital ubimus technologies. This area presents interesting engineering challenges that demand new implementation strategies to enable fast prototyping while enforcing the reduction of hardware costs. This proposal shares part of its targets and methods with the DIY ubimus design initiatives and may also have a positive impact on the implementation of the IoMusT. Alongside these, several open questions remain regarding the IoMusT, web audio technologies and crossadaptive performance targets, applicability, and the social implications of their deployments.

While the main objective of this book is not to present an exhaustive description of case studies or to furnish ready-made examples to be used as a guide for field deployments, there are plenty of sources that provide detailed information on ubimus methods (Brown et al., 2014, Keller, 2018, Keller et al., 2010, Lima et al., 2012). Keller et al. (2010) present their findings through various deployments of the time-tagging metaphor for creative action in transitional settings. Lima et al. (2012) report two case studies that engaged both musicians and non-musicians in educational settings, situated in Porto Alegre. Brown et al. (2014) describe their educational experiences with aboriginal communities in Queensland, Australia, targeting the evaluation of meaningful engagements. Keller (2018) describes a study of lay-musician interaction involving casual participants deployed in an audio-equipment store in Rio Branco, Brazil. Aliel and Keller implemented a series of artistic projects involving the design and deployment of ubimus technologies within the context of multimodal ecologies. The results are documented in (Aliel et al., 2019, 2018, Keller et al., 2019).

The reports on the educational applications of ubimus indicate highly promising and diversified approaches that may yield significant results both in well-established educational systems – such as the Norwegian case – as well as in under-funded or marginalised educational systems – as it is currently the case in Brazil, with a public educational system under the attack of a neoliberal government. Both feature success stories that point to interesting developments targeting dialogical group-creativity and computational-thinking approaches. These strategies may prove useful not only for the expansion of the students cognitive abilities but also as ways to deal with the social demands of an increasingly conflict-ridden and materially unfair world.

## Notes

1  This situation of dependence on technology for social interaction has exploded with the world pandemic. How to support social cohesion while enforcing physical distancing has become an urgent necesssity to be addressed.
2  New Instruments for Musical Expression. *Instruments* was later modified to *Interfaces*.
3  See for instance his writings from the 1940s onwards, collected in Schaeffer (2017).

4 This issue has not been actively pursued in ubimus projects – though Brown's research should be noted (Brown et al., 2018) – but it is definitely an aspect worth exploring.

5 No instructions, ideas, or technical notes on live electronics are recorded in the published score (a facsimile of the manuscript) If Boulez had original ideas about the electronics, one would expect some indications or hints there. As it is, new performances of the work depend on non-published, separately documented instructions. This betrays an attitude that places the *dots on the page* as having a first-class status and the live electronics as a secondary concern. So much for a highly-celebrated *live electronics* work!

6 The term *preset warrior*, as used in some sub-cultures of electronic music, is reserved for these cases.

7 https://elk.audio/.

8 If we take Latin America as an example, the right-wing governments' policies of budget cuts to the arts, science and open-access technologies has had a negative impact on many ongoing initiatives, pushing multiple artists and scientists to exile.

## Bibliography

Abolhasani, M., S. Oakes, and H. Oakes (2017). Music in advertising and consumer identity: The search for heideggerian authenticity. *Marketing Theory 17*(4), 473–490.

Aliel, L., D. Keller, and V. Alvim (2019). A soundtrack for atravessamentos: Expanding ecologically grounded methods for ubiquitous music collaborations. In *Proceedings of the Workshop on Ubiquitous Music (UbiMus 2019)*, pp. 652–662. Marseille: Ubiquitous Music Group and CMMR.

Aliel, L., D. Keller, and R. Costa (2018). The maxwell demon: A proposal for modeling in ecological synthesis in art practices. *Música Hodie 18*(1), 103–116.

Barrass, S. (2015). The musification of furniture in the form of a pouf-doodle. In *Anais do Workshop em Música Ubiqua / Proceedings of the Ubiquitous Music Workshop (UbiMus 2015)*. Vaxjo: Ubiquitous Music Group.

Basanta, A. (2010, August). Syntax as sign: The use of ecological models within a semiotic approach to electroacoustic composition. *Organised Sound 15*(2), 125–132.

Bernardo, F., P. Pestana, and L. Martins (2015). The smart stage: Designing 3d interaction metaphors for immersive and ubiquitous music systems. In *Proceedings of the International Conference on New Music Concepts*. Treviso, Italy.

Bhagwati, S. (2013). Towards interactive onscreen notations for comprovisation in large ensembles. In P. de Assis, W. Brooks, and K. Coessens (Eds.), *Sound & Score: Essays on Sound, Score and Notation*, pp. 143–177. Brussels: Leuven University Press.

Blacking, J. (1973). *How Musical Is Man?* Seattle: University of Washington Press.

Brown, A. R. (2015). Engaging in a sound musicianship. In G. E. McPherson (Ed.), *The Child as Musician: A Handbook of Musical Development*, pp. 208–220. Oxford: Oxford University Press.

Brown, A. R., D. Keller, and M. H. de Lima (2018). How ubiquitous technologies support ubiquitous music. In B.-L. Bartleet and L. Higgins (Eds.), *The Oxford Handbook of Community Music*, pp. 131–151. New York: Oxford University Press.

Brown, A. R., D. Stewart, A. Hansen, and A. Stewart (2014). Making meaningful musical experiences accessible using the iPad. In D. Keller, V. Lazzarini, and M. Pimenta (Eds.), *Ubiquitous Music*, Computational Music Science, pp. 65–81. Berlin: Springer.

Burtner, M. (2005, 4). Ecoacoustic and shamanic technologies for multimedia composition and performance. *Organised Sound 10*(1), 3–19.

Camporez, H. A. F., T. S. R. Mota, E. M. V. Astorga, M. V. M. Neves, H. Rocha, and L. L. Costalonga (2018). Robomus: Uma plataforma para performances musicais robóticas. In D. Keller and M. H. Lima (Eds.), *Applications in Ubiquitous Music*. São Paulo, SP: Editora ANPPOM.

Connors, T. M. (2015). Audiovisual installation as ecological performativity. In *Proceedings of the 21st International Symposium on Electronic Art (ISEA2015)*. Vancouver: ISEA.

Di Scipio, A. (2008). Émergence du son, son d'emergence: Essai d'épistémologie expérimentale par un compositeur. *Intellectica 48–49*, 221–249.

Emmerson, S. (2001, March). From dance! to "dance": Distance and digits. *Computer Music Journal 25*(1), 13–20.

Farias, F. M., D. Keller, V. Lazzarini, and M. H. Lima (2015). Bringing aesthetic interaction into creativity-centered design: The second generation of mixdroid prototypes. *Journal of Cases on Information Technology 4*(17), 53–72.

Gomes, J., N. Pinho, F. Lopes, G. Costa, R. Dias, D. Tudela, and l. Barbosa (2014). Capture and transformation of urban soundscape data for artistic creation. *Journal of Science and Technology of the Arts 6*(1), 97–109.

Harrison, S., D. Tatar, and P. Sengers (2007). The three paradigms of hci. In *Proceedings of the ACM CHI Conference on Human Factors in Computing Systems (CHI 2007)*, pp. 1–18. San Jose, California.

Ingold, T. (2013). *Making: Anthropology, Archaeology, Art and Architecture*. New York, NY: Routledge.

Jung, H., E. Stolterman, W. Ryan, T. Thompson, and M. Siegel (2008). Toward a framework for ecologies of artifacts: How are digital artifacts interconnected within a personal life? In *Proceedings of the 5th Nordic conference on Human-computer interaction: building bridges*, NordiCHI '08, New York, NY, pp. 201–210. ACM.

Keller, D. (1998). "... soretes de punta.". In *Harangue II [Compact Disc]*. Vancouver, BC: New Westminster, BC: Earsay Productions.

Keller, D. (2000). Compositional processes from an ecological perspective. *Leonardo Music Journal 10*, 55–60.

Keller, D. (2004, September). *Paititi: A Multimodal Journey to El Dorado*. Doctor in musical arts thesis, Stanford University, CA, USA. [AAI3145550].

Keller, D. (2018). Challenges for a second decade of ubimus research: Knowledge transfer in ubimus activities. *Música Hodie 18*(1), 148–165.

Keller, D., D. L. Barreiro, M. Queiroz, and M. S. Pimenta (2010). Anchoring in ubiquitous musical activities. In *Proceedings of the International Computer Music Conference (ICMC 2010)*, pp. 319–326. Ann Arbor: MPublishing, University of Michigan Library.

Keller, D. and A. Capasso (2006). New concepts and techniques in eco-composition. *Organised Sound 11*(1), 55–62.

Keller, D., L. Flores, M. Pimenta, A. Capasso, and P. Tinajero (2011). Convergent trends toward ubiquitous music. *Journal of New Music Research 40*(3), 265–276.

Keller, D., C. Gomes, and L. Aliel (2019). The handy metaphor: Bimanual, touchless interaction for the internet of musical things. *Journal of New Music Research 48*(4), 385–396.

Keller, D. and V. Lazzarini (2017). Theoretical approaches to musical creativity: The ubimus perspective. *Musica Theorica 2*(1), 1–53.

Keller, D., V. Lazzarini, and M. Pimenta (2014a). Prologue – ubiquitous music: A manifesto. In D. Keller, V. Lazzarini, and M. Pimenta (Eds.), *Ubiquitous Music*, pp. xi–xxiii. Berlin: Springer.

Keller, D., V. Lazzarini, and M. Pimenta (2014b). *Ubiquitous Music.* Berlin: Springer.

Keller, D. and M. H. Lima (2016). Supporting everyday creativity in ubiquitous music making. In P. Kostagiolas, K. Martzoukou, and C. Lavranos (Eds.), *Trends in Music Information Seeking, Behavior, and Retrieval for Creativity*, Chapter 5, pp. 78–99. Vancouver, BC: IGI Global Press.

Lazzarini, V. (2017a). *Computer Music Instruments: Foundations, Design and Development.* Berlin: Springer.

Lazzarini, V. (2017b). Towards a gradus ad parnassum for computer music. In L. Poitier (Ed.), *Innovative Tools and Methods for Teaching Music and Signal Processing*, pp. 97–117. Paris: Presses des Mines.

Lazzarini, V., D. Keller, C. Kuhn, M. Pimenta, and J. Timoney (2015). Prototyping of ubiquitous music ecosystems. *Journal of Cases on Information Technology 17*(4), 73–85.

Lazzarini, V., D. Keller, M. Pimenta, and J. Timoney (2014). Ubiquitous music ecosystems: Faust programs in csound. In D. Keller, V. Lazzarini, and M. Pimenta (Eds.), *Ubiquitous Music*, Computational Music Science, pp. 129–150. Berlin and Heidelberg: Springer International Publishing.

Lazzarini, V., J. Timoney, and S. Byrne (2015). Embedded sound synthesis. In *Proceedings of the Linux Audio Conference*. Mainz, Germany.

Lazzarini, V., S. Yi, J. Heintz, Ø. Brandtsegg, and I. McCurdy (2016). *Csound: A Sound and Music Computing System.* Berlin: Springer.

Lazzarini, V., S. Yi, J. Timoney, D. Keller, and M. S. Pimenta (2012). The mobile csound platform. In *Proceedings of the International Computer Music Conference*, pp. 163–167. ICMA: Ann Arbor: MPublishing, University of Michigan Library.

Lewis, G. (2000). Too many notes: Computers, complexity and culture in voyager. *Leonardo Music Journal 10*, 33–39.

Lima, M. H., D. Keller, L. V. Flores, and E. Ferreira (2017). Ubiquitous music research: Everyday musical phenomena and their multidisciplinary implications for creativity and education. *Journal of Music, Technology and Education 10*(1), 73–92.

Lima, M. H. D., D. Keller, M. S. Pimenta, V. Lazzarini, and E. M. Miletto (2012). Creativity-centred design for ubiquitous musical activities: Two case studies. *Journal of Music, Technology and Education 5*(2), 195–222.

Manning, E. and B. Massumi (2014, 01). *Thought in the Act: Passages in the Ecology of Experience.* Minneapolis: University of Minnesota Press.

McPherson, A. and V. Zappi (2015). An environment for Submillisecond-Latency audio and sensor processing on BeagleBone black. In *Audio Engineering Society Convention 138*. New York: Audio Engineering Society.

Messina, M. and L. Aliel (2019). Ubiquitous music, gelassenheit and the metaphysics of presence: Hijacking the live score piece ntrallazzu 4. In *Proceedings of the Workshop on Ubiquitous Music (UbiMus2019)*, Marseille, pp. 685–695.

Miletto, E., M. Pimenta, F. Bouchet, J. Sansonnet, and D. Keller (2011). Principles for music creation by novices in networked music environments. *Journal of New Music Research 40*(3), 205–216.

Nance, R. (2018). Music as a plastic art: An ecological strategy facilitating emergence in an instrumental composition ecology. In *Proceedings of the Ubiquitous Music Workshop (UbiMus 2018)*. São João del Rei, MG: Ubiquitous Music Group.

Oakes, S., D. Brownlie, and N. Dennis (2014). Ubiquitous music: A summary and future research agenda. *Marketing Theory 14*(2), 141–145.

Opie, T. and A. Brown (2006). An introduction to eco-structuralism. In *Proceedings of the International Computer Music Conference (ICMC 2006)*, pp. 9–12. Ann Arbor: MPublishing, University of Michigan Library.

Palaigeorgiou, G. and C. Pouloulis (2018, January). Orchestrating tangible music interfaces for in-classroom music learning through a fairy tale: The case of improvischool. *Education and Information Technologies 23*(1), 373–392.

Pimenta, M., D. Keller, L. Flores, M. de Lima, and V. Lazzarini (2014). *Methods in Creativity-Centred Design for Ubiquitous Musical Activities*, pp. 25–48. Berlin: Springer.

Quiñones, M., A. Kassabian, and E. Bosch (2013). *Ubiquitous Musics: The Everyday Sounds that We Don't Always Notice*. London: Routledge.

Schaeffer, P. (2017). *Treatise on Musical Objects, An Essay Across Disciplines*. Oakland: University of California Press.

Schafer, R. M. (1977). *The Tuning of the World*. New York, NY: Knopf.

Small, C. (1986). Performance as ritual: Sketch for an enquiry into the true nature of a symphony concert. *The Sociological Review 34*(S1), 6–32.

Stolfi, A. S., A. Milo, and M. Barthet (2019). Playsound.space: Improvising in the browser with semantic sound objects. *Journal of New Music Research 48*(4), 366–384.

Thorgersen, C. F. (2014). Lose control, listen to each other, and create - understanding cooperative music making from a chiasmatic perspective. *Reconstruction 14*(2), 1–16.

Truax, B. (2015, 4). Paradigm shifts and electroacoustic music: Some personal reflections. *Organised Sound 20*, 105–110.

Trueman, D. (2007). Why a laptop orchestra? *Organised Sound 12*(2), 171–179.

Turchet, L. (2019). Smart Musical Instruments: Vision, design principles, and future directions. *IEEE Access 7*, 8944–8963.

Turchet, L. and M. Barthet (2019). An ubiquitous smart guitar system for collaborative musical practice. *Journal of New Music Research 48*(4), 352–365.

Turchet, L., C. Fischione, G. Essl, D. Keller, and M. Barthet (2018). Internet of Musical Things: Vision and Challenges. *IEEE Access 6*, 61994–62017.

Turchet, L., J. Pauwels, C. Fischione, and G. Fazekas (2019). Cloud-smart musical instrument interactions: Querying a large music collection with a smart guitar. ACM Transactions on the Internet of Things. submitted *1*(3), 1–29.

Weiser, M. (1991). The computer for the 21st century. *Scientific American 265*(3), 94–105.

Wen-Chung, C. (1966). Open rather than bounded. *Perspectives of New Music 5*(1), 1–6.

Wessel, D. and M. Wright (2002, September). Problems and prospects for intimate musical control of computers. *Computer Music Journal 26*(3), 11–22.

Wyse, L. and S. Subramanian (2013). The Viability of the Web Browser as a Computer Music Platform. *Computer Music Journal 37*(4), 10–23.

Yi, S., V. Lazzarini, and E. Costello (2018). WebAssembly AudioWorklet Csound. In *4th Web Audio Conference, TU Berlin, Berlin*.

# 2 Everyday musical creativity

*Damián Keller*

Ubimus has pushed the boundaries of creative practice, embracing non-musicians as creative partners and fostering the use of everyday settings for artistic and educational endeavours. These two factors – the mundane settings and the untrained participants – have raised the bar of the requirements for music making, consequently triggering a shift in methods, concepts and targets of musical research. Rather than adopting established compositional methods that in some cases demand long periods of training, ubimus perspectives target the enhancement of the creative potential through new ways of conceiving and supporting creativity. This shift in emphasis – from the musical products to the development of creativity – entails the incorporation of alternative frameworks that serve as a jumping board towards material and technological changes. One of these frameworks is everyday musical creativity (or *little-c music*).

## 2.1 Introduction

In this chapter I propose a journey into little-c music land by visiting milestones of what is probably one of the least known objects of ubimus research. The concept of little-c music is fairly recent, but it shares a common set of demands with the related concept of general everyday creativity (Keller and Lima, 2016). While it is true that the material of music – sound – establishes specific constraints and affordances for technological development and for social exchanges, a very common mistake in musical interaction research is to take for granted that the only way to make music is by playing an instrument. Musical instruments, whether acoustic or digital, are the standard tools for musicians. Sometimes they foster creativity, particularly when used as venues for explorations of performance-centred music making. But most often than not, they enforce preconceived notions of sound making; their use demands a crisp separation between the acts of composing, playing and listening to music; and they are projected to be deployed in artistic venues, such as the stage or the studio. These characteristics provide the social and material grounding necessary for a currently hegemonic perspective on musical interaction, the acoustic-instrumental paradigm (Tanaka, 2009, Wessel and Wright, 2002).

The acoustic-instrumental approach not only involves the use of instruments, but also fosters the adoption of protocols and interaction procedures based on the European tradition of written instrumental music. For musicians that regularly deal with symbolic notation, periodic rhythms and pitch organised as chords and scales, there is nothing wrong with enforcing this particular mind-set for music making. But instrumentally oriented interaction proposals fall apart when the participants are not musically trained or when the settings are not tailored for artistic ends (Keller et al., 2011). Thus, this restrictive view of creative practice may not be amenable to the target public and to some of the locations embraced by ubimus activities. Hence, the first stop in our journey will be the concept of general everyday creativity and its relationship to ubimus practice.

### 2.1.1   *Resource qualities*

Technological support for pervasive musical activities increases the difficulty of the design task on two fronts. Ubimus ecosystems may enhance the users' creative potential by providing access to material and social resources. But a wider accessibility to resources could introduce unintended complexities that narrow the access to a small user base. Thus, one challenge to ubimus design-ers is to provide intuitive tools for complex creative tasks. Nevertheless, attain-ing this objective does not guarantee wide accessibility. Custom-made, special purpose hardware interfaces – such as those proposed by research in tangible user interface design (Fitzmaurice et al., 1995) – may fill the requirements of transparency and naturalness reducing the cognitive load of complex tasks. In this case, the catch lies in the financial toll. Special-purpose systems are diffi-cult to distribute and maintain. Consequently, the user base is narrowed by the increased costs of the hardware. A set of strategies adopted in ubimus research may provide solutions to the problem of sustainability without a negative impact on usability. Two proposed techniques are hardware repurposing and rapid prototyping (Lazzarini et al., 2015). Consumer-class mobile devices – such as cellular telephones and portable tablets – have been used to develop creative musical tools. Given the lack of standard support for audio and musi-cal data formats, the initial developments for mobile platforms were feasible but cumbersome (Flores et al., 2010, Keller et al., 2010, Radanovitsck et al., 2011). Later advances paved the way to a wider usage within the computer music community (Brinkmann, 2012, Lazzarini et al., 2012). Within an iter-ative approach to design – involving creative musical activities and usability assessments – rapid prototyping techniques were tailored for ubimus contexts. Since ubimus research targets both interaction and signal processing, flaws that arise from coordination among these two processes can be readily diag-nosed. Furthermore, on-site usage in full-blown musical activities uncovers opportunities for creative exploration of the software and of the environment.

Since the early ubimus endeavours, ubimus initiatives have relied on network infrastructure and distributed technological resources (Miletto et al., 2011).

The use of the internet has enabled the flourishing of both synchronous and asynchronous musical exchanges through various means. This form of music making encourages new modes of social interaction and engagement but it also entails new challenges. For instance, an emergent tool for ubimus activities is the Internet of Musical Things (IoMusT) (Keller and Lazzarini, 2017a, Turchet et al., 2018). The IoMusT has been proposed as a hub of objects and services that can be accessed by multiple agents for music making. There is a strong resemblance between the initial definitions of ubimus and the recent conceptualisations of the IoMusT. But there are some differences in emphasis. While the study and development of the IoMusT targets concepts and tools linked to the infrastructure needed for musical activities, ubimus research focuses on the processes of music making. These two aspects are complementary. Sometimes ubimus endeavours will take advantage of local resources and preexisting technological means through opportunistic design strategies (Keller et al., 2013). Other times ubimus projects will demand the development of custom, network-based technology aligned with the objectives of the IoMusT initiatives (Zawacki and Johann, 2012). Thus, we envision a dynamic of mutual enrichment between these two fields; ubimus experiences trigger the development of new IoMusT technology and as IoMusT resources become available they foster opportunities for innovative applications in ubimus practice. Given the potentially massive presence of the internet of things in everyday settings, a careful consideration of the requirements and the affordances of IoMusT components may clear the ground for their usage in ubiquitous musical activities. So our second stop will target the implications of the usage and selection of local, remote, persistent or volatile resources in little-c musical activities.

### 2.1.2 *Knowledge heterogeneity*

An issue to be considered in ubimus practice is the impact of the participation of the untrained subjects. Some cases can be excluded from this area of research. Musical activities for which lay participants can be trained (within reasonable periods), and musical projects in which lay engagement is fully scripted usually leave little margin for creative initiatives. Hence, little-c manifestations may include both musicians and lay participants doing music in everyday settings while targeting an active engagement in the aesthetic decisions by the untrained stakeholders. As we will see when we discuss specific cases, these scenarios may involve limited time for training (i.e., casual participation) and/or open musical forms that entail either on-the-fly decisions or extensive epistemic activity. Therefore, the third stop of our little-c journey will be *knowledge heterogeneity*.

The choice of settings not only impacts the access of the stakeholders to the creative resources, but also modifies the expectations of the participants towards the creative activities. This is particularly critical when the agents are not musically trained and consequently cannot rely on a repository of preexisting and shared implicit knowledge. Multiple ubimus experiments have shown that it is possible to provide effective support for the engagement of lay people in creative music making (Keller et al., 2014b). These initiatives are qualitatively different from other musical proposals targeted to amateurs. For instance, choir singing is adopted by some communities that foster social bonding while dismissing creative individuality. Many institutions that enforce vertical and authoritarian social structures – the Church and the Army are the two obvious examples – use group music making as a tool to infuse an esprit de corps in their membership. The participation in these groups entails the adoption of a strict hierarchy involving a separation of the roles of leaders and followers. Sometimes notation is used as a scaffold for knowledge transfer but more frequently training occurs by mechanical imitation. Usual strategies include the adoption of simplified rhythmic and pitch sequences, a shared and more or less fixed repertoire of songs or hymns and training by example-based imitative sessions involving mechanical repetitions. These top-down practices stand at the opposite end of the initiatives that foster the development of the creative potential – see (Emmerson, 2001, Keller, 2000, Lewis, 2000) for alternative, bottom-up, creativity-oriented proposals.

The ubimus experiences involving diverse combinations of agents and resources have unveiled specific challenges when the stakeholders come from different backgrounds: Given a shared set of musical goals, how can we boost the creative potential of lay participants while avoiding to limit the musical outcomes of the professional partners? We have gathered the ensuing results under the label *lay-musician interaction* (Ferreira et al., 2016, Keller, 2018). At first sight, it would seem that the activities that involve trained participants could be based on the established views on musical interaction. This would be true if the target practice adopted the hierarchical modus operandi described in the previous paragraph. But when the aesthetic objectives involve individuality and creativity, the demands for interaction support by the untrained partners are hardly met by the top-down methods.

### 2.1.3   Fast knowledge transfer

The lack of previous preparation plus the use of non-specific settings create very stringent demands for effective support of little-c musical activities. But these requirements are not uniform across all contexts. For instance, domestic settings are ideal for activities involving iterative engagement and persistent focus. In a way, this venue is similar to the studio but may furnish a more intimate and friendly context fostering relaxed approaches to music making. Contrastingly, transitional settings are not conducive to long-lasting engagements and are prone to the social pressures typical of public venues. These sharp differences in the affordances of both places point to a search for location-oriented strategies to make up for the absence of resources and to increase the creative opportunities when the resources become available. Diverse techniques have been adopted with varying impact on the creative outcomes, on the participants' engagement and on their ability to deal with decision-making in unfamiliar contexts or tasks. Some of these strategies are light-weight, demanding little temporal investment on training or production. We group them under the label *fast knowledge-transfer* approaches. Our last stop visits these methods and furnishes concrete examples of their usage.

Summing up, this chapter proposes an initial journey into an emergent phenomenon of ubimus activity: everyday musical creativity. Everyday musical creativity is situated within the context of creativity studies as a manifestation of general creativity targeting sonic outcomes (Keller and Lima, 2016). While embracing sound as a central element of cutting-edge musical endeavours, everyday musical creativity also encompasses the material, the temporal and the socio-cognitive dimensions of knowledge that lie beyond the sonic content (Glăveanu, 2013). Without making claims of completeness, I chose three aspects of little-c music making that have been unveiled by the results of ubimus field studies: resource qualities, knowledge heterogeneity and fast knowledge transfer. These three stops in the journey are complemented by glimpses of possible territories to be uncovered by future ubimus explorations. The next section will deal with little-c music phenomena situated at the edge of artistic practice and general creativity.

## 2.2 Ground zero: situating little-c music within the field of creativity studies

A cursory look at the recent production in creativity research unveils a persistent separation between the domain-specific manifestations of creativity and the theoretical frameworks employed to explain creative phenomena. This distance between current creative practice and creativity studies has two major consequences. On the one hand, creative practices rely on ad hoc proposals that are usually prescriptive and not applicable outside of specific aesthetic realms – see (Keller and Lazzarini, 2017b) for a discussion of weaknesses and strengths of music-theoretical approaches applicable to ubimus. On the other hand, current theoretically oriented work on creativity suffers from limited empirical support partially due to the aforementioned divorce between theory and praxis.

Within the ubimus community, we are working on integrating up-to-date approaches in creativity studies with data-collection methods applicable to a wide variety of emergent musical practices. The use of the term *emergent* in this context is neither arbitrary nor accidental. A recent survey by Keller and Barreiro (2018) highlights two forces of attraction in ubimus research. Ubiquitous musical activities are not limited to traditional artistic venues and are meant to be deployed throughout a wide range of contexts, including transitional, leisure-oriented, work-oriented and domestic settings. This versatility has powered the development of creative support strategies based on mobile or embedded devices, using light-weight prototyping techniques that take advantage of the extant web technologies. Consequently, music-making has been adopted for informal and formal educational contexts as a strategy to boost the stakeholders' creative engagement (Lima et al., 2012, 2017). This ubimus force of attraction is related to the availability of creative music making outside of the studio and the concert hall.

Another force of attraction mentioned by Keller and Barreiro (2018) is tilted towards the musically trained participants (though it may also be adopted by the lay public). Novel forms of sonic organisation and musical interaction have been enabled by the creative methods developed in ubimus. According to Connors (2017, 66), the proposals laid out "at the Amazon Centre for Music Research, in conjunction with the ubiquitous music group (g-ubimus) Keller and Lazzarini (2017a), [have] summarised the current trends in ecologically grounded methodologies [suggesting] that ecological approaches to creative practice may provide an alternative to the mainstream anthropocentric and disembodied acoustic-instrumental paradigms". The acoustic-instrumental perspective is built upon domain-specific concepts, rooted in rituals imported from the European 19th-century instrumental tradition – such as the adoption of the Italian stage, or the application of hierarchical social norms based on the model of the orchestra, or the incorporation of highly periodic forms of temporal organisation involving the use of the beat and its rhythmic subdivisions, or the usage of pitch as the central components of musical organisation based on equal-temperament and handled through scales and chords – see (Bown et al., 2009, Gurevich and Treviño, 2007) for critical discussions of these shortcomings in musical interaction). Contrastingly, the ecologically grounded creative initiatives underline the need for more flexible methods, applicable to multiple forms of artistic practice ranging from sound-oriented to collaborative and mixed artistic formats (Keller and Lazzarini, 2017a).

A first step in this direction is the development of frameworks that tackle both the musical practices based on acoustic instruments as sonic sources and the creative procedures usually linked to electroacoustic formats. The large diversity of creative practices that have been enabled by digital technologies challenges the validity and generality of concepts such as the note, the beat or the instrument, heavily anchored in theories from the 19th century. As attested by the musical projects conceived for remote locations (Burtner, 2011, Huron, 2008, Keller, 2004), restrictive notions of sonic usage are not good starting points for music making in the wild. For instance, Schaefferian reduced listening is based on the repeated reproduction of a sonic excerpt[1] (Kane, 2007). This procedure is not easily applicable to improvisatory or comprovisational practices. Hence, it is useful for acousmatic composition but it is not well suited to music making based on local or volatile sonic resources (Keller, 2014). Serial procedures – widely adopted in academic circles during the second half of the 20th century – employ discrete values as operational units (Boulez, 1986). Notational symbolic systems involving discrete parameters – e.g., pitch, duration or static dynamics – enable operations such as the inversion, the retrograde or the inverted retrograde of a series. But what happens when the variables are multidimensional or continuous (as it is the case in sonic textures[2])? Or what should composers do when the materials encompass an unlimited number of elements (as it occurs in the generative fractal processes)? Unless the serial operations remain at a fairly high level of abstraction, completely divorced from the sonic qualities, their usage drastically reduces the creative potential of the procedures.

The two examples above form part of a tendency towards prescriptive approaches that pervades many discussions on creative music practice of the second half of the last century – see (Parmar, 2012, Windsor, 1995) for critical appraisals. Another factor that may have played against a fluid dialogue between creativity theories and creative music making is the scant engagement of most psychologists with concrete artistic goals and procedures. One exception is (Ivcevic, 2007, 273) analysis of everyday vs. artistic creativity. According to Ivcevic, people readily attach the label of everyday creativity to phenomena that closely resemble the professional artistic manifestations. General everyday creativity refers to innovative features in daily activities, interpersonal life, work pursuits, sometimes involving problem solving (Richards, 2007, Richards et al., 1988). Some individual attributes are common to multiple domains and are usually tied to specific personality dimensions, such as openness to experience. According to McCrae and Costa (1996), this personality trait incorporates the motivations to pursue diverse experiences and ideas, it involves social non-conformism and it is related to cognitive styles characterised by originality, flexibility and playfulness. Complementarily, the psychologists Root-Bernstein and Root-Bernstein (2004) characterise everyday-creative personalities by traits such as keen observation (attention to detail), the ability to reach abstractions and the easiness to recognise patterns and to establish analogies. It is interesting to note that these traits are prone to be developed by long-term engagement with music making (Herholz and Zatorre, 2012).

Ivcevic (2007) suggests that the differences among artistic and general creativity domains come from two sources: (1) domain-specific knowledge or skill and (2) psychological states that facilitate the creative processes (Ivcevic, 2007). She states that knowledge and skill are essential to recognise what is creative, to build on the available resources and to go beyond the extant knowledge within the domain. Artistic creative endeavours demand long temporal investments. Apparently, they are rare when compared to the manifestations of general everyday creativity. While artistic creativity may lead to social recognition, everyday creativity usually remains private. According to Ivcevic, general everyday creativity refers to products or behaviours considered original and appropriate by the creator or by a relatively small group of people within the person's entourage. Everyday creativity becomes entrained in daily activities, such as creating a comfortable living environment, handling everyday issues, managing interpersonal relationships, doing crafts or structuring leisure time.

Ivcevic used an act-frequency approach, involving the realisation and identification of creative actions, to examine artistic and everyday creative behaviours while focusing on the similarities and differences between these two creative modalities in relation to personality traits and psychological health. Studies 1 and 2 showed that lay people are able to identify and distinguish between acts of artistic and everyday creativity. Study 3 showed that the two domains of creativity are moderately correlated, suggesting that everyday creativity is likely to accompany artistic creativity. Ivcevic states that in the symbiosis of these modalities, specialised creativity may benefit from the observations that take place during daily endeavours, such as when some artists depict everyday objects in their work or when everyday interactions become a point of departure for an artistic project.

I think her conclusions can be carried further. Artistic and general everyday creativity may rest on mechanisms that are dependent on the stakeholders access to the appropriate resources. All art triggers reflective processes which in some cases may take several years to come to fruition.[3] While it is true that the professional manifestations of creativity rely on extensive temporal investment in training, there are some forms of artistic practice that require little or no preparation. For instance, live coding demands a good grasp of programming skills combined with experience on specific audio synthesis techniques. Building this knowledge pool may take from many months to many years of study. But the action of coding itself is necessarily *live*, indicating that the process of decision-making is comparable to the execution of daily tasks. The differences between little and pro creativity are less related to the temporal investment in the activity than to the access to knowledge during the process of aesthetic decision-making. By reducing the amount of domain-specific knowledge needed to achieve an artistic result, the artistic practice may be compared to a daily chore. Despite demanding particular settings plus special cognitive and social conditions, this type of creative activity does not lie beyond the grasp of newcomers. This is what I mean by little-c music making.

## 2.3   Milestone 1: resource qualities

The material dimension of creativity has gained a central place in ubimus practices. Keller et al. (2014a) discuss current creativity models from a ubimus perspective highlighting the need for actual grounding on materiality. The *place factor* (Rhodes, 1961) is unpacked through the observation of the flux of local resources, encompassing aspects such as the ecological constraints arising from the attunement of the stakeholders to the local conditions (Gibson, 1977, Keller, 2000) and yielding adjustments with direct impact on the behavioural ecologies (Keller and Lazzarini, 2017a, Nance, 2018) and the ecological niche. Furthermore, the central role of materiality unveils the need to consider the dynamic aspects of the flux of resources, related to their availability and to their creative potential when shared within a community of practice. Two design qualities have been proposed to deal with these issues: volatility and rivalry (Keller, 2014).

### 2.3.1 Temporality

Ubimus phenomena involve both the locally available objects and the remote materials accessible through technological infrastructure. Two types of resources should be considered: (1) The resources present on site, defined in the creativity literature as the *place factor*; (2) The materials accessed through creativity support infrastructure which may or may not be collocated (Keller, 2014). Iannis Xenakis (1971/1992) suggested that creative musical activities may occur in-time or out-of-time (Xenakis, 1992). This idea has been adopted by the human-computer interaction literature under the labels of synchronous and asynchronous activities. Some materials may only become available during the creative activity and cannot be recycled for future use. Other resources may be repeatedly used during iterative creative work.

The improvisatory performances based on network infrastructure are a case in point. Each participant's action depends on the sonic cues provided synchronously by the other participants. These sonic cues are only available at the moment of the performance, therefore they can be classified as volatile material resources. Other resources can be incorporated in the context of iterative cycles of creative activity. A good example is the musical prototype (Miletto et al., 2011). A musical prototype is a data structure that supports actions by multiple users through network infrastructure. A single creative product is shared by the participants collaborating throughout the creative cycle. Participants access the musical prototype remotely and cooperate by doing direct modifications and by providing comments on their actions and on their partners' actions. Creative decisions are the result of a cumulative process of material exchanges that can last from a few hours to several months. Hence, we can say that a musical prototype is *a non-volatile or persistent material resource*.

How does volatility impact everyday creative activities? Volatility may be caused by the social dynamics fostered by the musical proposal. For instance, casual participation involves the engagement of agents that are not necessarily acquainted with the resources available for the activity. This limitation imposes very high demands on the usability of the support infrastructure, including designs that target small investments on installation, configuration or preprocessing of resources by end-users. These requirements can be bypassed by interaction strategies – described as multi-tier approaches – that distribute the functionality among various groups of participants who enter the creative cycle at different stages, providing pieces of knowledge that add value to the resources. Thus, multi-tier approaches may be applicable to casual participation in everyday contexts when the stockholders possess different levels of expertise (see also the milestone heterogeneous knowledge).

### 2.3.2 Rivalry

Kozbelt et al. (2010) classify general creativity theories into ten categories: developmental, psychometric, economic, stage-componential process, ideational, problem solving, problem finding, evolutionary, typological, systemic (systems). Economically oriented approaches to creativity furnish opportunities for observation and quantification of resources that are hard to assess or that are not available to other paradigms (Rubenson and Runco, 1992, 1995, Sternberg and Lubart, 1991). By observing the flux of consumption and production of resources, quantitative predictions may be linked to specific conditions and the resources become quantifiable. The effectiveness of a creative strategy can be assessed by comparing the resource usage with the creative yield. The creative outcomes may be predicted by analysing the quality and quantity of the resources and how they are handled and shared by the stakeholders. The ratio between resource consumption and creative waste can be used to assess the sustainability of the creative ecosystem under observation. Consequently, creative potentials and creative performance become linked to specific variables that can be studied through empirical work. Observable resources become the focus of the field experiments, opening a window to quantitative comparisons among different strategies for support of creative activities.

From an economy-oriented perspective, material resources may be *rival, non-rival or anti-rival*. Rival resources lose value when shared. Non-rival resources can be widely distributed without losing value. Information is a good example of a non-rival resource. Information can be freely shared without any impact on its social value. Contrastingly, if a food stock is partitioned within a community its value is reduced proportionally to its depletion rate. An empty food stock has no social value. Anti-rival resources gain value proportionally to their spread within the community.

There are some interesting observations to be gathered through the application of the quality of rivalry in ubimus. Resources for creative activities can be characterised by their level of relevance and originality (Weisberg, 1993). In the context of group activities, these two factors constitute opposite forces (Ferraz and Keller, 2014). Creative resources that are unique and that have not been shared among group members keep their creative potential while featuring a high level of originality. Through sharing, original resources lose their creative potential but gain acceptance among group members. The most relevant resources are the ones most widely distributed which feature the highest social acceptance. Therefore since creative rival resources lose value through social acceptance, they can negatively impact originality. On the other hand, creative non-rival resources can be freely distributed without affecting originality. When widely shared, the non-rival c-resources can attain higher levels of relevance than the rival c-resources.

Sound samples can be classified as creative rival resources. The novelty of the creative products that use samples decreases proportionally to the number of copies in the sonic result. Deterministic synthesis models generate the same sound for the same set of parameters, so they can also be classified as rival c-resources. Given that physical objects produce different sonic results each time they are excited, the events they produce can be classified as non-rival c-resources. On a similar vein, stochastic synthesis algorithms such as ecological modelling[4] can render multiple events without producing repeated instances (Haworth, 2015, Keller and Truax, 1998). Musical sources based on timbre manipulations – such as the use of processed guitar sounds – are also the examples of non-rival c-resources.[5]

Summing up, creative rival resources do not add value to the creative product when shared. Therefore, distribution of copies of creative rival resources among group members should be reduced to a minimum. This limitation does not apply to the case of creative non-rival resources. These resources can be shared without imposing a steep reduction on the originality of the stakeholders' creative products. Anti-rival resources gain value proportionally to their distribution among the stakeholders.

Regarding their temporality, material resources can be classified along a continuum from persistent to volatile. Persistent resources provide firm referents for everyday musical activities because they tend to be available throughout the activity. The volatile resources' accessibility is limited since their life cycle tends to be shorter than the duration of the activity. Acoustic-instrumental improvisational practices feature sonic resources that only become available at the moment of sharing and that cannot be retrieved after they occur without resorting to technological support. Recycling and re-usage are built into digital systems through their data structures. Given the casual nature of most interactions occurring in everyday contexts, a balance between volatility and persistence may be necessary to enable diverse musical practices. Storage and processing power of mobile and embedded devices is usually enough for individual needs during short creative sessions. But when the number of stakeholders increases or when the creative activity extends for long durations, the amount of computational resources may require the implementation of a persistent managing system.

## 2.4   Milestone 2: knowledge heterogeneity

Creative decision-making demands knowledge of the existing resources and knowledge of the intentions of the creative partners. With the advent of the IoMusT (Keller and Lazzarini, 2017a, Turchet et al., 2018)), the awareness of the available resources may depend on ongoing exchanges of information between the stakeholders and on the features of the support infrastructure. The acquisition of data from physical objects is becoming feasible through the deployment of sensors. But to be useful for decision-making, this data needs to make sense to the participants of the creative activity. An issue to be addressed is how to provide meaningful ways to handle the resources in ubiquitous musical ecosystems under the stringent conditions of everyday settings.

Since Polanyi (1958) initial formulation of the concept of tacit knowledge, the idea that some forms of knowledge are not amenable for sharing has increasingly gained acceptance. Based on a survey of 60 papers from the area of knowledge management, Grant (2007) analyses the impact of the tacit knowledge concept and formulates a model based on Polanyi's work. Grant's model adopts Polanyi's basic precept that all knowledge includes a degree of tacitness. Grant's survey indicates that the adoption of an overly simplistic view of the tacit/explicit dimension leads to significant failures in knowledge management practice, especially in IT-related projects. Hence, he proposes a continuum between tacit and explicit knowledge: from contexts suitable for stakeholders with a limited background experience, with little tacit knowledge; through settings where experts with shared backgrounds and experience make full usage of a shared tacit-knowledge pool; and including situations in which personal knowledge can hardly be made explicit; to contexts where the stakeholders cannot articulate their knowledge, hence the label "ineffable".

Rather than equating tacit to implicit knowledge, Grant suggests that implicit knowledge might be described as tacit knowledge that has the potential to be made explicit. The use of explicit representations – such as verbal explanations, graphic depictions or the implementation of symbolic systems – depends on the level of specialisation of the shared resources. To complement this knowledge, experts within a field have a large pool of shared tacit resources. Beginners, on the other hand, demand broadly shared knowledge, such as natural language, to eventually gain access to implicit resources. So, some forms of explicit representations may serve as doors to access specialised resources.

The field of creativity studies has addressed some aspects of the processes involved in the production of new knowledge (Kozbelt et al., 2010, 23). A recent categorisation of general creativity magnitudes fits well within the dimensions of knowledge proposed by Grant and Polanyi. Four levels have been proposed: eminent creativity (*Big-c*), professional creativity (*pro-c*), everyday creativity (*little-c*) and personal creativity (*mini-c*) (Table 2.1) (Beghetto and Kaufman, 2007, Kaufman and Beghetto, 2009). Big-c or eminent creativity refers to the socially established, paradigmatic examples of creative results, such as published works of art and scientific theories. Eminent creativity manifestations involve creative products that are prone to wide social exposure. Contrastingly, personal experiences leading to creative products fall within the class of little-c phenomena (Richards et al., 1988). Mini-c is characterised by internal, subjective and emotional aspects of everyday creativity. And the little-c label is reserved for creative manifestations targeting

*Table 2.1* Creativity magnitudes: the four-c model

| Label | Scope | Description |
| --- | --- | --- |
| Big-c | Eminent creativity | Socially acknowledged creative performance |
| Pro-c | Professional creativity | Creative performance that attains widespread recognition |
| little-c | Everyday creativity | Personal creative performance |
| mini-c | Subjective creativity | Personal creative potential |

See Keller et al. (2014a) for a discussion of these magnitudes within ubimus.

products. Between little-c and Big-c phenomena, Kaufman and Beghetto (2009) propose another class – professional creativity or pro-c – encompassing creative achievements that do not attain the eminence of Big-c manifestations. Both pro-c and Big-c processes demand knowledge only accessible to experts. The differences between these two magnitudes can be gauged by their social impact. Big-c musical products are usually surrounded by a large pool of explicit knowledge that includes written discussions, analyses and extramusical resources (Simonton, 1990). While this pool of knowledge facilitates the access to the musical experience by a broad public, it does not guarantee access to creative music making. Pro-c products feature a fair amount of technical knowledge targeting musicians. The requirement of implicit knowledge involving specialised skills in listening and sound making separates this category from everyday musical manifestations.

Where is musical knowledge situated within the tacit/explicit dimension? According to Keller and Brown (2017), the answer depends on the type of musical knowledge in focus. The acoustic-instrumental paradigm deals with musical experiences based on symbolic or mechanical resources tailored for the use of acoustic musical instruments. Thus, its designs usually rely on common-practice musical notation and digital emulations of acoustic instruments. When dealing with emergent music making in everyday venues and when targeting non-musicians, to demand domain-specific knowledge means to exclude casual and untrained participants. Hence, while acoustic-instrumental designs aim at virtuosic performances (Wessel and Wright, 2002), ubimus designs embrace manifestations of everyday creativity. The type of knowledge required by these two approaches is very different. Acoustic-instrumental designs rest on the usage of symbolic notation and on extensive exposure to specialised instrumental practice. Ubimus designs rely on local and opportunistic usage of social and material resources, featuring the repurposing of extant technologies, such as embedded, mobile and networked devices, the world wide web and the internet of musical things.

### 2.4.1 Dialogics

Another factor that impacts the creative processes targeting everyday settings is the diversity of the profile of the participants. Sawyer and DeZutter (2009) analysis of the exchanges of improvisatory theatre-groups sessions adheres to an ecologically grounded perspective on creative practice. In their conclusions, the authors suggest that hierarchically structured groups rely on the creativity of the individual that directs the group, while non-hierarchical organisations disseminate the creative processes among the group members. Thus, each social configuration demands a specific method of study.

> The creativity of an orchestra performance resides, in large part, in the creativity of the composer and of the conductor. The creativity of a centrally managed business team resides in large part in the autocratic leader. Such individuals, and their creative processes, can be successfully

studied using individualistic methods. However, to the extent that a group manifests collaborative emergence, it will be more likely to require inter-action analysis to explain processes of distributed creativity.

(Sawyer and DeZutter, 2009, 91)

This issue raises the question: What support mechanisms are appropriate to target emergent, distributed, heterarchical, improvisatory and dialogical forms of group creative practice?

In line with other socially oriented perspectives, the dialogical approach to ubimus is based on the premise that knowledge is socially constructed (Lima et al., 2012, 2017). Pioneered by Helena Lima, this philosophical and method-ological proposal is based on Paulo Freire's conceptions (Shor and Freire, 1987). Since the early sixties, Freire's educational praxis changes the teacher's purpose from a mere conduit of technical-theoretical information to a listener and proponent of the active and conscious engagement of the students in the construction of knowledge. Thus, the educator encourages the pupils to assume a protagonist role in the creative processes, through a critical reflection of their choices and their consequences. Hence, knowledge is considered the basis for the dialogical and reflective actions that take place within a commu-nity of practice (Wenger, 2010).

The dialogical conception highlights the role of the local cultural refer-ents as resources to build experiential knowledge grounded on personal engagements with the local context. By establishing connections between their previous experiences and the new contexts, the participants may become contributors to the creative processes. An aspect emphasised by Freire is the need for care and respect for diversity. The knowledge contributed by the student and the new resources brought by the educator should target a conscious and respectful attitude towards each other's beliefs, experiences and tastes. Hence, dialogical processes support exchanges without confrontation fostering a space of coexistence for diverse and sometimes seemingly incom-patible worldviews.[6]

Dialogical methods are focused on social interaction, adopting an iterative cycle of exchanges to foster individual and collective reflections. This concep-tion stands apart from the perspectives that target creativity as a purely mental process – see (Keller et al., 2014a) for a detailed discussion of the limitations of disembodied and out-of-context approaches to creativity. Through hands-on activity and social interaction among peers, the participants are stimulated to evaluate their proposals, developing a critical view on their creative products and fostering a sharp perspective of the impact of their actions on the local reality.

What are the implications of ubimus dialogics for everyday music making? A strong reliance on local resources has been one of the trademarks of the ubimus initiatives. Time-tagging employs environmental cues as scaffolds for aesthetic decision-making (Keller et al., 2010, Pinheiro da Silva et al., 2013). Graphic-procedimental tagging uses foraged pictorial elements as referents for comprovisational decisions (Aliel et al., 2015, Melo and Keller, 2013). The Sound Sphere metaphor for creative action incorporates user-defined semantic descriptors to handle timbre operations (Bessa et al., 2015, Keller, 2018, Pereira et al., 2018). Playsound.space proposes the retrieval of sonic resources through user-driven semantic tokens (Stolfi et al., 2019). All these strategies rest on the stakeholders' knowledge of graphical or sonic materials as they relate to collective decision-making. Hence, they are based on cycles of foraging, sharing and selection involving non-hierarchical decisions. These processes yield two by-products that characterise the dialogical communities. On the one hand, group music-making lets the stakeholders build a shared knowledge pool that allows them to reach consensual decisions. On the other hand, the participants' usage of their local referents ensures the persistence of diverse components within this shared pool.

Professional musical activities rest on established practices built on domain-specific explicit knowledge and on a large reservoir of tacit knowledge. Tapping into this knowledge demands investments on long periods of training and on the production of domain-specific resources such as scores, electroacoustic soundtracks and pushes the design towards the usage of emulations of musical instruments. These procedures are best exploited in venues prepared for artistic performances, establishing a clear separation between the audience and the artists. These conditions are seldom met when musical activities take place in transitional, leisure-oriented, work-oriented or domestic spaces. Contrastingly, creative music making in everyday contexts involves the active engagement of participants with little or no previous preparation or mutual contact, together with the active pursuit of scaffolds for aesthetic decision-making based on local resources. These sharp differences of technical background among little-c music stakeholders can be gathered under the rubric of *heterogeneous knowledge or knowledge heterogeneity*.

## 2.5 Milestone 3: fast knowledge transfer

Our journey so far – beyond the ground zero represented by the conceptual push and pull of domain-specific vs. general creative factors – has included two milestones, usage of resources and knowledge heterogeneity. Both are by-products of the constraints and opportunities introduced by the engagement of creative participants that do not belong to the artistic milieu and by the occupation of spaces that previously were considered barren for creative endeavours. We have discussed the implications of materiality and temporality in ubimus design, proposing categories such as volatile and persistent ubimus resources. We have also explored the consequences of sharing within the context of group-oriented creative initiatives, highlighting the impact of a new design quality: rivalry.

Regarding the social dimension, we have discussed the implications of individualistic and vertical social organisations – historically linked to the acoustic-instrumental practices – for contexts that demand flexible and fluid forms of musical interaction. An aspect to be considered when designing for everyday music making is the role of general creativity. Designs based on domain-specific knowledge may enforce long periods of preparation and involve resources that are usually unavailable in little-c contexts. Furthermore, the diverse profiles of the stakeholders imply a knowledge base containing contrasting levels of expertise. Rather than adopting a centralised model of decision-making, consensus-building among participants entails accessing and understanding the shared resources and the partners intentions. By building upon the inclusive practices fostered by Freire and other educators working at peripheral countries, a design philosophy based on dialogics seems to provide a path to overcome part of these caveats.

The two milestones that we have visited provide a glimpse of the issues to be encountered when designing for everyday musical activities. Nevertheless, this short journey into little-c music land would not be complete if we did not tackle examples of the strategies used to explore this fuzzy territory. How can we deal with knowledge heterogeneity? What is the impact of adopting volatile or persistent resources? How can we approach the implications of rivalry and how does this design quality relate to the characteristics of a shared knowledge pool? There are more questions than answers at this stage of the research on little-c music phenomena. But part of the design techniques developed during the last decade of ubimus practice may furnish solutions for some of these issues. To begin with, let us consider temporality.

### 2.5.1   Temporality

Time-tagging is a metaphor for creative action that has emerged as a means to avoid the computational burden of the visually oriented approaches to audio mixing (Keller et al., 2010). This metaphor encouraged musical experiences in everyday settings while boosting the participation of non-musicians (Keller et al., 2013, Pinheiro da Silva et al., 2013). Two generations of prototypes were designed and deployed (Farias et al., 2015, Radanovitsck et al., 2011). Keller et al. (2009) used an emulation of a first-generation mixDroid prototype (mixDroid 1G) for the creation of a complete musical work. The initial objective was to test whether the interaction technique was suitable for a complete creative cycle: from the initial state – defined as a collection of unordered sound samples, to the final state – a time-based organised sonic product. The procedure encompassed several mixing sessions. The mixDroid 1G prototype was used in the emulation mode on a laptop computer and was activated with an optical mouse. The result was a seven-minute stereo sound work – *Green Canopy On The Road* – the first documented ubimus work, premiered at the Brazilian Symposium on Computer Music held in Recife, Brazil (Keller et al., 2009).

After this initial validation, two complementary studies were conducted. Focusing on the demands of naive participants in everyday contexts, a second study was carried out in transitional settings (at a shopping mall, at a busy street and in a quiet outdoor area featuring biophonic sounds) and in private settings (at the home of each participant and at a studio facility) (Pinheiro da Silva et al., 2013). Six subjects participated in 47 mixing sessions using samples comprising urban sounds and biophonic sources. Creativity support was evaluated by means of a creative-experience assessment protocol encompassing six factors: productivity, expressiveness, explorability, enjoyment, concentration and collaboration (CSI[7] v. 0.1 – (Keller et al., 2011)). Outdoor sessions yielded higher scores in productivity, explorability, concentration and collaboration when compared to studio sessions.

A third study made use of recorded vocal samples created by the participants (Keller et al., 2013). In order to untangle the effects of place and activity type, three conditions were studied: place, including domestic and commercial settings; activity type, i.e. imitative mixes and original creations; and body posture, realising the mix while standing or sitting. Ten subjects took part in an experiment encompassing 40 interaction sessions using mixDroid 1G. Subjects created mixes and assessed their experiences through the CSI-NAP protocol v. 0.2 (Keller et al., 2011). Explorability and collaboration factors yielded superior scores when the activities were carried out in domestic settings.

The results highlighted the impact of the venue on the support of the creative experiences. The outdoor spaces were preferred by the participants of the second study, but the domestic settings got slightly higher ratings in the third study. While the profile of the subjects impacted the outcome of the third study, this trend was not confirmed by the second study's results. Hence, the main conclusions to be drawn from these studies point to the impact of the venue on the subjects' evaluation of the experience. Both their ability to explore the potential of the support metaphor and their ability to collaborate were boosted by domestic settings and outdoor settings.

These conclusions reinforce the need for strategies to establish bridges between the local resources and the process of aesthetic decision-making. Time-tagging explores the temporality provided by the local acoustic cues opening a path to the design of metaphors for creative action based on the temporal features of everyday resources and activities. These features do not need to be exclusively sonic and can be obtained as by-products of events occurring in other modalities. Their temporal scale can be adjusted according to the needs of the creative activity and the extracted information may be shared by means of creative surrogates (Keller et al., 2015). Examples of the musical techniques applicable to ubimus contexts are provided by Opie and Brown (2006) and Gomes et al. (2014). An interesting avenue of development could use behavioural patterns elicited by the architectural characteristics of urban spaces, involving the application of concepts such as *place-temporality* (Wunderlich, 2013).

### 2.5.2  Semantics

Another avenue to explore the material dimension of little-c music entails a broader access to local referents by means of meta-resources, paving the way to generalised strategies of creative interaction through semantics. This initiative rests on the assumption that natural (spoken or written) language constitutes a widespread channel for knowledge-sharing among literate stakeholders. Literacy, in this context, should be qualified as a reasonable grasp of abstract concepts and a basic acquaintance with information technology. Thus, semantics-based interaction demands using a common spoken language, involving shared cultural traits and having (at least temporary) access to electronic devices. These requirements are usually met in urban contexts by school-aged or older populations. So, in principle, no specialised training is necessary.

Semantics-based musical interaction has a historical precedent in verbal-notational practices. Verbal scores were widely adopted by the experimental practitioners of the fifties and sixties, for instance by the performance-oriented artist collective Fluxus, featuring composers such as La Monte Young and performance artists such as George Maciunas and Joseph Beuys. At the time, the computational infrastructure was restricted to large companies and research centres. So the adoption of computational tools would have involved constraining the artistic practices to specialised venues – a requirement that went against the grain of the proposals championed by Fluxus.

Contrastingly, the current tendencies in creative music making indicate that computational resources are employed at some stage in almost all artistic practices (see a historical overview of technology-based music making in Keller and Costa (2018). But these resources are not always available to lay participants and various design challenges forfeit the full engagement with creative activities outside of the specialised venues. Given this context, semantics-based musical interaction may furnish a way to promote musical knowledge transfer without resorting to traditional notation. Two ubimus proposals illustrate this strategy: Playsound.space (PS) and the Sound Sphere Metaphor (Bessa et al., 2015, Pereira et al., 2018, Stolfi et al., 2019). The Sound Sphere Metaphor for Creative Action will be the focus of several upcoming publications. Preliminary results and the long series of prototypes in development since 2015 are available online.[8] Let us deal with Playsound.space to address whether this tool could eventually be incorporated into everyday music creation.

Stolfi et al. (2019) describe Playsound.space as an online music-making tool, an open platform to play with Creative-Commons audio content from the Freesound database using semantic queries and supporting sound selections informed by spectrogram representations. The tool features the integration of a multi-user chat system with embedded language translation. Based on the Web Audio library,[9] it features some functionalities of audio editing and processing. Stolfi and partners report the results of two studies targeting (1) free improvisation and (2) soundscape composition.

The first study featured six sessions involving various combinations of acoustic instrumental performances[10] with one or two PS players. The improvisations lasted from 2:30 to almost 15 minutes and were preceded by exploratory sessions of 3 to 8 minutes. Only three participants out of a total of eight filled the survey. The results indicated the usage of a small amount of audio samples and the exploratory usage of audio processing on PS. The participants comments included positive appraisals of the large amount of available sounds (despite choosing to work on a small subset) and of the possibility to avoid deliberate choices, while using very broad categories in their sound search, for instance, employing terms like "non-musical sounds". Negative evaluations included technical issues, such as the delays due to the slow internet connection, and the musicians' unfulfilled expectations regarding the prototype's functionalities.

The second study targeted soundscape-oriented activities involving 17 college students with previous experience and training in music and sound (12 subjects) and without previous domain-specific training (5 subjects). A target activity involved creating a one-minute audio composition over a period of three weeks, using a set of four tools including PS. The students had to produce a report on their technical and aesthetic decisions. All of them participated in an anonymous online survey to evaluate the tools. The assessments on usability were positive but left space for improvement. The creativity-support factors yielded the highest scores for exploration, expressiveness and results-worth-the-effort. But the overall results were not very positive. According to Stolfi and coauthors, given that most of the compositional activities were based on audio editors, the participants tended to prefer the tools that were integrated with DAWs. Most of the negative comments targeted lack of support for audio operations such as editing and processing and questioned some of the interface design choices (in particular, aesthetic appearance and usability). The positive assessments highlighted the adoption of the spectrogram as a reliable carrier of sonic information and the ability to create quick sketches of multiple sonic combinations (a functionality that is usually cumbersome for novices when using traditional digital audio workstations, or DAWs).

Leaving the technical drawbacks aside – which can be addressed in future iterations of the tool – PS presents an interesting application of semantics-based interaction for selecting sonic resources. While the cycle of search-choose-deploy presented some problems for free improvisers, it seemed to fulfil the needs for a quick-sketching tool for soundscape-oriented participants. Improvisers indicated the need of a *preview* option before sharing the individual results with the group. They also reported that the dependence on searches – imposed by the design of PS – may sometimes impact negatively on the creative flow. Nevertheless, the uncertainty of the search results and the ability to tap into a very large pool of resources were seen as very exciting boosters of creativity. These results are aligned with the proposal to include Gelassenheit factors in the design of ubimus systems, as suggested by Aliel and coauthors (Aliel et al., 2015, 2018). In this case, uncertainty is introduced by the mismatch between the semantic descriptors and the sonic targets. This mismatch widens the epistemic field for decision-making (Ferraz and Keller, 2014) which in turn enhances the knowledge pool, pushing the creative processes towards new paths.

An issue that was negatively evaluated by the participants of the compositional task – the lack of integration with standard DAWs – should be analysed within the context of the efforts to expand the capabilities of current ubimus ecosystems (Lazzarini et al., 2015). Here we can identify two trends. One trend gives priority to the maintenance and expansion of the accumulated knowledge gathered around a stable tool set. A central piece of this tool set is the Digital Audio Workstation, with various accessories for interacting with sound and musical data. Another trend pushes for the expansion of interaction strategies by means of the incorporation of post-DAW technologies, for instance, the internet, browsers, wireless protocols, mobile devices, embedded devices or the internet of things. While this criticism could be dismissed purely on technological grounds – as the tools become more capable we need to adjust our practices to the new capabilities – the social affordances of new resources and behaviours (their potential for social action) have to be carefully considered. The semantics-based selection of parameters for audio processing has been investigated by Stables et al. (2014). In a sense, this approach is comparable to the retrieval of audio samples proposed in PS. But Stables and coauthors propose the implementation of plug-ins for standard DAW interfaces. Given a typical studio infrastructure, centred around the desktop with optional internet access, both approaches (DAW and browser-based) are equivalent. But the DAW-based proposal breaks down once we move outside of the studio, into territories populated with mobile and embedded technologies with little screen real estate and with unreliable internet connectivity. As a down side of the browser-based approach, basing the functionality of the system on permanent internet access is prone to failure. It is reasonable to expect access to internet-based resources at various stages of the creative cycle (for instance, for resource foraging, community sharing of resources and for publishing of creative products). But a demand of reliable internet access throughout the creative activity suffers from various limitations (Barbosa, 2010). As a negative aspect of DAW-based tools, typical ubimus activities involve noisy settings and target the usage of a variety of personal devices with limited computational capabilities and with small surfaces for interaction. Hence, strategies that do not rely on large displays, large amounts of random-access memory (RAM) or niche technologies (i.e., technologies that are not supported by most platforms) have a better chance to achieve a sustainable life cycle.[11]

## 2.6 Conclusions and glimpses of future developments

Manifestations of everyday musical creativity involve new ways to use creative resources. Until the end of the 20th century, music creation was predominantly done by highly trained individuals and the musical products were usually restricted to specialised venues. The widespread availability of technological assets combined with a slowly changing set of social expectations on what constitutes art have provided the necessary impulse for the emergence of ubimus practices.

From a design perspective, ubimus experiments assess the resource usage through observations of creative products and material resources. While some creative techniques provide a high product yield with a small ecological footprint, other practices tend to produce high levels of creative waste. Therefore, assessments of material usage may furnish a window to the resource flow mechanics and its impact on ubimus ecosystems, employing creative waste, resources and products as observables of everyday music making. Among the design aspects to be considered, we discussed rivalry, temporality, dialogics, modalities of engagement, modalities of knowledge and knowledge heterogeneity as design qualities present in little-c manifestations (Table 2.2).

Another aspect to be considered is the potential for enhanced forms of participation in decision-making by the untrained stakeholders, fostered by social knowledge construction. Part of the experimental results discussed in this chapter pointed to increased levels of engagement when the musical activities involved a mix of novices and professional musicians (Ferreira et al., 2016). The motivations are unclear, but they may be related to a tendency to equate extant practices to musical relevance. Given the lack of an everyday-oriented musical tradition, lay participants may be using criteria extracted from their

*Table 2.2* Design qualities highlighted by ubimus experiments that target little-c manifestations

| Design quality | Target | Description | Design categories |
| --- | --- | --- | --- |
| Rivalry | Material resources | Impact of sharing on the creative potential of the knowledge pool | Rival, anti-rival, non-rival |
| Temporality | Material and behavioural resources | Temporal features of resources used for creative purposes | Volatile, persistent, iterative |
| Dialogics | Behavioural resources | Exchanges for knowledge building and transfer within a community of practice | Non-hierarchical, decentralised, dialogical |
| Modalities of engagement | Behavioural resources | Participation in a community of practice | Iterative, casual, continuous |
| Modalities of knowledge | Meta-resources | Qualities of the resources available in a community of practice | Tacit, implicit, explicit and derivatives |
| Knowledge heterogeneity | Social resources | Characteristics of the stakeholders profiles, with possible impact on the collective creative potential | Homogeneous, heterogeneous and derivatives |

familiar forms of music making to assess their creative products and processes. When these products and processes differ from their expectations, their interest is diminished. This is a very difficult obstacle to circumvent. Familiarity is a highly reliable predictor for the subjective quality of cultural resources and products. The implementation of mechanisms to introduce novelty without disrupting the novices' musical experience is among the open issues to explore in future ubimus projects.[12]

### 2.6.1  *Temporality*

Ubimus research suggests that the resources' temporality should be taken into account when designing for everyday contexts. Methodologically, the volatility of the material resources is a design quality that can be applied to gauge the level of potential creative support. Persistent resources, such as network-shared musical data allied to consistent metaphors for interaction, may prove useful to support creative activities that involve multiple devices and asynchronous access by multiple stakeholders. Volatile resources gain importance in everyday music practices that target synchronous interaction.

### 2.6.2  *Rivalry*

Collaborative strategies, highlighting the socially distributed nature of the creative resources, put in evidence the need to understand the impact of sharing on creativity. Relevance and originality are closely tied to the spread or concentration of resources in the stakeholders' hands. The concept of rivalry establishes a bridge between sharing and the creative potential of the pooled resources. Some resources gain creative value when shared while others are negatively impacted by a relaxed distribution policy. A third type of resources affords sharing without reducing its potential for creative outcomes. Because everyday musical endeavours may take place in public spaces where participants freely join and leave the creative activity, a careful analysis of the dynamics of sharing and selection should be promoted. Furthermore, little-c musical activities are not constrained to the use of resources available on site. Remote access to resources and to collaborators may become available through the use of infrastructure such as the internet of musical things. How to strike a balance between presence and remote engagement is an open avenue for ubimus research.

### 2.6.3  *Knowledge heterogeneity*

Everyday music making expands a tendency to include lay participants in creative music making that emerged in the mid 20th century and only recently gained a reliable technological support base. This tendency is represented by diverse initiatives that entail a shift from the hierarchical partitioning and the strict separation of roles promoted by the acoustic-instrumental paradigm. Hence, previous social organisations that enforced a clear stratification between leaders and followers are not well suited to the needs of horizontal knowledge-sharing among participants with highly diverse profiles in unstructured contexts. Knowledge heterogeneity may demand support strategies tailored for diverse technical profiles, non-hierarchical social exchanges and opportunistic resource usage.

### 2.6.4 Dialogics

A strong candidate to support fluid and flexible forms of social organisation in everyday music making is the dialogical proposal laid out by Lima and coworkers (Lima et al., 2012). This approach – grounded on community knowledge-building, with a respect for diversity, and fostering the use of local referents to develop a critical assessment of the social implications of artistic and design practices – is backed by effective results in multiple cultural contexts (Ehn, 1988, Shor and Freire, 1987).

### 2.6.5 Fast knowledge transfer

The three dimensions of creative practice that emerge from recent creativity theories and methods encompass material, socio-cognitive and temporal factors. We believe that these dimensions are interrelated and that any effective creative-practice framework has to deal not only with the elements of the three dimensions, but also needs to account for their relational properties (Keller et al., 2015). An emerging approach to ubimus design involves the adoption of light-weight resources, combined with the usage of local referents. In line with the opportunistic design strategies, the proposed techniques foster fast knowledge construction while relying on general creative factors to encourage the participation of casual stakeholders. Whether these methods will provide a firm ground to develop technologies for musical practices in everyday settings is still an open question. But the initial results look promising.

### Acknowledgements

This project was partially supported by a Productivity Research Grant funded by the Brazilian Research Council (CNPq). Special thanks to Victor Lazzarini for his comments on an early draft of the text.

### Notes

1 An in-depth discussion of compositional units such as the note, the musical object, the operational object or the multimodal event is beyond the scope of this chapter, but it should be addressed to advance towards a workable framework for the analysis of by-products of ubimus practice.
2 Smalley (1986, 82) attempts to describe texture as opposed to gesture, "where gesture is interventionist, texture is laissez-faire; where gesture is occupied with growth and progress, texture is rapt in contemplation; where gesture presses forward, texture marks time; where gesture is carried by external shape, texture turns

to internal activity; where gesture encourages higher-level focus, texture encourages lower-level focus". This poetic depiction is hard to operationalise. Texture depends on persistent conditions that are typical of environmental sounds or synthesised emulations. These conditions can be mimicked by some instrumental techniques, closing the gap between texture-based sound-making and gesture-oriented syntaxes (see Lachenmann's work for multiple examples).

3 Several researchers have argued that artistic proficiency demands a very long temporal investment, exemplified by the ten-thousand hour rule indicated by the studies in technical expertise.

4 Haworth (2015) provides an interesting discussion of the political implications of the adoption of ecologically grounded creative practice.

5 This example was suggested at the UbiMus 2014 by an anonymous reviewer.

6 The persistent censorship and exclusion of the Freirean ideas from the educational public systems in extreme-right regimes is a response to the reflective growth championed by the Brazilian educational movement.

7 Since the initial deployments in 2009, the CSI protocol has gone through several adjustments, including changes in the Likert scale, in the assessment factors and in the support information for the analysis of the data. The tool was relabelled CSI-NAP.

8 https://soundsphere.com.br/beta.

9 See Chapter 10 for details on this and other related technologies.

10 Voice, flute, sax, violin, bass, piano and percussion, including live processing.

11 Current electronic consumer devices tend to last on average two years, with new models and features appearing every six months. This is one of the reasons why ubimus designs need to target sustainability as a key priority. Ten years seems to be a minimum period to test and deploy a technological proposal. But given the current rate of innovation it is hard to say whether a proposal could achieve that horizon.

12 The design of anticipatory strategies for little-c music making might provide a path to deal with the paradox of novelty-in-familiarity. This issue has not been addressed by current musical theories centred on creative practices, so it may constitute one of the challenges for the second wave of ubimus initiatives.

## Bibliography

Aliel, L., D. Keller, and R. Costa (2015). Comprovisation: An approach from aesthetic heuristics in ecocomposition. In *Proceedings of the Brazilian Symposium on Computer Music (SBCM 2015)*, pp. 169–180. Campinas, SP: SBC.

Aliel, L., D. Keller, and R. Costa (2018). The maxwell demon: A proposal for modeling in ecological synthesis in art practices. *Música Hodie 18*(1), 103–116.

Barbosa, L. (2010). Network music performance (performance musical em rede). In D. Keller and R. Budasz (Eds.), *Musical creation and technologies: Interdisciplinary theory and practice*, pp. 180–200. Goiânia, GO: Editora ANPPOM.

Beghetto, R. A. and J. C. Kaufman (2007). Toward a broader conception of creativity: A case for "mini-c" creativity. *Psychology of Aesthetics Creativity and the Arts 1*(2), 73–79.

Bessa, W. R. B., D. Keller, F. M. Farias, E. Ferreira, F. Pinheiro da Silva, and V. S. Pereira (2015). Soundsphere v. 1.0: Documentation and analysis of the initial tests. In F. Z. Oliveira, D. Keller, J. T. de Souza Mendes da Silva, and G. F. Benetti (Eds.), *Proceedings of the Amazon International Symposium on Music (SIMA2015)*. Porto Velho, RO: UNIR.

Boulez, P. (1986). *Orientations: Collected Writings*. London: Faber and Faber.

Bown, O., A. Eldridge, and J. McCormack (2009). Understanding interaction in contemporary digital music: From instruments to behavioural objects. *Organised Sound 14*(2), 188–196.

Brinkmann, P. (2012). *Making Musical Apps: Using the Libpd Sound Engine*. O'Reilly & Associates Incorporated. Sebastopol, CA.

Burtner, M. (2011). Ecosono: Adventures in interactive ecoacoustics in the world. *Organised Sound 16*(3), 234–244.

Ehn, P. (1988). *Work-Oriented Design of Computer Artifacts*. Stockholm: Arbetslivscentrum.

Emmerson, S. (2001, March). From dance! to "dance": Distance and digits. *Computer Music Journal 25*(1), 13–20.

Farias, F. M., D. Keller, V. Lazzarini, and M. H. Lima (2015). Bringing aesthetic interaction into creativity-centered design: The second generation of mixdroid prototypes. *Journal of Cases on Information Technology 4*(17), 53–72.

Ferraz, S. and D. Keller (2014). Preliminary proposal of the in-group, out-group model of collective creation. *Cadernos de Informática 8*(2), 57–67.

Ferreira, E., D. Keller, and M. H. Lima (2016). Sonic sketches in ubiquitous music: Educational perspectives. *Sonic Ideas 8*(15), 12. Electronic paper number: 12.

Fitzmaurice, G., H. Ishii, and W. Buxton (1995). Bricks: Laying the foundations for graspable user interfaces. In *Proceedings of the ACM SIGCHI Conference on Human Factors in Computing Systems (CHI'95)*, pp. 442–449. Denver, Colorado.

Flores, L. V., M. S. Pimenta, E. R. Miranda, E. A. A. Radanovitsck, and D. Keller (2010). Patterns for the design of musical interaction with everyday mobile devices. In *Proceedings of the IX Symposium on Human Factors in Computing Systems*, IHC '10, Belo Horizonte, MG: SBC, pp. 121–128. Belo Horizonte, MG: SBC.

Gibson, J. J. (1977). The theory of affordances. In R. Shaw and J. Bransford (Eds.), *Perceiving, Acting, and Knowing: Toward an Ecological Psychology*, pp. 67–82. Mahwah, NJ: Lawrence Erlbaum Associates.

Glăveanu, V. P. (2013, March). Rewriting the language of creativity: The five a's framework. *Review of General Psychology 17*(1), 69–81.

Gomes, J., N. Pinho, F. Lopes, G. Costa, R. Dias, D. Tudela, and Á. Barbosa (2014). Capture and transformation of urban soundscape data for artistic creation. *Journal of Science and Technology of the Arts 6*(1), 97–109.

Grant, K. A. (2007). Tacit knowledge revisited: We can still learn from polanyi. *The Electronic Journal of Knowledge Management 5*(2), 173–180.

Gurevich, M. and J. R. Treviño (2007). Expression and its discontents: Toward an ecology of musical creation. In *Proceedings of the 7th International Conference on New Interfaces For Musical Expression (NIME '07)*, NIME '07, New York, NY, USA, pp. 106–111. New York, NY: ACM.

Haworth, C. (2015, March). Sound synthesis procedures as texts: An ontological politics in electroacoustic and computer music. *Computer Music Journal 39*(1), 41–58.

Herholz, S. C. and R. J. Zatorre (2012). Musical training as a framework for brain plasticity: Behavior, function, and structure. *Neuron 76*(3), 486 – 502.

Huron, D. (2008, May 21). Lost in music. *Nature 453*, 456–458.

Ivcevic, Z. (2007). Artistic and everyday creativity: An act-frequency approach. *The Journal of Creative Behavior 41*(4), 271–290.

Kane, B. (2007, 4). L'objet sonore maintenant: Pierre schaeffer, sound objects and the phenomenological reduction. *Organised Sound 12*, 15–24.

Kaufman, J. C. and R. A. Beghetto (2009). Beyond big and little: The four c model of creativity. *Review of General Psychology 13*(1), 1–12.

Keller, D. (2000, December). Compositional processes from an ecological perspective. *Leonardo Music Journal 10*, 55–60.

Keller, D. (2004, September). *Paititi: A Multimodal Journey to El Dorado*. Doctor in musical arts thesis, Stanford, CA, USA. [AAI3145550].

Keller, D. (2014). Characterizing resources in ubimus research: Volatility and rivalry. In *Proceedings of the V Workshop in Ubiquitous Music (V UbiMus)*. Vitória, ES: Ubiquitous Music Group.

Keller, D. (2018). Challenges for a second decade of ubimus research: Knowledge transfer in ubimus activities. *Música Hodie 18*(1), 148–165.

Keller, D., D. L. Barreiro, M. Queiroz, and M. S. Pimenta (2010). Anchoring in ubiquitous musical activities. In *Proceedings of the International Computer Music Conference (ICMC 2010)*, pp. 319–326. Ann Arbor, MI: MPublishing, University of Michigan Library.

Keller, D., A. E. B. Barros, F. M. Farias, R. V. Nascimento, M. S. Pimenta, L. V. Flores, E. M. Miletto, E. A. A. Radanovitsck, R. O. Serafini, and J. F. Barraza (2009). Ubiquitous music: Concept and background. In *Proceedings of the National Association of Music Research and Post-Graduation Congress - ANPPOM*, Curitiba, PR: ANPPOM, pp. 539–542. National Association of Music Research and Post-Graduation (ANPPOM): Goiânia, GO: ANPPOM.

Keller, D. and A. R. Brown (2017). Knowledge transfer in ubiquitous musical activities. In *Proceedings of the Brazilian Symposium on Music Research*. Goiania, Brazil.

Keller, D. and R. Costa (2018). Special issue música hodie: Contributions of sound and music computing to current musical and artistic knowledge. *Música Hodie 18*(1), 03–15.

Keller, D., E. Ferreira da Silva, F. Pinheiro da Silva, M. H. Lima, M. S. Pimenta, and V. Lazzarini (2013). Everyday musical creativity: An exploratory study with vocal percussion. In *Proceedings of the National Association of Music Research and Post-Graduation Congress*. Natal, RN: ANPPOM.

Keller, D., L. V. Flores, M. S. Pimenta, A. Capasso, and P. Tinajero (2011). Convergent trends toward ubiquitous music. *Journal of New Music Research 40*(3), 265–276.

Keller, D. and V. Lazzarini (2017a). Ecologically grounded creative practices in ubiquitous music. *Organised Sound 22*(1), 61–72.

Keller, D. and V. Lazzarini (2017b). Theoretical approaches to musical creativity: The ubimus perspective. *Musica Theorica 2*(1), 1–53.

Keller, D., V. Lazzarini, and M. S. Pimenta (2014a). Ubimus through the lens of creativity theories. In D. Keller, V. Lazzarini, and M. S. Pimenta (Eds.), *Ubiquitous Music*, Computational Music Science, pp. 3–23. Berlin: Springer.

Keller, D., V. Lazzarini, and M. S. Pimenta (2014b). *Ubiquitous Music*, Volume XXVIII of *Computation Music Series*. Berlin: Springer.

Keller, D. and M. H. Lima (2016). Supporting everyday creativity in ubiquitous music making. In P. Kostagiolas, K. Martzoukou, and C. Lavranos (Eds.), *Trends in Music Information Seeking, Behavior, and Retrieval for Creativity*, Chapter 5, pp. 78–99. Vancouver, BC: IGI Global Press.

Keller, D., N. Otero, V. Lazzarini, M. S. Pimenta, M. H. Lima, M. Johann, and L. L. Costalonga (2015). Interaction aesthetics and ubiquitous music. In N. Zagalo and P. Blanco (Eds.), *Creativity in the Digital Age*, Series on Cultural Computing, pp. 91–105. London: Springer.

Keller, D., F. Pinheiro da Silva, E. Ferreira, V. Lazzarini, and M. S. Pimenta (2013). Opportunistic design of ubiquitous music systems: The impact of anchoring on creativity. In E. Ferneda, G. Cabral, and D. Keller (Eds.), *Proceedings of the XIV Brazilian Symposium on Computer Music (SBCM 2013)*. Brasília, DF: SBC.

Keller, D., F. Pinheiro da Silva, B. Giorni, M. S. Pimenta, and M. Queiroz (2011). Spatial tagging: An exploratory study. In L. Costalonga, M. S. Pimenta, M. Queiroz, J. Manzolli, M. Gimenes, D. Keller, and R. R. Faria (Eds.), *Proceedings of the 13th Brazilian Symposium on Computer Music (SBCM 2011)*. Vitória, ES: SBC.

Keller, D. and B. Truax (1998). Ecologically based granular synthesis. In *Proceedings of the International Computer Music Conference*, pp. 117–120. Ann Arbor, MI: MPublishing, University of Michigan Library.

Kozbelt, A., R. A. Beghetto, and M. A. Runco (2010). Theories of creativity. In J. C. Kaufman and R. J. Sternberg (Eds.), *The Cambridge Handbook of Creativity*, Volume The Cambridge Handbook of Creativity of *Cambridge Handbooks in Psychology*, pp. 20–47. Cambridge: Cambridge University Press.

Lazzarini, V., D. Keller, C. Kuhn, M. Pimenta, and J. Timoney (2015). Prototyping of ubiquitous music ecosystems. *Journal of Cases on Information Technology 17*(4), 73–85.

Lazzarini, V., S. Yi, J. Timoney, D. Keller, and M. S. Pimenta (2012). The mobile csound platform. In *Proceedings of the International Computer Music Conference*, Ljubljana, pp. 163–167. ICMA: Ann Arbor: MPublishing, University of Michigan Library.

Lewis, G. E. (2000, December). Too many notes: Computers, complexity and culture in voyager. *Leonardo Music Journal 10*, 33–39.

Lima, M. H., D. Keller, M. S. Pimenta, V. Lazzarini, and E. M. Miletto (2012). Creativity-centred design for ubiquitous musical activities: Two case studies. *Journal of Music, Technology and Education 5*(2), 195–222.

Lima, M. H., D. Keller, and L. V. Flores (2017). Ecocomposition and everyday creative musical practices: Theory and practice experience in ubiquitous music research at ufrgs application school with high school students in and out classroom. In *Proceedings of the 1st International Conference of Music for and by Children: Perspectives from children, composers, performers and educators (Musichildren 2017)*. University of Aveiro, Portugal.

McCrae, R. and P. Costa (1996). Toward a new generation of personality theories: Theoretical contexts for the five-factor model. In J. S. Wiggins (Ed.), *The Five-Factor Model of Personality: Theoretical Perspectives*, pp. 51–87. New York, NY: Guilford Press.

Melo, M. T. S. and D. Keller (2013, November). Tocaflor: Exploration of the graphic-procedural metaphor in a mixed media artwork. In D. Keller and M. A. Scarpellini (Eds.), *Proceedings of the Amazon International Symposium on Music (SIMA2013)*. Rio Branco, AC: EDUFAC.

Miletto, E. M., M. S. Pimenta, F. Bouchet, J.-P. Sansonnet, and D. Keller (2011). Principles for music creation by novices in networked music environments. *Journal of New Music Research 40*(3), 205–216.

Nance, R. (2018). Music as a plastic art: An ecological strategy facilitating emergence in an instrumental composition ecology. In *Proceedings of the Ubiquitous Music Workshop (UbiMus 2018)*. São João del Rei, MG: Ubiquitous Music Group.

Opie, T. and A. Brown (2006). An introduction to eco-structuralism. In *Proceedings of the International Computer Music Conference (ICMC 2006)*, New Orleans, LO, pp. 9–12. Ann Arbor: MPublishing, University of Michigan Library.

Parmar, R. (2012). The garden of adumbrations: Reimagining environmental composition. *Organised Sound 17*(3), 202–210.

Pereira, V. S., S. L. Silva, W. R. B. Bessa, T. R. Alcântara-Silva, and D. Keller (2018). Soundsphere: Participatory design as a strategy to develop sustainable technologies in ubiquitous music. *Sonic Ideas 10*(19), 7–44. Electronic paper number 7.

Pinheiro da Silva, F., D. Keller, E. Ferreira, M. S. Pimenta, and V. Lazzarini (2013). Everyday musical creativity: Exploratory study of ubiquitous musical activities. *Música Hodie 13*, 64–79.

Polanyi, M. (1958). *Personal Knowledge: Towards a Post-critical Philosophy*. Harper torchbooks. London: Routledge.

Radanovitsck, E. A. A., D. Keller, L. V. Flores, M. S. Pimenta, and M. Queiroz (2011). mixdroid: Time tagging for creative activities. In L. Costalonga, M. S. Pimenta, M. Queiroz, J. Manzolli, M. Gimenes, D. Keller, and R. R. Farias (Eds.), *Proceedings of the XIII Brazilian Symposium on Computer Music (SBCM 2011)*, Vitória, ES: SBC. Vitória, ES: SBC.

Rhodes, M. (1961). An analysis of creativity. *The Phi Delta Kappan 42*, 305–311.

Richards, R. (2007). Everyday creativity and the arts. *World Futures 63*(7), 500–525.

Richards, R., D. K. Kinney, M. Benet, and A. P. Merzel (1988). Assessing everyday creativity: Characteristics of the lifetime creativity scales and validation with three large samples. *Journal of Personality and Social Psychology 54*, 476–485.

Root-Bernstein, R. and M. Root-Bernstein (2004). Artistic scientists and scientific artists: The link between polymathy and creativity. In R. J. Sternberg, E. L. Grigorenko, and J. L. Singer (Eds.), *Creativity: From Potential to Realization*, Chapter 8, pp. 127–151. Washington, DC, US: American Psychological Association.

Rubenson, D. L. and M. A. Runco (1992). The psychoeconomic approach to creativity. *New Ideas in Psychology 10*(2), 131–147.

Rubenson, D. L. and M. A. Runco (1995). The psychoeconomic view of creative work in groups and organizations. *Creativity and Innovation Management 4*(4), 232–241.

Sawyer, K. and S. DeZutter (2009, 05). Distributed creativity: How collective creations emerge from collaboration. *Psychology of Aesthetics, Creativity, and the Arts 3*, 81–92.

Shor, I. and P. Freire (1987). What is the 'dialogical method' of teaching? *Journal of Education 169*(3), 11–31.

Simonton, D. K. (1990). History, chemistry, psychology, and genius: An intellectual autobiography of historiometry. In M. A. Runco and R. S. Albert (Eds.), *Theories of Creativity*, pp. 92–115. Newbury Park, CA: Sage.

Smalley, D. (1986). Spectro-morphology and structuring processes. In S. Emmerson (Ed.), *The Language of Electroacoustic Music*. London: Palgrave Macmillan.

Stables, R., S. Enderby, B. D. Man, G. Fazekas, and J. D. Reiss (2014). Safe: A system for the extraction and retrieval of semantic audio descriptors. In *Proceedings of the 15th International Society for Music Information Retrieval Conference (ISMIR 2014)*. Taipei, Taiwan: ISMIR.

Sternberg, R. and T. Lubart (1991). An investment theory of creativity and its development. *Human Development 34*(1), 1–31.

Stolfi, A. S., A. Milo, and M. Barthet (2019). Playsound.space: Improvising in the browser with semantic sound objects. *Journal of New Music Research 48*(4), 366–384.

Tanaka, A. (2009). Sensor-based musical instruments and interactive music. In R. T. Dean (Ed.), *The Oxford Handbook of Computer Music*, Oxford Handbooks, Chapter 12, pp. 233–257. New York, NY: Oxford University Press.

Turchet, L., C. Fischione, G. Essl, D. Keller, and M. Barthet (2018). Internet of musical things: Vision and challenges. *IEEE Access 6*, 61994–62017.

Weisberg, R. W. (1993). *Creativity: Beyond the Myth of Genius*. Books in psychology. New York, NY: W. H. Freeman.

Wenger, E. (2010). Communities of practice and social learning systems: The career of a concept. In C. Blackmore (Ed.), *Social Learning Systems and Communities of Practice*, pp. 179–198. London: Springer.

Wessel, D. and M. Wright (2002, September). Problems and prospects for intimate musical control of computers. *Computer Music Journal 26*(3), 11–22.

Windsor, W. L. (1995). *A Perceptual Approach to the Description and Analysis of Acousmatic Music*. Doctoral thesis in music, London: City University.

Wunderlich, F. M. (2013). Place-temporality and urban place-rhythms in urban analysis and design: An aesthetic akin to music. *Journal of Urban Design 18*(3), 383–408.

Xenakis, I. (1992). *Formalized Music: Thought and Mathematics in Composition*. Harmonologia series. Hillsdale, NY: Pendragon Press.

Zawacki, L. and M. Johann (2012). A prospective analysis of analog audio recording with web servers. In *Anais do Workshop em Música Ubíqua / Proceedings of the Ubiquitous Music Workshop (UbiMus 2012)*. São Paulo, SP: Ubiquitous Music Group.

# 3   DIY electronics for ubiquitous music ecosystems

*Joseph Timoney, Victor Lazzarini, and Damián Keller*

Many of the innovations in electronic musical instruments have for a long time had a strong link with the phenomenon of DIY (Do-It-Yourself) electronics. Since the early days of electronic music, composers, instrumentalists, and inventors had to forge a creative relationship in order to realise their particular ideas and ambitions, which went beyond the established practice. Such innovations eventually took a foothold in mainstream culture, supported by an interest in home-made electronics, spawning successful commercial enterprises, some of which still exist today. Particularly, starting in the post-second world war period, some of these developments in DIY electronics have strongly influenced the musical landscape. More recently, the DIY culture has not only become pervasive, but is also fuelling a new wave in interactive electronic art, as it fosters major technological shifts.

This new impetus for DIY hardware has been powered by the appearance of low-cost microcontroller units that are easily programmable using high-level languages. Furthermore, new computer interfacing standards such as the Universal Serial Bus (USB), which is present in most modern platforms, have greatly simplified some of the technical requirements for software transfer and peripheral communications. This, allied with free, libre, and open-source (FLOSS) (DiBona and Ockman, 1999) sharing of computer code, has lowered significantly the level of expertise required for practitioners.

New low-cost general-purpose hardware platforms such as the Arduino, Raspberry PI, Intel Galileo and Edison, and BeagleBone Black have allowed the development of custom, and sometimes novel, sound synthesisers, effects units, and controllers. The imagination of an individual designer combined with a certain level of technical facility can reap the benefits of a wide range of possibilities offered by the home music electronics workshop. Furthermore, the adoption of FLOSS principles means that ideas can be shared and modified to both the individual's and the community's requirements. This potential suggests a fertile ground for ubimus exploration and development. As an instance of this, composers and musicians are now able to access and manipulate these technologies for their own creative applications very successfully, as reported in Chapter 4.

In this chapter, we will examine briefly the relationship between the history of electronic musical instruments and DIY hardware. This will be followed by an assessment of the ties and tensions between analogue and digital technologies. We then look at the possibilities of the currently available microcontroller technologies, discussing some of its musical applications. In complement to this we look at DIY electronics as a platform, within the scope of ubimus.

## 3.1 DIY musical hardware: an abridged history

The early days of electronic instrument design were dominated by individual inventors who pursued their original ideas in a home-industry environment, as they were not initially supported by the established music instrument industry. Together with the pioneers of new mechanical instruments, such as the Futurists (Russolo, 1967), they developed new designs that were largely free of the constraints of existing forms of music-making. Some of these novel home-made instruments enjoyed a reasonable level of success and were eventually produced commercially in small numbers by some manufacturers. An early example of this was the *Theremin* (Theremin, 1928), created by Leon Theremin in the early twenties, and then licensed to the RCA Corporation for commercial exploitation. In France, another such instrument was the *Ondes Martenot* (Russcol, 1972), invented by Maurice Martenot in the same decade, which was adopted by some composers as a new component of the orchestral palette. The *Trautonium* (Holmes, 2008), developed by Friedrich Trautwein in Germany, also gained some prominence, being later produced by Telefunken.

These three instruments provided innovative approaches to sound production and control. The Theremin, a box fitted with two aerials used to control amplitude and pitch, allowed players to interact with thin air to control these parameters, whereas the other two used physical contacts between performer and instrument: a combination of a ribbon for pitch and switch for amplitude in the case of the Ondes Martenot, and a resistor-wire metal plate in the Trautonium. These early examples provided a measure of how the medium of electronics could be exploited in very original ways and have been a continuous source of inspiration for many electronic music practitioners along the years.

Apart from individual efforts such as these, experimentation with non-standard electronic sound-making devices in the period before the second world war was limited to some larger organisations with research interests in the area. For instance, at Bell Telephone Laboratories, two important inventions were developed, the voder and the vocoder (Dudley, 1938). These were early attempts to create speech synthesisers that could be used for telephone communications, and their principles were used many years later in a number of audio processing designs. It is clear that access to affordable hardware and to technical know-how was very limited, which curtailed any widespread developments in electronics for sound and music until the establishment of a strong DIY electronics movement.

### 3.1.1  The post-second world war beginnings

The history of post-second world war electronic musical tools is linked with a DIY electronics subculture that grew up alongside it. Two factors were important for this: an incipient usage of electronic sound by composers and musicians, and a general absence of commercial electronic instruments. In addition, much of the existing sound amplification and recording equipment was fairly expensive and difficult to maintain. A few organisations were able to provide access to these sonic studios, as in the case of Musique Concrète and Elektronische Musik studios set up by Radio France and the West German Radio, in Europe, and the Columbia-Princeton Electronic Music Centre in the United States (Cross, 1968). In general, however, in the immediate post-war period, access to electronic music-making devices was limited to the few musicians that possessed the musical training and had access to institutional support.

In North America, a group of musicians embraced the DIY principles in a very dedicated way, forming a group sometimes referred to as "Music for Magnetic Tape", led by the seminal composer John Cage. Their musical practice was mostly organised around tape editing and mixing, but also involved the building of custom devices. From this group emerged the celebrated partnership of Louis and Bebe Barron, who wrote the score for the 1956 sci-fi movie *Forbidden Planet* (Wierzbicki, 2005). This was the first completely electronic film score, created using their own homemade sound generators, and was in general very innovative in the way new sounds were incorporated into a movie soundtrack. In a more conventional musical setting, another custom-instrument pioneer was Raymond Scott, credited with the development of the *electronium*, and acknowledged as the designer of the first electronic sequencer (Blom and Winner, 2000).

In a separate development, DIY kits for electronic amplifiers were introduced by a number of companies from the late 1940s, targeting primarily the hi-fi hobbyist market. Examples of such companies were Heathkit (Kaeding, 2015) and Dynaco (Dunn, 2001), whose founder, David Hafler, was interested in selling entire amplifiers as build-it-yourself kits, a somewhat novel approach. The average hi-fi enthusiast was generally provided with a schematic, a choice of output transformer (which determined the power of the final amplifier), and selected parts and tubes, hand-crafting his/her unique components on a homemade chassis. Hafler's idea was to supply preassembled, tested circuit boards which only needed to be connected to the transformers, controls and power supply to produce a working unit. From the user perspective, the attraction of buying a kit and assembling it oneself was cost: it was the most economical option to good-quality audio equipment.

The development of the music electronics DIY market in the fifties is illustrated by the appearance of Theremin kits. The Theremin, although not having a widespread adoption in concert or popular music, had been used in a number of motion picture soundtracks which followed in the wake of the Barrons' pioneer work, and became a popular instrument for the hobbyist. Robert

Moog's first product was such a kit (Wepman, 2000) before he embarked on developing the principles of voltage-controlled modules and synthesisers, which became the basis of many electronic musical instruments produced in the sixties and seventies. The use of control voltage (CV) to regulate device parameters and to carry signals between various components of an instrument was an important breakthrough of this era, allowing for the first time a standard means of interfacing electronic musical instruments.

During the sixties, popular music helped bring the experience of electronic sound to a wider audience. The widespread use of electric instruments by musicians such as Jimi Hendrix (Murray, 2005), and the experimental use of newly developed sound devices, such as custom effects circuits and studio equipment, provided a strong motivation for the electronics DIY enthusiast. By the early seventies, affordable commercially made electronic devices became available, which led to their popularity spreading quickly among musicians (Pinch and Trocco, 2004). DIY electronics continued to develop alongside this, with companies such as PAiA providing full synthesiser kits (PAiA Corporation, 2015), and hobbyist magazines publishing circuit designs. In particular, a variety of sound processing algorithms (such as distortion, filters, and phase shifters) were made popular through these publications, most of which were of a complexity level at the reach of the non-specialist. Some aspects of sound tools construction, however, remained less straightforward than others. For instance, while assembling a sound generating circuit was generally accessible, constructing controllers such as keyboards was still a significant hurdle.

### 3.1.2   The eighties and decline

The end of the seventies was a turning point in synthesiser designs as the first instrument with a full microprocessor control appeared, the Sequential Circuits' *Prophet 5* (Vail, 2000). This was a significant development for electronic music instruments. Within a few years, the musical instrument digital interface (MIDI) protocol was developed and introduced by a consortium of music companies. Designed for communications between electronic instruments, it became, and still is, an industry standard (Manning, 2004). MIDI opened up a completely new set of possibilities for interaction with a variety of devices. In particular, as microcomputer-powered personal computers (PCs) became widespread, it enabled music instruments to be easily controlled by software. Furthermore, as a standard protocol, MIDI opened a gateway to the musical use of devices that were not originally designed for artistic purposes.

This era saw a decline in the popularity of music instrument kit building, for a number of reasons. One of these was that the popularity of the PC meant that writing programs for musical purposes became more attractive than hardware electronics. Music software sidestepped many problems and limitations including cost, and it also offered ease of debugging and flexibility to change. Additionally, as synthesisers became reliant on microprocessors, building these required specialised skills such as assembly language programming. From the music instrument industry perspective, falling production prices, with the development of low-cost assembly-line processes for mass-produced electronics, made finished products more affordable. This, in turn, reduced the motivation to offer cost-saving alternatives to these instruments and devices.

Another practical difficulty was the introduction of a surface mount integrated circuit (IC) components. Printed circuit boards (PCBs) using these ICs are hard to assemble by hand. Consequently, through-hole parts, which were preferred by kit builders, became more expensive as surface mount parts were favoured by industry. Lastly, the growing popularity of application specific integrated circuits (ASICs), particularly in digital equipment, means that fewer designs were based solely on standard off-the-shelf components that could be obtained by non-specialists.

### 3.1.3   FLOSS software

In tandem with the decline in the popularity of DIY hardware, there was a significant development of music and media software for general-purpose microprocessor computers. This was helped by the nascent FLOSS movement, and by the changes in communication, information sharing, and education opportunities, offered by the internet and the word-wide web (WWW). The enormous breadth of access to, and interactions with, millions of people, the low cost of storage, and the ease of distribution of software artefacts allowed for the development of code communities, whose practice was analogous to the DIY hardware hobbyists of previous decades.

While access to open-source software and sharing of code had been a common practice since the early days of music computing (Lazzarini, 2013), the great accessibility hurdle to software use (especially in areas such as music and creative arts) was only overcome by the presence of affordable hardware platforms, and reliable information sources. With these two elements in place, the FLOSS movement flourished, giving rise to a community of programmers, *coders*, who did not necessarily stem from the traditional computer science training route. Also, as sound-making devices, computers became less cumbersome and finally more realtime capable, which enabled a migration away from outboard MIDI-controlled instruments towards computer-generated audio.

The impacts of the FLOSS DIY software communities have been multiple. They fostered the means of disseminating ideas and sharing programs, providing an infrastructure that has allowed new procedures to flourish. In music software, there are many successful packages whose development stems from these communities, which are broadly equivalent to commercially available software, and also in some cases offer features that are beyond these. A remarkable example of such communities in terms of their level of activity is the one centred on audio and music software for the Linux operating system (Phillips, 2000). The proliferation of eager programmers, high-quality development tools, and a wide user base providing constant feedback allow FLOSS communities to be both sources of innovation and sustainability.

### 3.1.4   Rebirth of DIY hardware

In recent years there has been a significant resurgence in DIY hardware, and this trend has been mirrored within electronic music. It began with projects such as MidiBox (Klose, 2019), and followed on with the desire to recreate the older analogue instruments that had been long discontinued by the commercial manufacturers. The developments in low cost and easily programmable microcontroller platforms have provided further impetus. This initial thrust has been further enhanced by drivers such as internet videos and publications like the Make magazine (Dougherty and Huss, 2015), with its associated *maker movement* (Dougherty and Maxwell, 2012).

The MidiBox project started in the late nineties and aimed to provide a strictly open-source platform for the development of MIDI controller devices. The primary application was a sequencer, introduced at a time many music instrument companies significantly scaled back on the production of such devices. Its design is modular: there is a MidiBox core along with various analogue and digital input and output board designs, providing a flexible set of modules that could be freely combined. The core system is powered by a microcontroller, for which a MidiBox operating system code is freely available for adaptation to particular projects. To support this, an internet forum infrastructure, similar to that used for FLOSS, has been employed by the user community for sharing code and configurations. This type of flexibility made the MidiBox platform very popular and provided a model that has been adopted by many other DIY communities.

For some applications, MIDI was superseded by Open Sound Control (OSC), which is a newer protocol for the control of media devices. One of the advantages of OSC is that it does not rely on dedicated hardware, and it is normally implemented using the internet protocol (IP), by means of the user datagram transport protocol (UDP) (Wright and Freed, 1997). As many of the music platforms already employed some form of network connectivity via IP, OSC became a very good fit. It also provides, as the name indicates, a more open and flexible means of sending control messages, including much better precision beyond what the original MIDI protocol can deliver. In critical applications, such as the ones described in Chapter 11, OSC is essential, as it is the only means capable of transmitting the kind of data required by crossadaptive processing.

Another phenomenon that took place since the early years of the new century has been the return of analogue synthesiser instruments. While in the seventies most devices were of the subtractive type using analogue voicing circuits, in the eighties, there was a prevalence of digital instruments. The introduction of these began with frequency modulation (FM)-based synthesisers and continued with the development of samplers, sample-playback, and other methods of digital signal processing (DSP) for sound generation (Russ, 2012). In the nineties, as subtractive synthesis became popular again with musicians and manufacturers, synthesisers were still mostly built using DSP ICs.

This was followed by nostalgia for older the analogue equipment, with many users asserting that digital equipment was not of the same high audio quality standard. Reinforcing this trend, some popular music genres, such as electronic dance music (EDM), had been employing analogue instruments from an early stage. As much of the music instrument industry had discontinued the production of analogue equipment, access to these instruments was limited to the second-hand market, pushing their costs outside the financial reach of many musicians.

While companies refused to contemplate a return to analogue, a group of home professionals and new kit companies appeared in response to the demand. A prime example is the xOxbOx, which reproduced the Roland TB-303 bass synthesiser (Fried, 2015). Its continuing popularity, even after the original kits were taken off production, led other small companies to provide the necessary PCBs and parts, as well as completely finished units. Fuelled by a similar interest in rediscovering the sound of classic effects units of the past, small suppliers started to make analogue guitar-effects pedals (Tonepad, 2015).

From a practical perspective, in general, most new kits will eschew surface mount parts, sticking with through-hole components only. When the surface mount ICs are used, they are often pre-mounted on a PCB or the assembly using them will be pre-wired to prevent damage from poor construction. The phenomenon of the internet video has been a key contributor to the rebirth of DIY hardware, as it has facilitated the quick dissemination of information through detailed demonstration. The video medium has never been particularly important for the FLOSS software movement, but for the practicalities of constructing electronics projects, it has been a significant educational tool.

As we noted before, this rise in the interest of DIY hardware for audio and music is part of a wider maker movement (Blikstein, 2013). The Make magazine, first published in 2005, began in 2006 to promote events known as Maker Faires, which have been embraced by communities interested in sharing and celebrating DIY and open-source technology and projects. Many of these initiatives combine hardware and software elements, sometimes referred to as *physical computing* (O'Sullivan and Igoe, 2004), and have been facilitated by the great improvements in microcontroller technologies, particularly in terms of their ease of programmability. In fact, the FLOSS movement has been influential to the new hardware enthusiasts, who adopted much of the dissemination infrastructure set up and used by the software community. The rebirth of DIY hardware has been combined with the advances in FLOSS, allowing new programmable musical devices to exist beyond the traditional general-purpose desktop and laptop platforms.

## 3.2   Analogue and digital hardware

The DIY hardware revival has not solely been concerned with implementing new versions of the older analogue technology. In fact, a number of designs for DIY digital instruments and effects also appeared. However, the profile and popularity of analogue hardware has been higher. This can be attributed to a number of factors. Firstly, by the end of the nineties much of the musical instrument industry had shifted towards digital implementations, making it easy and affordable to purchase commercial standard, ready-made digital devices. Secondly, many of the new analogue instruments and devices have not been placed at an affordable price range for artists and hobbyists. Additionally, many companies, such as Roland, did not return to marketing analogue products, and their classic designs were still not widely available.

A more abstract aspect was the debate on the sound differences between analogue and digital instruments. This parallels the audiophile phenomenon, where some musicians and enthusiasts would argue that analogue hardware produces a superior warmth and *fatness* (an uncertain qualitative assessment involving timbral depth and sound body). The relative rarity of analogue devices in the commercial marketplace meant that these qualities were never assessed precisely and gained a mythical status amongst users. Part of this debate has not been very well informed, confounding questions of musical quality, creativity, and hardware tools. It can be argued that a well-made digital instrument can provide as much musical scope as an analogue one. But the issues involved cannot be settled through assessments of musical products or by fulfilling support infrastructure requirements. Recent advances in ubimus research point to a complex set of factors to be considered (Keller et al., 2014b).

It is worth considering how long such preference for the sounds of older analogue equipment will last. As digital emulations get better and better, the next generation of users may not care as much for the *real thing* as the *current* one, and instead may have a completely different set of musical priorities. In fact, it is possible that artists become more interested in emerging qualities produced by the combination of local environmental features enhanced by mobile and distributed resources than in the fixed set of sonic possibilities provided by the acoustic-instrumental model (Burtner, 2011, Di Scipio, 2014, Keller et al., 2011). Moreover, many practitioners of electronic music have been absorbed with building their own custom tools rather than using ready-made instruments, something that has been supported by the appearance of a new wave of microcontroller technologies, allowing the development of the physical computing practice.

## 3.3 Microcontroller technologies

A microcontroller is a kind of microprocessor that, in addition to the central processing unit (CPU), also includes random-access memory (RAM), modifiable read-only memory (flash ROM) memory, digital input and output (I/O), analogue-to-digital converters, and even comparators, on a single die/package. Originally, microcontrollers could only be programmed using assembly language. However, most software developers prefer programming in high-level languages, which motivated vendors to provide tools for this, in particular C language compilers and libraries. The early development practice would involve users building a complete supporting circuit around the bare microcontroller IC, rather than employing a more or less complete board, which could simply be programmed. Before the widespread use of flash memory, such systems depended on earlier types of programmable ROM (e.g. electronically erasable programmable ROM, EEPROM), for which the required peripheral hardware (programmer devices) was beyond the reach of the hobbyist or artist.

The first proper microcontroller board for hobbyists appeared in the nineties with the introduction of the BASIC Stamp (Paralax Corporation, 2015). This is a microcontroller with a small, specialised BASIC language interpreter (PBASIC) built into its ROM, making it easy to program. The peripheral interface controller (PIC) microcontroller family was also released around the same time (Verle, 2008). PICs had a modifiable flash ROM that could be programmed in assembly language. A complete board based version, the PICAXE, the PIC alternative to the BASIC stamp, appeared around the turn of the century. The PICAXE microcontrollers are pre-programmed with an interpreter (PICAXE, 2015) similar to the BASIC Stamp but using internal EEPROM instead, thus reducing cost. This also allows downloads to be made with a simple serial connection eliminating the need for a dedicated PIC programmer hardware.

The BASIC Stamp and the PIC have been used by a number of hobbyists to build MIDI controllers. The MidiBox project discussed in Section 3.1.4 is one of them, which was originally built using PIC microcontrollers. Since then the design has shifted to using an STM32F4 microcontroller, and more recently NXP's LPC1769 module. Another useful application of the PIC has been to build MIDI-to-CV converters to control analogue synth circuits. The PICAXE interestingly has not been used by hobbyists for any well-known DIY musical tools.

Neither the Basic Stamp nor the medium price-range PICs (such as the PIC16F84) were particularly suited to simultaneous MIDI reception and transmission as they do not support buffered serial communications. On the Basic Stamp II, any MIDI data coming in while the Stamp is processing will be lost. On a PIC, the code must be carefully designed to interleave serial reads and other processing at the sub-MIDI bit level to avoid loss of data. In addition to such MIDI issues, the complicated nature of these devices has been a barrier to their general uptake. They require a good technical background, with hardware and software skills to be used effectively. This eliminates the casual hobbyist and those with an idea but lacking the know-how.

### 3.3.1    The Arduino development board

Arduino started in 2005 as a student project at the Design Institute of Ivrea, Italy (Arduino, 2019). The original motivation was to have a lower-cost alternative to the BASIC Stamp. The original Arduino board consists of an Atmel 8-bit AVR microcontroller with complementary components to facilitate programming and incorporation into other circuits. The Atmel Company was set up in the mid-1980s and the AVR range was introduced in the mid-1990s (Atmel Corporation, 2015). These products were very popular with hobbyists because of a few key features, which include ease of programming, strong cross-platform development support, low cost, through-hole availability, a good set of peripherals, and low power consumption.

The integrated development environment (IDE) for the Arduino system is based on the AVR C Compiler and an implementation of the Wiring library (Noble and Joshua, 2009). The IDE is cross-platform and the use of Wiring provides a high-level programming system that is easier for novices to use than plain C, and the applications (known as sketches) are very small. Input and output operations are simple to write, and the board design allows direct access to the I/O pins of the microcontroller. Thus connecting it to items such as external sensors and displays is straightforward. The I/O pins are separated into digital inputs and outputs and analogue inputs and outputs. A drawback is that analogue output is only possible through a pulse-wave modulation (PWM) waveform. An important aspect of the Arduino is the standard way that connectors are exposed, allowing the CPU board to be connected to a variety of interchangeable add-on module boards known as shields. Some shields communicate with the Arduino board directly over various pins, but many shields are individually addressable via an $I^2C$ serial bus, allowing many shields to be stacked and used in parallel.

## 3.4 Low-cost general-purpose computing devices

In addition to the microcontroller boards, a recent development has been the availability of very small, low-cost, general-purpose computers. These are generally based on low-power CPUs and are provided in bare development boards, to which peripherals such as keyboards, monitors, and sound cards can be added. Unlike the microcontrollers discussed in Section 3.3, these devices run full operating system software, generally based on the Linux kernel, providing more computing power and wider support for programming languages. This means that such boards can take advantage of existing music software (synthesisers, music programming languages), which can be easily ported to the platform.

### 3.4.1  Raspberry PI

The Raspberry PI is a low cost credit card-sized computer running Linux (Upton, 2015). It comes with a version of the Debian software distribution named *Raspbian*, but it is capable of operating with other distributions. The first version had a 32-bit ARM-architecture (arm-v6) processor System-on-a-Chip[1] (SoC), running at 700 MHz. The board includes a number of IO connections: composite video out, analogue audio out, external USB port, Ethernet port, and High-Definition Multimedia Interface (HDMI) connector. OS software and user disk can be provided via an SD card. Updated versions of the PI have been released since 2015, shipping with increasingly more powerful processors with multiple cores and running at higher clock rates.

Hybrid boards integrating Arduino support to the Raspberry PI computer have also been released, allowing the fitting of Raspberry PI to Arduino shields. These include, for instance, the Gertduino board (van Loo, 2015), which has the additional features of a real-time clock, 16MHz oscillator, infrared data access (IRDA) interface, serial port (RS232) level converter, and a battery back-up power supply for the Atmega-48 microcontroller. Combinations of Arduino and Raspberry PI are also very common, and applications can be quite varied. One good example is the development of modules for synthesisers, where synthesis software running on the Raspberry PI can take advantage of the interfacing capabilities of Arduino (Ikenberry and Lim, 2013).

### 3.4.2   BeagleBone black

The BeagleBone black is a device launched in April 2013 (Beaglebone, 2015), which uses a 1GHz Sitara ARM Cortex-A8 processor. It also runs OSs based on the Linux kernel (Ubuntu, Android). It is an alternative to the Raspberry PI, which can be easier to set up, also featuring better connectivity. It has a faster processor, but its graphics and audio performance are poorer. Due to a much smaller user community, it has less available options for add-on boards, and support is not as widely present as for the Raspberry PI. However, there are various interesting music projects based on this hardware, such as the one reported in (Batchelor and Wignall, 2013). Similarly to the Raspberry PI, these computers are capable of running standard Linux distributions, or variations of these, which facilitates the porting of desktop applications.

### 3.4.3   Intel Galileo and Edison

The Intel Galileo board (Intel Corporation, 2015b) is an embedded systems development board based on the Quark system-on-chip (SoC), which includes an Arduino-like functionality (and compatibility with some existing extension shields and software). The board can be used as a straight replacement for the Arduino Uno boards, with a customised Arduino IDE that allows programming of sketches using the Wiring library. The Galileo, however, runs under a Linux-based operating system, and thus allows other modes of application that are not restricted to Arduino IDE sketches, and which can take more complete advantage of the board capabilities.

The Galileo has been produced in two models (GEN1 and GEN2). The two share some basic attributes that include a Quark processor, which has the same instruction set to the Pentium, or i586, CPU, and contains a single core running at 400 MHz (also known as "Clanton"), 10/100Mbit ethernet, PCI Express, USB 2.0 device and host interfaces, and microSD card reader. GEN1 boards have a 3.5-mm RS-232 connector, whereas GEN2 replaces this with a six-pin Transistor-Transistor Logic (TTL) Universal asynchronous receiver-transmitter (UART) header that is compatible with standard adaptors. The Galileo has been demonstrated as a platform for ubimus in (Lazzarini et al., 2015), where a case study for an embedded audio synthesiser is discussed, and a number of potential applications are shown.

The Intel edison (Intel Corporation, 2015a) is an even smaller system, which is provided as a 35.5 by 25.0 mm board. This includes the complete computer (an Intel Atom-based SoC), 1 GB memory, 4 GB flash storage, a wireless network (WiFi) interface, and Arduino connectivity. For development and debugging, it can be plugged to a Galileo-size breakout board with headers for all the different IO elements, plus USB and power supply inputs. It can also be plugged to other small-size boards to give access to the various types of connectivity as needed (maintaining the overall size of the system to a minimum). The Atom processor, running also at 500 MHz, provides more processing power than the Galileo.

As in the other cases, the fact that these boards are fully operational Linux computers allow them to be used as the core of a general-purpose digital musical instrument, seizing the power of systems such as Csound (Lazzarini et al., 2016). With this software, complete programmable music tools can be built. Good-quality and low-latency audio can be achieved via the use of USB audio interfaces, and a realtime preemptive kernel, both of which are available to users. Also, the small size of these computing devices allows artists to consider various ways of deployment for ubimus activities (in installations, wearables, etc).

### 3.4.4  Hard-realtime platforms

While the technology of DIY platforms has enabled a variety of approaches in the creation of music-making instruments, much of it was not purposely designed for these applications. As we have noted, for example, Raspberry PI and Galileo/Edison boards are general-purpose computing platforms, and likewise, Arduino-type hardware provides support for a broad range of connectivity applications. In general, it is possible to say that they have not been designed particularly with a hard-realtime constraint, which is a key aspect in the design of performance-oriented computer music instruments. This enables lower latency in audio processing, providing a faster reaction time. In McPherson (2016), a number of DIY platforms have been tested with regards to this and shown not to perform very reactively. In particular, the threshold of 10 ms latency, which has been established as a test benchmark (Wessel and Wright, 2002) was not achieved by many of the systems tested. We should note that depending on the context, latencies not exceeding 4 ms may be required (Rubine and McAvinney, 1990).

It is clear that reactive music performance systems based on DIY hardware need to be supported by a custom-designed platform. An example of this is the Bela platform (McPherson and Zappi, 2015), which is a low-latency audio and sensor platform designed to be plugged to a general-purpose computing platform (the BeagleBone Black computer, cf. Section 3.4.2). The Bela is in part a hardware platform, providing audio, as well as control analogue and digital, IO, and software, comprising of a custom real-time Linux kernel, based on the Xenomai framework (Brown and Martin, 2010). This allows a preemptive audio task that can use very small buffers for ultra-low latency (buffering can be as short as 46 µs). The Bela platform represents the other end of the spectrum from the typical repurposing attitude of DIY instrument-building. Here, instead of making do with general-purpose or adapted technologies, we have a highly customised platform that allows the design of specialised instruments, whose performance may be compared to engineered off-the-shelf solutions. Bela provides support for user-developed C++ programs and for music programming languages such as Csound.

Similarly, the ELK platform MindMusicLabs (2019), presented as a music application operating system, is a hard-realtime environment also based on Linux and Xenomai. It is deployable in a variety of computing hardware, from Raspberry PI to more specialised devices. The system guarantees 1-ms round-trip latencies, which makes it very reactive and suitable for most of the demanding applications. The system is designed to work with the VST plugin standard (Steinberg, 2019), as it is centred around a host software, called *sushi*, that is described as a headless (i.e., with no graphical user interface) digital audio workstation (DAW). It has support for the Csound language via plugins created with Cabbage (a plugin generator that wraps Csound code inside a VST).

### 3.5   DIY electronics in the ubimus context

In the light of what has been presented here, it is now possible to speak of a DIY movement, which originated in Engineering, but is now firmly grounded in the Creative Industries. The crossover from a strictly hobbyist concern to an artistic and creative one has followed the development of increasingly flexible, and programmable, devices and components. The design of these has been characterised by an open, general-purpose, approach that provides plenty of scope for innovation. In this scenario, we can see that two particular aspects become significant for the concerns of ubimus: the use of DIY electronics as a platform for creativity, and the emergence of an Internet of Musical Things (IoMusT) (Keller and Lazzarini, 2017, Lazzarini et al., 2015, Turchet et al., 2018). It follows from these that we can think of a ubimus ecosystem that is not only composed of off-the-shelf production devices, on which custom software is run but of an open range of hardware and software configurations that can be assembled from scratch.

### 3.5.1 DIY as a creativity exploration platform

Creativity in DIY electronics can be seen from a twofold perspective. First, there is the innovation in the design of the *instrument*, the device or devices that will be employed in an artistic setting. Secondly, we have the artwork in which this instrument is inserted. One of the more salient aspects of these two creative actions is how they are intertwined. While we have seen examples of this throughout the history of music (one can think of the work of the Futurist composers in designing and composing for new instruments), the electronics DIY environment fosters this dual role of the artist in creating a piece of art through the integrated design of tools and the work in which they are used. In many cases, it is impossible to distinguish these two components of the work as discrete steps in the artistic process.

The role of the artist is now less strictly defined, and we have moved on from the tradition of very specialised roles (e.g. the *composer*, the *performer*, the *technician*), into a practice that embraces a variety of interconnected skills. As a counterpart to this, there is scope for exploring creativity in this continuum of activities. It is a trait of the maker movement (Dougherty, 2012) that creative actions are recognised from a variety of angles beyond what was considered purely *the artistic*, influencing and shaping education, business and government affairs. As a platform, DIY provides a wide scope for the development of everyday creativity (see Chapter 2).

The use of computers in music had already opened up new possibilities for musicians and amateurs, and the presence of mobile devices also played an important part on these developments (Pimenta et al., 2014). The addition of a means of tweaking, designing, and creating computing devices and their software expands these existing possibilities into a scenario where all aspects of the process are open to invention and intervention. While some of the work that uses these resources has stayed grounded on traditional approaches to music making (e.g. beats, defined pitch scales, repetitive patterns), it is clear for many practitioners that the DIY electronics as a platform provides a gateway to a substantially expanded musical universe. It is, in essence, agnostic with regards to concepts, interfaces, and symbols, and it can be easily taken and manipulated that way.

### 3.5.2 An Internet of Musical Things

An important aspect of the latest wave of developments in DIY electronics is how devices can now take advantage of the internet infrastructure and be *connected* over a wide area. Examples of use can be seen in how small computing units devices can be remotely controlled, and how they can be used to gather input data, to provide output, to be interactive with people and the environment, etc. This gives the possibility of extending *instruments*, or the conceptual ubimus devices, over a wide area that can be of geographical significance, if required. It also facilitates the distribution of computing load between a variety of units, without the explicit need of creating dedicated networking infrastructure (ubimus riding on the ubiquitous presence of the internet).

An analysis of all the potential implications of the emergence of IoMusT, first proposed in Lazzarini et al. (2015), is beyond the scope of this article, but this topic is explored in Chapter 9 (see also Keller and Lazzarini (2017), Turchet et al. (2018)). It is possible to anticipate a change in the way musicians and audiences interact with music-making devices. It also opens an even wider range of possibilities for a multimedia integration of various artistic concerns, and for the delivery of education projects that have an artistic intent.

There is also significant scope for ecologically grounded creative practice, as discussed in (Keller et al., 2014a). For instance, since location and environment can be used in, and designed for, an IoMusT ubimus system, we can take advantage of the constructs observed in the creative phases (*potential, performance*, and *outcome*), while dealing with cognitive resources, material and social resources, social interaction, and ecological niche profile.

### 3.5.3    *The ubimus ecosystem*

The context in which ubimus ecologies have so far been discussed can be described as one consisting of off-the-shelf hardware devices and technology, sometimes involving repurposing of hardware through customised, issue-specific, finely tuned, software solutions. Examples of this approach can be found in earlier discussions of ubimus (Flores et al., 2010, McGlynn et al., 2012, van Troyer, 2014). For instance, typically we would have web, mobile, and desktop platforms, as discrete elements, plus a combination of these, in a given ubimus system. Software can be designed to take advantage of the specific infrastructure, and, when the need arises, peripheral hardware can be added to it. In this scenario, there are some limitations in terms of the size of the computing platform, its granularity (e.g. we could discuss systems that are made up of a hundred mobile phones, but we have not yet considered thousands of little wearable devices, and scalability.

If we bring DIY electronics platforms into consideration as an extension of what originally was taken as the playground for ubimus, we start to move into a much wider ecosystem. Many of the original ideas of Ubiquitous Computing (Weiser, 1995) begin to become more tangible, as devices start to disappear into our surroundings. We can think of a combinations of ready-made and custom components, which cooperate in a given system where there is no peripheral-computer dichotomy. The granularity of such a system can be brought down to the microcontroller-based circuit. With the modern SoC designs, complete computing platforms can be based on a small piece of hardware, that can interact with an unspecified number of other computational elements of various sizes and dispositions, only limited by the temporal and spatial constraints of the type of application.

This extended ubimus ecosystem is therefore open to both hardware and software intervention; creativity becomes a feature of both the system design and its use. In such scenario, the sharing of ideas through an open-source environment emanates from the norm in artistic practice: learning from example, and advancing the field by contributing your own solutions. In ubimus ecosystems, the boundaries between the hitherto separate categories of system design, artistic concept, technical realisation, and performance are blurred into a single entity.

## 3.6 Conclusions

In this chapter, we explored the history and technology of DIY electronics for music making, and attempted to contextualise its practice within ubimus. The use of electronics in music stretches back to the beginning of the 20th century with pioneer music instrument designs, such as the Theremin. With the development of the electronics component industry and a specialised hobbyist market, the practice of making kit-based DIY sound and music devices was popularised. After the microcomputer revolution in the eighties and nineties, and the widespread use of personal computers for music, a resurgence of DIY electronics took place aided by the simplification of microcontroller-programming and use.

Focusing on current uses of DIY electronics, we have considered the ways in which this approach is significant to the concerns of ubimus. In particular, we have noted its importance as a platform for the development of creativity. One playground is provided by the emergence of an Internet of Musical Things, which can be seized for artistic and educational ends. Another avenue for research has been opened by the application of embedded systems. Rather than designing isolated components, ubimus ecosystems can be deployed as subsystems that incorporate functionality depending on the local availability of components. Finally, we have shown how DIY electronics have become a significant element of the ubimus ecosystems, extending the possibilities for invention/intervention to the hardware components of a computing system. A number of examples of this are reported in Chapter 4, which demonstrate the impact of DIY systems in musical creation.

## Note

1 A system that fully integrates all common components of a computer on a single chip.

## Bibliography

Arduino (2019). Arduino - home. http://www.arduino.cc/.
Atmel Corporation (2015). Atmel - home. http://www.atmel.com.

Batchelor, P. and T. Wignall (2013).    Beaglepi.    *Csound Journal 18*, 1–12. http://csoundjournal.com/issue18/beagle_pi.html.

Beaglebone (2015). Beaglebone black. http://beagleboard.org/BLACK.

Blikstein, P. (2013). Digital fabrication and 'making' in education: The democratization of invention. In J. Walter-Herrmann, and C. Büching (Eds.), *FabLabs: Of Machines, Makers and Inventors.* Bielefeld: Transcript Publishers.

Blom, G.-J. and J. Winner (2000). *Manhattan Research Inc.* Holland: Basta Audio/Visuals.

Brown, J. H. and B. Martin (2010). How fast is fast enough? Choosing between xenomai and linux for realtime applications. In *Proceedings of the Real Time Linux Workshops*, pp. 25–27. Nairobi, Kenya.

Burtner, M. (2011).    Ecosono: Adventures in interactive ecoacoustics in the world. *Organised Sound 16*(03), 234–244.

Cross, L. (1968). Electronic music, 1948–1953. *Perspectives of New Music 7*(1), pp. 32–65.

Di Scipio, A. (2014). The place and meaning of computing in a sound relationship of man, machines, and environment. In *Proceedings ICMC/SMC/2014*, Athens, Greece, pp. 47–53.

DiBona, C. and S. Ockman (1999). *Open Sources: Voices from the Open Source Revolution.* Sebastopol, CA: O'Reilly Media.

Dougherty, D. (2012). The maker movement. *Innovations 7*(3), 11–14.

Dougherty, D. and S. Huss (2015). Make magazine. http://makezine.com.

Dougherty, D. and K. Maxwell (2012). Diy producer society. *Innovations 7*(3), 3–10.

Dudley, H. (1938). System for the artificial production of vocal or other sounds. US Patent 2,121,142.

Dunn, G. (2001).    Dynaco company history.    http://home.indy.net/ gregdunn/dynaco/history.html.

Flores, L. V., M. S. Pimenta, and D. Keller (2010). Patterns for the design of musical interaction with everyday mobile devices. In *Proceedings of the 9th Brazilian Symposium on Human Factors in Computing Systems*, Belo Horizonte, Brazil.

Fried, L. (2015). xoxbox. http://www.ladyada.net/make/x0xb0x/.

Holmes, T. (2008). *Electronic and Experimental Music: Technology, Music, and Culture.* London: Routledge.

Ikenberry, A. and J. Lim (2013). Csound eurorack module. *Csound Journal 18*, 1–12. http://csoundjournal.com/issue18/eurorack.html.

Intel Corporation (2015a).    Intel edison? One tiny platform, endless possibility. http://www.intel.com/content/www/us/en/do-it-yourself/edison.html.

Intel Corporation (2015b).    Intel galileo gen 2 development board - empower your prototype.    http://www.intel.com/content/www/us/en/do-it-yourself/galileo-maker-quark-board.html.

Kaeding, R. (2015).    A heathkit story (past & present).    http://www.heathkit-museum.com/hvmhstory.shtml.

Keller, D., L. V. Flores, M. S. Pimenta, A. Capasso, and P. Tinajero (2011). Convergent trends toward ubiquitous music. *Journal of New Music Research 40*(3), 265–276.

Keller, D. and V. Lazzarini (2017). Ecologically grounded creative practices in ubiquitous music. *Organised Sound 22*(1), 61–72.

Keller, D., V. Lazzarini, and M. S. Pimenta (2014a). Ubimus through the lens of creativity theories. In D. Keller, V. Lazzarini, and M. S. Pimenta (Eds.), *Ubiquitous Music*, Computational Music Science, pp. 3–23. Berlin: Springer.

Keller, D., V. Lazzarini, and M. S. Pimenta (2014b). *Ubiquitous Music*. Berlin: Springer.

Klose, T. (2019). Midibox blog. http://www.midibox.org.

Lazzarini, V. (2013). The development of computer music programming systems. *Journal of New Music Research 42*(1), 97–110.

Lazzarini, V., J. Timoney, and S. Byrne (2015). Embedded sound synthesis. In *Proceedings of the Linux Audio Conference 2015*, Johannes Gutenberg University, Mainz, Germany, pp. to appear.

Lazzarini, V., S. Yi, J. ffitch, J. Heintz, Ø. Brandtsegg, and I. McCurdy (2016). *Csound: A Sound and Music Computing System*. Berlin: Springer.

Manning, P. (2004). *Electronic and Computer Music*. Oxford: Oxford University Press.

McGlynn, P., V. Lazzarini, G. Delap, and X. Chen (2012, May). Recontextualizing the multi-touch surface. In G. Essl, B. Gillespie, M. Gurevich, and S. O'Modhrain (Eds.), *Proceedings of the International Conference on New Interfaces for Musical Expression*, Ann Arbor: University of Michigan.

McPherson, A., R. Jack, and G. Moro (2016). Action-sound latency: Are our tools fast enough? In *Proceedings of NIME 2016*, pp. 1–6. Brisbane, Australia.

McPherson, A. and V. Zappi (2015, May). An environment for submillisecond-latency audio and sensor processing on beaglebone black. In *Audio Engineering Society Convention 138*. New York.

MindMusicLabs (2019). Elk development kit. https://github.com/elk-audio/elk-docs.

Murray, C. S. (2005). *Crosstown Traffic: Jimi Hendrix and the Post-War Pop*. London: Faber.

Noble, J. and N. Joshua (2009). *Programming Interactivity: A Designer's Guide to Processing, Arduino, and Openframeworks* (1st ed.). Sebastopol, CA: O'Reilly Media, Inc.

O'Sullivan, D. and T. Igoe (2004). *Physical Computing: Sensing and Controlling the Physical World with Computers*. Boston, MA: Course Technology Press.

PAiA Corporation (2015). Paia - home. http://www.paia.com/.

Paralax Corporation (2015). The original basic stamp microcontroller. https://www.parallax.com/microcontrollers/basic-stamp.

Phillips, D. (2000). *Linux Music & Sound*. San Francisco, CA: No Starch Press.

PICAXE (2015). Home - PICAXE. http://www.picaxe.com/.

Pimenta, M. S., D. Keller, and V. Lazzarini (2014). Ubiquitous music - a manifesto. In D. Keller, V. Lazzarini, and M. S. Pimenta (Eds.), *Ubiquitous Music*, Computational Music Science, pp. xi–xxiii. Berlin: Springer.

Pinch, T. and F. Trocco (2004). *Analog Days*. Cambridge, MA: Harvard University Press.

Rubine, D. and P. McAvinney (1990). Programmable finger-tracking instrument controllers. *Computer Music Journal 14*(1), 26–41.

Russ, M. (2012). *Sound Synthesis and Sampling*. Music technology series. London, UK: Taylor & Francis.

Russcol, H. (1972). *The Liberation of Sound*. Englewood Cliffs, NJ: Prentice-Hall.

Russolo, L. (1967). *The Art of Noise*. New York, NY: Something Else Press.

Steinberg (2019). VST SDK 3.6.x. https://github.com/steinbergmedia/vst3sdk.

Theremin, L. S. (1928). Method of and apparatus for the generation of sounds. US Patent 1,661,058.

Tonepad (2015). Tonepad, a resource for diy music. http://www.tonepad.com.

Turchet, L., C. Fischione, G. Essl, D. Keller, and M. Barthet (2018). Internet of musical things: Vision and challenges. *IEEE Access 6*, 61994–62017.

Upton, E. (2015). Raspberry pi. http://www.raspberrypi.org.

Vail, M. (2000). *Keyboard Magazine Presents Vintage Synthesizers: Pioneering Designers, Groundbreaking Instruments, Collecting Tips, Mutants of Technology*. Book Series. San Francisco, CA: Miller Freeman Books.

van Loo, G. (2015). Gertduino. http://www.raspberrypi.org/introducing-gertduino/.

van Troyer, A. (2014). Repertoire remix in the context of festival city. In D. Keller, V. Lazzarini, and M. S. Pimenta (Eds.), *Ubiquitous Music*, Computational Music Science, pp. 51–63. Berlin: Springer.

Verle, M. (2008). *PIC Microcontrollers*. Belgrad: mikroElektronika.

Weiser, M. (1995). The computer for the 21st century. In R. M. Baecker, J. Grudin, W. A. S. Buxton, and S. Greenberg (Eds.), *Human-computer Interaction*, pp. 933–940. San Francisco, CA : Morgan Kaufmann Publishers Inc.

Wepman, D. (2000). Moog, robert. http://www.anb.org/articles/13/13-02679.html.

Wessel, D. and M. Wright (2002, September). Problems and prospects for intimate musical control of computers. *Computer Music Journal 26*(3), 11–22.

Wierzbicki, J. (2005). *Louis and Bebe Barron's Forbidden Planet: A Film Score Guide*. Film Score Guides. Lanham, ML: Scarecrow Press.

Wright, M. and A. Freed (1997). Open sound control: A new protocol for communicating with sound synthesizers. In *Proceedings of the ICMC*, Thessaloniki, Greece, pp. 101–104.

# 4  A brief report from the land of DIY

*Koka Nikoladze*

When you are born, one of the first things that we receive is a name that we carry until we die. A name is the most personal human belonging I can think of. Your name is the first thing we share when we introduce ourselves, with our profession often following next – as if our professional title was our second name – the second most personal human belonging.

My birth name is Koka and until I was 18 years old I introduced myself as a violinist. There were periods when I was more of a "violinist" than "Koka". Later I introduced myself as a composer, which often required additional clarification, such as the style and category of composition practice I exercised. The more I drifted into music technology, the more I had to clarify, until recently, when I realised that I was unable to define my profession with a name.

I feel like I am at work all day every day and my work includes activities that at first sight do not fit together in any meaningful way. I still compose on paper, which makes sense because of my degree in composition, but then I drift into making programs for automation, sound generation and processing, making and modifying different controllers for interfacing with those programs, designing hardware and producing hardware – working with wood and metal. There are days when I work as a sourcing agent, lost in data sheets of electronic components, then making circuit boards and running long marathons of soldering hundreds of those components.

There were periods when I used to take strong painkillers before taking the stage because of the unbearable pain caused by working as a technician for the setup of the performance, installing dozens of mechanical hammers and motors around the concert hall, but it has not always been like that.

Just several years ago I was a composition student with a prominent interest in music programming, but with very little skills or interest in making hardware. I always thought I needed an engineering degree to even start thinking of building something reasonable, but once in a while I sketched down ideas of expressive musical instruments to build in some distant future. These sketches included a design of a violin bow sensor made from an optical mouse that would measure the velocity and the direction of a moving bow and let me use my violinist skills for playing virtual instruments.

One day I just stumbled upon a cheap optical mouse at an electronics shop in Oslo, disassembled it and made a quick prototype, which worked right away. That led me to a local *maker space* to search for somebody to commission a small plastic enclosure for my prototype. That evening has shifted my peaceful professional life into a totally unexpected direction.

Jensa – one of the key members at Bitraf (Bitraf, 2019), the maker space, opened the door. There was a party going on and he was a bit drunk. He invited me in, gave me a tour around the workshop and upon hearing my request, playfully pushed me to sit down and make it myself, instead of recommending someone who could make my enclosure for me. At first, I thought it was a joke, but when he made me revive my superficial knowledge of SketchUp – a simple 3D design software – then how to use a calliper – all the while supervising the design process – I realised it was a possibility. Then he quickly showed me how to prepare 3D models for printing, explained how to use a 3D printer in five minutes and in about two hours from arrival, I had produced my first mechanical part.

That very evening I made several more prototypes and optimised the design. I could hardly believe that I was designing and 3D-printing myself. On my way home I held the plastic part in my hand and looked at it every minute, I just could not let it go. I put it next to my bed before going to sleep so that it was the first thing I saw in the morning. Next day I went to Bitraf again.

Since then I spend most of my time at Bitraf, learning engineering and electronics from members, including children, who have made robotic toys with microcontrollers. I learned by observing and doing, mostly from members who were keen on sharing their knowledge of how to use a laser cutter, a metal lathe, CNC router, power tools, etc.

Bitraf is a diverse community of more than a thousand members, including amateur hobbyists and skilled professionals of mechanical and electronic engineering, robotics, industrial design, architecture and numerous other fields. It is a maker-shelter in the middle of Oslo, where DIY is not only a fun way of accomplishing everyday goals, but rather an ideology – the way of being. Every instrument I have built at Bitraf is a byproduct of artistic curiosity, interaction with members, fascination with new fabrication possibilities and learning them. This is why most of my instruments are built with leftover materials from other people's projects.

## 4.1   Following the trails vs off the beaten track

Until Bitraf I knew very little about the world outside of musical academia and even though I worked in the field of experimental contemporary music for years, I feel I have always had a certain amount of comfort of following the trails. From today's perspective, even the experiments, which I was proud of and thought were bold when I studied or worked at the academia, seem to have been following prescribed manufacturing procedures and have been carried out in a relatively safe space. This is of course no criticism of academia, which I consider as my second home, it is rather a personal observation based on subjective experience.

Bitraf was *off the beaten track*. At Bitraf I was not surrounded by my dearest musician friends and colleagues, so when it came to music, I was free to experiment in every possible direction, embrace different aesthetics without anyone caring too much about it. At Bitraf I had no ambitions. I knew nothing about making instruments, so every new project was an unguided journey with numerous challenges and no prescribed solutions. I just had to collect bits and pieces of helpful information on the fly and fit them together for achieving the goal, and every achieved goal felt like climbing another mountain. Bitraf members were always there to help without judging my goals and those included some of the best engineers in Norway.

At Bitraf I first learned to collaborate with the material. Using leftovers from other people's projects has largely conditioned the way I build instruments. Such workflow never allowed me to come up with complete ideas and then materialise them. I rather had to examine materials first and then tailor my designs around them. For example, for as long as I can remember, I wanted to make a mechanical device that played acoustic beats just like a synthesiser, but I never got round to making one until I found sheets of some quality plywood and brass rods in the free material section. I would have made the machine bigger, but its size and overall shape was limited by the amount of material I found.

### 4.1.1 Beat Machine No. 1

The *Beat Machine No. 1* is a 32-step, hand-cranked, programmable mechanical sequencer. It plays eight small objects that are mounted on a wooden box in front of a sequencer wheel. Patterns can be easily reprogrammed by re-arranging plywood teeth in a wheel, which pluck the objects. Sound is produced acoustically and gets amplified if the machine is placed on a larger resonator box. When a microphone is placed close to the machine, because of the proximity effect, a plucked ruler starts to sound like a deep bass drum, so with simple amplification, the machine successfully mimics a large drum kit (Figure 4.1).

The objects mounted on the Beat Machine No. 1 include a ruler, a small wooden box with some grains of rice in it, an extension spring, a bent brass rod, several metal parts milled out of a brass sheet, a safety pin and a metal fork. Most of these objects were found at Bitraf, with a fork stolen from my own kitchen.

Beat Machine No. 1 was made with the intention of giving it to my friend, who was a rapper, for his street performances, but before I was done, my friend stopped rapping and took a job at an oil company, so I was left with the Beat Machine No. 1. With every beat machine I had a fun practical end-goal in mind, but when I completed them, it always came out different from what was originally planned. The Beat Machine No. 1 was repeatedly requested for gallery displays, but no rapper has yet requested it for accompaniment.

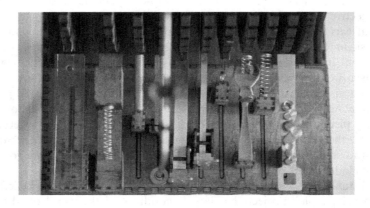

*Figure 4.1* Beat Machine No. 1

### 4.1.2   Beat Machine No. 2

The *Beat Machine No. 2* is an electromechanical instrument with four electromagnets and four objects mounted on a wooden box. The electromagnets get triggered by a microcontroller inside the box and hit the mounted objects. Each of those objects mimic an element of a modern drum kit. A coil holder from a soldering iron mimics a kick drum, a piece of thin plywood with attached springs mimics a snare drum, a glass tube with some sand in it was supposed to mimic something resembling an open high hat, but it turned out to sound precisely like a glass tube with some sand in it and a metal rod carries the function of a closed hi-hat when muted with a clamp and a ride cymbal when unmuted (Figure 4.2).

The Beat Machine No. 2 was also a vehicle-project for me to investigate the Arduino (Arduino, 2019) Nano microcontroller that I found at Bitraf (see Chapter 3 for a detailed introduction to this and other similar DIY hardware for ubimus). I decided to fully use the memory of the microcontroller and managed to program in eight complex rhythmic patterns. One fader on the side of the machine was originally used to morph between patterns to produce different grooves and another fader was used for setting tempo. The four switches on the same side correspond to the four objects mounted on the machine. They can mute and unmute corresponding electromagnets. Later I created another firmware for the machine that lets me control it from the Ableton Live digital audio workstation (DAW) to better synchronise the machine with other synthesisers. A blinking LED inside the machine was also included with a practical goal in mind. In rare cases where I would mute all four objects and continue singing or playing, I wanted to stay in tempo and have a visual cue until *dropping* back the beat.

*Figure 4.2* Beat Machine No. 2

My primary intention was to mount the Beat Machine No. 2 on a microphone stand or hold it next to my face so that I could sing a song with an acoustic beat and use a single microphone for amplification and mixing, but it turned out to be rather hard to fit my mouth and the machine together in front of a single microphone. Later the Beat Machine No. 2 was mainly requested by festivals, who wanted me to play with it live, but it turned out to be extremely complicated to amplify the machine on a big stage mainly because of feedback issues. The most memorable experience was the performance for TEDx Oslo, where I had to stand and perform in a very specific position on stage to avoid explosion of feedback, somehow damping certain frequencies with my body. The stressful part was that no one other than me knew this, so I was left to carry that great burden of responsibility alone. Miraculously, it worked.

### 4.1.3 Beat Machine No. 5

The *Beat Machine No. 5* is somewhat similar to No. 2, but here the bass drum is made out of a tea-candle and a syringe that blows tiny bursts of butane gas through open fire, causing miniature explosions. It was meant to mimic the iconic TR-808 kick. The machine also includes a DC motor on the side that is in tight contact with the wooden body and can play scales. The Beat Machine No. 5 produces relatively loud acoustic sound and can be easily amplified with one or two microphones. The day I was finished with the machine I thought I had finally made a stable instrument that I could use for several productions and maybe take on a tour, but it first melted a microphone that I used to record it for a demonstration video and then it was rejected by two venues in Germany because of fire safety concerns. It finally ended up sitting in my living room, where I set it up and play for fun once every couple of months (Figure 4.3).

*Figure 4.3* Beat Machine No. 5

## 4.2    Solenoid Orchestra

In-between beat machines production came larger-scale projects, such as the Solenoid Orchestra. Urban Liturgy – a piece for this mechanical orchestra – was commissioned by Ultima festival in 2017 to be performed at Youngstorget – a public square in Oslo. When I outlined the concept, I understood what I wanted to do, but did not have the technology to realise it. I wanted to perform with an orchestra or multiple heavy-duty hammers and motors playing acoustic percussion loud enough to fill a public square with sound. I enquired with two companies for the development and production prices – a German company wanted 44 euros and a Japanese company, 65 euros. At that moment that was not feasible by any stretch of imagination, so I decided to design and fabricate the orchestra myself at Bitraf.

Having spent a lot of time with machinery has led me all the way down to nuts and bolts, literally. I spent the entire summer manufacturing custom metal parts, modifying skateboard bearings, experimenting with folded frame structures made with an aluminium composite called Dibond, producing custom high-current circuit boards with different kinds of transistors and diodes. Bitraf machinery and community know-how turned out to be sufficient for producing a solenoid orchestra of twenty-four heavy-duty hammers and twenty-four motors, controlled over ethernet by a network of eight controllers from a single laptop. The only thing I did not consider was making the entire system waterproof.

On September 9th at 1 PM, the first performance of Urban Liturgy at Youngstorget was washed out by heavy unpredicted rain, ruining one-quarter of the Solenoid Orchestra. Instead of focusing on performance, I and the festival team ran around the square desperately trying to save as much of the hardware as we could. Even with an incomplete setup, the evening performance went well and it was one of the most rewarding experiences of my professional career, but after the festival I had to spend a full week inspecting and fixing damaged members of the orchestra.

The Solenoid Orchestra toured around Norway and Germany, but after several shows it found its place in our dark basement, hopelessly waiting for maintenance together with many other instruments that are hard to transport.

## 4.3 KOI

Another example of a complex project is KOI (Koka's Orchestra Interface). It was produced for a commission by PODIUM Esslingen to be used with Ensemble Resonanz at Elbphilharmonie in Hamburg. For this performance I wanted to interface with the ensemble in realtime via interactive note stands. From my doctoral project, which is about animated notation, I knew about different systems that used networks of tablets for displaying dynamic scores to musicians. I also knew that the amount of information to be displayed to musicians for sight-reading was limited by musicians themselves, so the ability of displaying diverse and complex material was not necessarily useful. Since I wanted to make my system easily scalable and also experiment with different approaches of dynamic notation, I decided to produce it myself.

KOI is a network of interactive note stands that can be daisy-chained together with ethernet cables. The network consists of A4-sized circuit boards that musicians can put on their note stands. Each board has a main grid of twenty-eight bright LEDs, a linear array of nineteen LEDs on the side, a four-LED visual metronome on top and a numeric display. Individual building blocks of a piece printed on paper can be laid over the circuit board. Then individual LEDs from the main grid can be triggered to indicate changes of notes, looping phrases or other elements. The nineteen-LED array on the side can be dimmed up and down to indicate changing dynamics, different numbers can be displayed on a seven-segment display and visual metronome patterns can be adjusted . All these parameters can be adjusted or automated individually for every stand from a single laptop. The simple interface was made with visual programming environment Max (Puckette, 2002) (Figure 4.4).

The KOI system uses Arduino Nano microcontrollers and RS 485 transmitters, which allow for very long cables between musicians and reliable transmission of data. The problem of powering the entire system via one single chain of ethernet cables was solved by running the whole network on high voltage and stepping it down at each individual note stand. In this way, branches of up to 32 stands can be connected in a daisy-chain, which transmits data and from which they are powered. For the performance at Elbphilharmonie, I used mainstream controllers, such as the ones produced by Novation and Korg, for reactive composition on stage. Different controllers were mapped to specific parameter changes that were displayed to musicians that they followed in realtime.

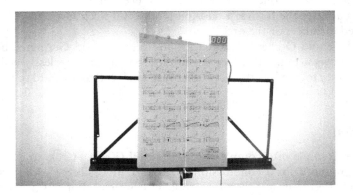

*Figure 4.4* Blinkscore panel

The performance at Elbphilharmonie was the first successful attempt of mine in manipulating a large ensemble on stage with buttons, knobs and faders, but shortly before the concert I was fixing some fallen-out components in my dressing room, soldering them back. I can probably successfully claim that I am the only artist who soldered at Elbphilharmonie Hamburg and yes, I brought my Weller soldering iron with me together with the score.

## 4.4   Conclusions

In this chapter, I have attempted to report a personal experience of the wide-ranging makers' universe, where I made a contact with some of the ideas of ubimus. The roles of the composer and the instrument maker are forever entangled in my daily practice, and this has had a significant impact on my work. Every year of my five years at Bitraf, I have had to throw away several large boxes of incomplete prototypes for the lack of storage space. These included custom pedals, electronic and mechanical sequencers, acoustic filters, wind and string instruments, etc. Because of constant absence of time I was unable to give them away. It was impossible to get everything to some functional state where anyone other than me could use them. At some point we were out of space at home and now there is no more room in our basement to store instruments.

I believe that every rewarding experience that has come making instruments on an everyday basis comes at an expense, and in my case that is constant chaos. I prefer to think that my instrument-making work is a highly satisfying process of sorting out immense chaos into tiny chunks of understandable order. For me, the process of making instruments has turned into a form of performance practice that is tightly integrated with everyday life. I am quite happy with the formulation of what I do, but this still far away from a single understandable name that would describe my profession, so that I could say it after I introduce myself.

During my second year at Bitraf , when the Beat Machine No. 2 became popular on social media, I got a number of friend requests from people who also made musical instruments and knew the field way better than I did, and I gradually became aware of a new world with rich presence and history. I feel incompetent to talk about how emerging of new musical instruments triggered epochal changes, but the overwhelming diversity of musical instruments and tools for creative expression all around the world, all the way from k'ni (Vietnamese mouth violin) to modern modular synthesisers makes me think that making and exploring new instruments is nearly an instinct. Quite early on, I made a conscious decision to never have the ambition to be an instrument maker, but to simply exercise spontaneous creativity in the field on an everyday basis.

Most of what I have learnt in the field of making instruments has not come from chrestomathic literature, but from social media and YouTube, which are relatively new forms of communication and learning that we yet have to explore. I am not willing to change this way of learning. I want to avoid a narrow expertise, and rather explore in a freestyle manner in order to always have enough headroom for creative *search*, rather than *research*. Social media pages, such as the Facebook *Mesmerising Instruments* and *Sounds, Rare and Strange Instruments* and Instagram channels, such as *Powwow, Orb Magazine* and similar, are endless sources of inspiration that keep me working all the time.

## Bibliography

Arduino (2019). Arduino - home. http://www.arduino.cc/.
Bitraf (2019). Bitraf wiki. https://bitraf.no/wiki/Forside.
Puckette, M. (2002). Max at seventeen. *Computer Music Journal 26*(4), 31–43.

# 5 Interactive systems and their documentation: a perspective on multimedia installation art

*Federica Bressan*

The darkness of the room was interrupted by intermittent and sudden flashes of light. I could hear a loud, low-pitched, irregular beat, accompanied by a high buzz. "Is that my heart?" I asked. "Yes, it is," I heard a voice answer. I recognised it as belonging to the gentleman who a few minutes earlier had secured my body with sensors to detect my heartbeat, breathing, and brain waves. I was a guinea pig for a new immersive and multisensory artistic performance called "Dissense," in which the performer's electrophysiological signals are recorded in real time and translated into vibrating objects, sounds, and lights. The audience would also get to feel what I felt, through tiny devices called VibroPixels attached to their bodies.

The lights came back on and I squinted to adjust my eyes. Gradually, I was able to focus on the members of the artistic and technical team, who looked satisfied with the outcome of the test. As the team went about their normal business, the strangeness of what I had just experienced clung to me. I had thought multimedia had exhausted its possibilities and could not be exciting anymore, but this was different. The use of electrophysiological signals – at once so personal and mysterious – in a skilfully designed immersive environment created a powerful experience. It touched me. It changed me. It forced me to rethink everything I thought I knew about expanded media and its potential for creating new expressive languages.

*Summer 2017, at UQAM in Montréal. Dissense is a piece by Chris Salter and TeZ*

Interaction with multimedia technology and sensory devices for artistic purposes is an intriguing domain, with strong links to the industrial sectors of virtual reality, gaming, medical rehabilitation, and learning. Since the early 2000s, there has been growing attention to a new genre of scholarship and practice focusing on the senses, art, design, and new technologies: immersive and multi-sensory installations and performances that challenge human perception by merging haptic (touch), visual, acoustic, and other sensory phenomena. These works embrace the all-pervasive and invisible computing present in our everyday lives and use it to design new *meaningful engagements* (Brown and Dillon, 2012). The process leading to their realisation normally involves a highly interdisciplinary team and its practice is informed by a range of different disciplines: theatre, architecture, visual art, computer music, perceptual psychology, cultural theory, and engineering.

The excitement in this field translates into much experimentation, from technological pioneering to new approaches to creativity, resulting in a big picture in constant evolution, fluid, as rich as it is fragmented. Artists do not go about their experimentations to make documentarists and historians happy, and they shouldn't. But it we agree that there is some value in documenting this particular field in this historical moment, that is, if we put ourselves in the shoes of the preservation expert, then we are confronted with a big problem: how to capture each of these works, and the overall landscape they form together, in an adequate way. Preservation theory is always a few steps behind what it tries to preserve, i.e. the products of its contemporary culture – just like, by its own nature, philosophy always "comes too late. Philosophy, as the thought of the world, does not appear until reality has completed its formative process, and made itself ready" (from the preface of Hegel's *Philosophy of right*).

We are currently failing to preserve the heritage constituted by interactive and multimedia art works – according to a definition of preservation that includes *contextual information*, i.e. information that will help people in the future make sense of the work in its context. Contextual information desirably includes a documentation of the creative process that led to the realisation of the work, providing valuable insight into the complex dynamics that shape the creative acts, and into the effects of technology, with all its attributes, on creativity. It's not that we are not trying, nor that it is an impossible task. These works elude, challenge, refuse to comply with existing archiving paradigms and documentation strategies. And for the most part, it takes the commitment of an institution, with a deployment of consistent resources, to set up a preservation system. It is not the effort of one. It is not something we can delegate to artists, either. This slows down the process of achieving a solution: besides identifying the solution, which is a challenge in itself, reality with its inertia needs to follow the change to accommodate the solution, and this is probably an even bigger challenge.

When expressing criticism for existing cataloguing standards, one should always be careful and consider that they exist in the real world, have been implemented in real-world institutions, and it is this, rather than how good or bad the cataloguing model is, that resists the change. That is also why there is a fracture between many theorists and real-world archives. Theorists can modify or discard an obsolete model and make up a new one, anytime they need. And it is a good thing that people of intellect have this freedom. On the other hand, we have archives and cultural institutions, which almost by definition move very slowly. And it is a good thing that they resist change. Their mission is to maintain and protect our collective memory: they should remain the same and transform much slower than the world does. However, this state of affairs often produces incommunicability between theorists who are much ahead and propose sophisticated solutions, and archives who fight funding cuts and struggle to keep up with the demands of routine software and hardware updates. Some problems are shared by all archival institutions, but obviously we are going to find very different situations depending on the size of the institution, its country, its history, and so on.

Therefore, when observing that existing cataloguing standards are inadequate, it should be clear that the problem is bigger than the cataloguing standards, and that it is not an attack on the institutions. Ideally, between the visionary theorists and conservative archivists, there would be a group of professionals who mediate information and narrow the tension caused by the gap.

Interactive multimedia installations and performances require a fundamental re-thinking of preservation and documentation, which should be based on events and processes rather than on fixed objecthood; consider context and decide how the new digital entities are going to be accessed, presented, displayed. What is wrong with existing cataloguing standards? Nothing *per se*. The problem is that they are being used to capture information about objects that are different than the ones that they were created for. So there is nothing wrong with the cataloguing standards, but with our expectation of them, and the use we make of them. It's a case of unsuccessful repurposing. Our loyalty to the tradition is greater than our capacity to acknowledge a new reality and adapt to it. Our minds also have inertia, and as a consequence many conservators attempt to "fix the processual and fluid nature of these works" (Dekker, 2013) to fit established cataloguing standards first designed for traditional beaux arts or documentary heritage.

The standards are not wrong across the board, or our attempt to repurpose them would not have worked at all. So, the extent to which these standards are inadequate should be made explicit. Clearly there is an overlap, and it shouldn't be minimised. What these cataloguing standards (or non standard: simply existing cataloguing strategies in use across the globe) capture very well are the physical parts of an installation or performance, which are normally maintained and preserved – because the main purpose of these catalogues is re-performance, re-staging. Besides the administrative data – very important for cultural institutions that manage budgets, operate loans, keep track of copyright issues, and therefore are managed a lot like a company – another aspect of the work that is normally well captured in the documentation is the work's aim, what the work is about, in the form of a narrative often told directly by the author. Zealous archivists and curators (in my entire career, I have not met one archivist who is not zealous and dedicated) sit down with the artist and take accurate notes during an interview. This practice of collecting information about a work is so common that Future project has developed the Variable Media Questionnaire to help systematise this process.[1]

The ability to document the author's intention in creating the work (what it is about, how it works), and all of its (physical) components, covers already a significant part of a work. Surely, it can be argued that we are *completely* failing to preserve these works. Many institutions will claim that they are preserving this type of works and proceed to show their database with all the tabs filled with the right metadata. And yet: something's missing. Those who call for new preservation models, new metadata to accommodate the new works, focus on that "something," that has to do with how the work is documented *and* presented (access). In a way it has to do with the "essence" of the work, referring to its dynamic, live, transient moment of existence. It is like documenting the costumes and the shoes of dancers, the size of the stage and the background...and not capturing the dance itself. The motion. This problem is at the core of interactive multimedia art: we can document each component, separately, hope to preserve some (regular physical objects), some not (software patches? organic materials?), but the work has meaning as a whole, when it's assembled, together, often participated (collaborative co-creation), and in action – in this moment in time.

Besides the philosophical idea of the *essence* of the work, which we all understand even if it's hard to articulate, there are way more concrete ways in which the interactive nature of installations and performances is translated. For example, most cataloguing standards require documents to be classified by homogeneous types and, consequently, that multimedia works are disassembled and their components grouped by type. But these works come as a *multidimensional* "assembly of artifacts" (Bowers et al., 2007), so the *documentary unity* must be (temporarily) violated during cataloguing. It is not always easy to re-assemble the parts and give the work its informational potential back, a potential that only resides in the relation of the parts. And this is a good scenario, when some documentation exists. Most works, of course, go undocumented (for any mundane reason, rarely for neglect).

Secondly, the essence of the work as in *how it works*, how meaning is acted out in the motion of the parts (and the users/performers), is hard to describe in a simple structured way, like in a grid, a list of fields to fill. How do we understand this motion? Dynamicity? Interaction? This information is normally contained in the text that the curator, or someone on his/her behalf, collects while interviewing the author(s). The problem with this text is that it is not easy to search. We want to interrogate a system with semantic queries, i.e. based on an *understanding* of semantic and structural information in the text. In order to structure information this way, we need to build a model of how we understand and classify interactive multimedia installations and performances.

During the past ten years, the academic community has grown awareness about the specific problems of preserving interaction, starting dedicated workshops and conferences. Many projects have been funded since the 1990s and many interesting ideas have been proposed. An incredible amount of effort has been devoted to finding a solution to the preservation and documentation of interactive multimedia installations and performances. What follows is a summary of some notable projects and initiatives.

As far as the documentation of the hardware (here in the broad sense, every tangible component of the work) and software components is concerned, a useful approach is to assign functional "significance to display equipment, its relation to the worlds identity based on conceptual, aesthetic and historical criteria, and the role the equipment plays in the work" (Laurenson and van Saaze, 2014). For each component, we can ask: is the equipment functional or is it (also) conceptually important? Is the equipment visible or hidden from view? The decision tree developed by the DOCAM Conservation and Preservation Committee[2] "allows stakeholders to identify the problems and potential solutions associated with preserving works that incorporate technological components," and can guide the decision making process at the time when problems with the maintenance of the equipment arise. Depending on the work and its specific problems, a simple replace with identical or equivalent parts might be the best solution. However, the long-term problems of preserving the work and the experience remain open.

Documentation can be seen as a *process* that spans across different stages of the work's life cycle: it includes information about the work's "condition, its content, its context, and the actions taken to preserve it" (Dekker, 2013). It is widely accepted that in most cases only the documentation will survive the work, thus acquiring a new importance as the [only] source of knowledge about the work, though not necessarily in competition with the work.

Besides the work in and of itself, the idea, the concept or [conceptual] model, the intention of the work, can be the object of preservation. The Variable Media Network (VMN) proposed a strategy where artists are encouraged to define their work independently from medium so that the work can be translated once its current medium becomes obsolete (Dekker, 2013). The artist's intention is considered by a number of international institutions as the guiding principle for their documentation (Hummelen, 2005), and audiovisual interviews are thought to optimise the process of capturing his or her intention during extensive interviews (often based on the interview model proposed by the Forging the Future project, mentioned a few paragraphs above). When the artist is uninterested, deceased, or unavailable for any reason, someone else is burdened with the responsibility of making decisions about the work's presentation and preservation with partial information at hand. Sometimes the restorer's domain needs to extend into the curatorial one. The decision tree mentioned above might give a sense of direction in situations of doubt, and shared (ideally standard) practices are preferable over individual efforts to "reinvent the wheel" under the virtuous name of "adapting existing practices."

Multi-layered models have also been devised to capture the complexity of these works in documentation. Rinehart's Media Art Notation System (MANS) (Rinehart, 2007) has three layers of implementation: the conceptual model of documentation, the preferred expression format (vocabulary) for the model, and the score, which serves as a record of the work that is database-processable. The core concepts form a "broad strokes" description of the work that can be used by the artist or museum at the time the work is created or collected. Further details can be filled in later in the life of the work, in line with the idea of documentation as a process.

A different model for preservation, that does not prescribe a model of the work, was introduced by Bressan and Canazza (2014). The model is organised in four layers, each of which serves as a container for specific types of documents. The layers are not in a hierarchical relation and were inspired by a methodological framework for the preservation of scientific data. They adopt the conceptual tools and the terminology of computer science: four levels of abstraction from the bits (any part of the original installation that can be preserved *as is*), to data (technical notes, comments about the realisation of the installation, including high-level descriptions of algorithms used), to record (any element that was modified or updated in respect of original installation in order to re-interpret the installation), to experience (any document that bears witness to some aspect of the human-machine interaction).

Summarising, the problems of preservation (and maintenance) of installations and performances, and their re-interpretation, can be formulated as follows:

1  Preservation and maintenance: whether the replacement of an element violates or *decreases* the authenticity of the piece, is a philosophical question. As such, it has no right or wrong answer. This does not legitimise us to inaction, on the contrary it calls us to take responsibility for our (informed, reasoned) choices, which should always be declared, owned, and documented.
2  Re-interpretation: whether it is vetted by the artist or it depends on someone else's choices, any new staging of a previous piece, that is not identical to it (and it rarely is, almost by definition) is to be considered a new version (in case it is vetted by the artist) and for all intents and purposes a new interpretation (vetted or not).

This also applies to preservation strategies that involve migration, emulation, and virtualisation, precisely because the ultimate question about authenticity cannot be answered (see the previous point), the *distance* or divergence from the *original* or previous cannot be objectively measured. It is undeniable, however, that there are better and worse approaches, where better is defined as informed, approved by a team of experts rather than a single individual, and aided by existing tool like the DOCAM decision tree, the Variable Media Questionnaire, and tools alike.

Taking into account the context where the work was created and exhibited complicates things because we often lack the historical distance to make objective assessments about our own cultural landscape, let alone a past one. An extreme, but intellectually legitimate, conclusion that may follow this observation is that ideal preservation is an impossible task, betrayal and bias are inevitable, and therefore we should not even try because any action results in fabrication. As a consequence, we should sit and watch a wealth of creative potential and intellectual labour crumble in front of our eyes. There is another, equally rational and legitimate, position, which moves from the same premise: *ideal* preservation is an impossible task. But then it activates a different set of ethical values: we acknowledge that reflecting upon *unarchivable* works, documenting our choices, working in teams, produces useful results both within and without preservation *per se*. It fosters an intellectual discussion, setting the conditions for the development of a stimulating cultural ethos that inevitably leads to academic advancement and artistic creativity. It prevents the complete loss of artefacts, practices, stories, and ultimately heritage goods, present and future memory and identity. It keeps us attentive, on guard for unintentional "fabrications," and thus actively engaged with the heritage.

## 5.1   Preservation

The ultimate objective of preservation is "to ensure the permanent accessibility of documentary heritage" (Edmondson, 2002), where permanent means "decades or centuries, or long enough to be concerned about the obsolescence of technology" (Hedstrom, 2002). The efforts of preservation are mainly aimed at slowing the process of degradation that inevitably affects all physical media as well as the process of obsolescence that affects all software, file formats, programming languages, etc.; at copying the information stored on degrading media onto new media, in order to extend its LE and to enable wider access.

In its most straightforward meaning, preservation assumes the existence of an object to preserve, of an artefact that coincides with the good of cultural significance, that is subject to physical decay over time. Physical decay seemed to be the main threat to all cultural goods until a relatively recent time, and despite the great excitement in the field, we are still in the process of letting go of old mental habits and of re-defining what preservation means, what it applies to, and how it can be effectively carried out. Digital technology is not helping this process, by presenting a narrative of *technological advancement* for a market where new devices appear every few months, intentionally limiting backward compatibility, thus shortening the LE of software and hardware, and ultimately of data and information, beyond any reasonable point, and certainly more than necessity would impose in terms of what technology can actually do. Users – that is what cultural institutions are with respect to commercial software – hardly have any power to change this state of affairs. But as preservation professionals they would be aware that however limited digital technology may be, its alleged instability and unreliability is sometimes exaggerated. An anxiety about digital technology serves the goals of the market, in a twisted way. There is no easy way out of this situation, but as preservation professionals we should know when the problem is actually technology, and when it is the policies about the use of a certain technology. Is this really a fragile medium? Or do we intentionally sabotage our technology to replace it with a new one as fast as it pleases the manufacturers?

With the advent of audiovisual materials – or rather, since we have become aware of their cultural significance, or alternatively since we have attributed it to them – the traditional paradigm with an object to preserve at its centre started to show its cracks. Audiovisual materials are fundamentally different animals with respect to traditional cultural heritage items, and for the sake of this dissertation, they are the middle link between those items and interactive performances and installations. They are different because:

- their LE can be measured in years or decades vs. centuries or millennia;
- there is *content* that can be separated from the *carrier* or container;
- mediation technology is required to access the content.

These differences have ontological as well as practical consequences. The first one, the short LE, results in the fact that preservation must be timely, sometimes urgent. But what does preservation address? Point two shows that there is a dichotomy between content and carrier: this means that content can be *saved* by being extracted from the carrier and transferred to another carrier. Depending on the type of carrier/technology, terms like re-mediation, digitisation, transcoding, etc. will be used. The third point is a requirement of the previous one, and its goal was simply to show that a full system, a technological setup, is necessary to access/preserve audiovisual heritage. All the problems deriving from the implications of content transfer pertain to the literature of audiovisual preservation and are beyond the scope of this dissertation.

Although audiovisual heritage undermines the traditional paradigm of preserving an object, and *the original* object at that, the presence of the carrier keeps these materials compatible with this approach, meaning that it can be extended to include them, without leading to a conceptual collapse. This partial compatibility, or maybe this misunderstanding, has some scholars wonder what the "object" of the preservation is (the carrier? the content? where is the line?), but it doesn't impede the practical work of digitisation and storage.

Installations and performances showed that the emperor has no clothes. Despite some hopeless attempt to archive a living thing "as is," some scholars have already acknowledged that these works are unarchivable (Ernst, 2010), and that the focus should shift from things to processes and intangibles. These works may be better defined as "a process of cultural participation involving the public, the work itself, and the museum," rather than as a unique piece created by an artist (Barbuto and Barreca, 2013).

Unarchivability is the necessary axiom upon which to build a new theory of preservation not centred around a (static) object. Here is where another semantic problem arises, that of preservation vs. documentation. Preservation, conservation, and documentation are terms that recur in the field of…preservation, but they are not entirely interchangeable. Focusing on preservation and documentation for the sake of this dissertation: preservation is a broad term, in its broader meaning it includes actions to raise awareness in the public, and it assumes the existence of an object to preserve, but loosely. In fact, it could be well intended as every action contributing to keeping alive an item of cultural, artistic, documentary significance – or the memory of such item. Documentation may be one of these actions, so in a way documentation is a subset of preservation. However, in this dissertation, it is important to make a distinction, because where we agree that there is no object to preserve *as is* (or a surrogate, as in the case of audiovisual materials), documentation assumes a central role and this has consequences. It is somehow beyond the scope of this dissertation to examine these consequences, but it is important to declare that with installations and performances we are not preserving or archiving an object, but rather we are trying to capture relevant aspects of the original work in a variety of formats and on a variety of carriers. There are several schools of thought about documentation, from those who think that documentation is an unsatisfactory solution because of the unbridgeable gap between the ephemerality of performances and the fixity of a document (see for example Phelan (1993)) to those who say that documentation is a way to continue the life of the performance, to continue its journey through time and space (see for example Auslander (2006)). Here, we assume that documentation is valuable (and better than the alternative, because rejecting documentation altogether leaves us with *nothing*.) But we also limit the focus of documentation to a specific aspect of performances of installations such that theoretical and semantic questions don't apply. In particular, we focus the attention on a specific class of installations and performances, that make use of electrophysiological stimuli as control signals for a multimedia and multi-sensory display.

## 5.2  Immersive and multi-sensory installations

A particular class of installations and performances exploits concepts and technology from *physiological computing*, a branch of computer science that studies how [human] sensory data can be captured, processed, and included in a technological system to trigger functions or to be displayed at the interface. Physiological computing focuses on sensory data like brainwaves, heartbeat, skin conductivity, eye tracking, and breathing – electrophysiological signals that are normally used to monitor biological functions and health (Salter, 2015). Examples are Haptic field by Chris Salter (2017)[3] and The body that carries me by Ernesto Neto (2014).[4] The impact of physiological computing goes well beyond the arts, with immediate spillovers in adjacent sectors such as social security, domotics, and education.

The technology employed in this field is sometimes bought in the store, but very often it is custom made. The VibroPixels (Hattwick et al., 2017, Ignoto, 2018) are a good example of custom-made sensors. This fascinating and very fast evolution is not really being tracked. In art preservation, the focus is on the entire work: what type of sensor is used is normally only relevant in relation to the technical scheme for the next exhibition. An archive of what kind of senses we *use* for creative purposes today, and what kind of sensors we use to detect and distribute them, is currently missing. Such archive would contribute to the documentation of the works, while tracing the evolution of this intriguing and fast-developing application field.

The way we document our reality will determine the questions that researchers will ask tomorrow.

(H. Kraemer)

The creation of the documents, and their potential for organisation, retrieval, and use in the future (Briet, 1951) constitute complementary problems in building a good body of documentation. The quality of the final *network*, which may or may not include the installation or performance itself, has to be predicated on a good conceptual model, and has to make sure that the format of each document is easily accessible, interoperable, and implements safety measures against tampering (Duranti, 2012).

This is an example of an aspect of multi-sensory installations and performances that current cataloguing standards entirely miss: what senses are considered, and what technology is used to detect, process, and display the multi-sensory information. It is worth noticing that even if this information were included in a text report, so it were not missed in a way, it would not be searchable. The importance of structured information cannot be stressed enough. Without structured information, it is impossible to query the system about that information – in this case, about the senses in multi-sensory installations. Considering that these works invest so much on this type of information, to ignore it seems to *miss the point* or miss the *essence* (see the previous section) of the work itself. The same can be said for interactive art: documenting all its physical parts but not representing (in a structured way) the *interactive* aspect of the work, is like documenting the duration of a music piece, the instruments that play, the key in which it is written, and ignore the melody. In fact, identifying the importance of documenting these core aspects of interactive art as well as multi-sensory installations, simply means importing into this domain a concept that has been well known in music information retrieval (MIR) for over two decades: content-based retrieval.

Queries (interrogations) are specific research criteria to retrieve (access) data in a database. They are normally based on keywords associated with the data itself, such as title and author. Content-based retrieval, or query by content, allows the user to interrogate the database with criteria related to the multimedia content, such as harmonic modulations in a song or brightness transitions in a movie scene. In order to achieve this, the data must be analysed to extract high-level information about its content. This practice has been long known in the field of music (Lerch, 2012), where Shazam is the most popular example of query by content: instead of retrieving a song by author and title, one can whistle the melody or input an audio stream to search for a match in the database – and in the field of still images. But only recently it has been applied to moving images, see the research project "The Sensory Moving Image Archive. Boosting Creative Reuse for Artistic Practice and Research" (SEMIA, 2017–2019), coordinated by Giovanna Fossati at the University of Amsterdam. The project investigates the application of deep learning techniques to explore sensory features found in digitised audiovisual archives such as movement, colour, and form.[5] Query by content has never been applied to multi-sensory data. What does this mean?

Following Kraemer's quote a couple of paragraphs earlier, this means that by not capturing certain information (in a structured way) we make it impossible to ask all the questions that would involve that information, and all the knowledge explicitly or implicitly contained in that information. In particular, without a database that stores sensory data used in immersive and multi-sensory installations (e.g. heartbeat, brainwave, skin conductivity of the performer/participants, obtained with biosensors) we cannot ask questions like: "Show me all the installations that use brainwaves to control sound equalisation," or "that combine muscle activity with accelerometers," or "where the heartbeat rate exceeds 140 beats-per-minute?"

Asking ourselves whether these are interesting questions or not is not the point. First off, it is easy to make a case that they are interesting, but the most important point is that by *allowing* for this information to be searched, we open up infinite possibilities to ask new questions that we cannot think of today. The meaning of the Kraemer's quote is that we have the responsibility to draw the boundaries of a playing field where other will play after us, matches or even games that we cannot imagine yet. And if we don't understand this responsibility and act accordingly, we sabotage the possibilities to access our own heritage, the heritage we claim to care for, and that we claim to be preserving to the best of our capabilities and with the investment of our best resources.

Building an archive that documents these parallel timelines (the senses used today and in the future; the technology to detect, process, and display these senses today and in the future) fills a specific gap of today's cataloguing systems. It could be constructed as an independent module, making it slightly easier to integrate in existing systems (see the problem of inertia in the previous section). It can be considered an improvement of existing cataloguing systems without actually modifying them, but by expanding them. For example, in the case of *Dissense* (described in the opening narrative in this chapter), the sensory data of the performer include the heartbeat (among others), which is detected with a wearable device attached to her finger; this heartbeat is mapped onto sound and tactile feedback which the audience receives via loudspeakers and the VibroPixels. The same installation, in the future, may detect the heartbeat by means of another type of device. Each sense is always linked to a specific technology for each installation or performance, and one may evolve over time while the other remains constant. Thus it will be possible to ask even more new questions about these works. It is worth noticing that besides the importance of modelling the information and structuring the data well, it is also important to collect a critical mass of data, and that accumulating data increases the value of the archive over time. Think of the query: "Show me all the performances produced between 2010 and 2015 that used brainwaves," or "all the installations in the database that make use of a Kinect." For each record in the database, information about new technology and new mapping strategies is added.

## 5.3 Conclusions

Much experimentation is observed in the field of interactive multimedia installations and performances, in particular those that explore the expressive potential of multi-sensory data thanks to a fast evolving sensory technology and ubiquitous computing. These works pose serious challenges to existing cataloguing standards, and in order to achieve a satisfactory solution, i.e. their effective preservation, a number of problems need to be solved at two levels: the identification of the solution, which means re-thinking our preservation and documentation strategies, and secondly winning the resistance to change unwillingly opposed by real-world institutions.

The good news is that the field is open to new ideas, and the sky is the limit. If we believe that the same excitement characterising technological experimentation can be brought into the intellectual domain, in terms of visionary ideas, radical re-design of preservation practices, etc. then it is not hard to see that instead of being discouraged by the current state of affairs, we have reasons to be exited about what will come.

Google has recently released the Google Arts and Culture site, a massive collection of photos, primary source documents, videos, virtual reality experiences, etc. dedicated to cataloguing and exploring art, performances, and music.[6] This platform impresses for its unprecedented way of delivering high-resolution contents via the browser, and it is interesting in that it comes from a giant tech company, that invests and leads the way in arts and culture, waving the banner of technology. It is often said that culture should lead the way, not technology, to the risk of some not well-defined threat of de-humanisation. In this case, technology is definitely flexing its muscles, but before we demonise the project, or dismiss it as a toy (in which case it would be a toy that Tate Gallery, the Rijksmuseum in Amsterdam, MoMA in New York, Uffizi in Florence, and many others, are happy to be associated with), we can try to see how this approach stimulates new ideas, pushes the boundaries of the possible, and helps the emergence of new building blocks for reality. It goes without saying, it is just as important that a different class of scholars and institutions *pulls back* and scrutinises every new idea. Concerns and skepticism are not undesirable, when they counterbalance a strong and almost aggressive force such as technological advancement. We need every voice out there to move forward as a society in a coherent way.

## Acknowledgments

I would like to thank George A. Dunn for helping with the editing of the opening narrative.

## Notes

1 Variable Media Questionnaire: http://variablemediaquestionnaire.net (last seen October 9, 2020).
2 DOCAM's Decision Tree: http://www.docam.ca/en/restoration-decisions/a-deci sion-making-model-the-decision-tree.html (last visit October 9, 2020).
3 Haptic field was originally designed for the Berliner Festspiele's Immersion program in 2017: http://www.chrissalter.com/haptic-field/ (last visited October 9, 2020).
4 The body that carries me was presented at the Guggenheim Museum in Bilbao: http://ernestoneto.guggenheim-bilbao.eus/en/ (last visited October 9, 2020).
5 http://sensorymovingimagearchive.humanities.uva.nl (last visited October 9, 2020).
6 Google Arts and Culture: https://performingarts.withgoogle.com/en (last visited October 9, 2020).

## Bibliography

Auslander, P. (2006). The performativity of performance documentation. *PAJ: A Journal of Performance and Art 28*(3), 1–10.

Barbuto, A. and L. Barreca (2013). Maxxi pilot tests regarding the documentation of installation art. *Preserving and exhibiting media art*, pp. 181–195. In Noordegraaf et al. (2013).

Bowers, J., L. Bannon, M. Fraser, J. Hindmarsh, S. Benford, C. Heath, G. Taxén, and L. Ciolfi (2007). From the disappearing computer to living exhibitions: Shaping inter-activity in Museum settings. *The Disappearing Computer*, Volume 4500 of *LNCS*, pp. 30–49. Berlin: Springer-Verlag.

Bressan, F. and S. Canazza (2014, December). The challenge of preserving Interactive Sound Art: A multi-level approach. *International Journal of Arts and Technology 7*(4), 294–315.

Briet, S. (2006 [1951]). *What Is Documentation? English Translation of the Classic French Text*. Toronto, ON: Scarecrow.

Brown, A. R. and S. Dillon (2012). Meaningful engagement with Music composition. In D. Collins (Ed.), *The Act of Musical Composition. Studies in the Creative Process*, p. 32. London, UK: Routledge.

Dekker, A. (2013). Methodologies of multimedial documentation and archiving. *Preserving and exhibiting media art*, pp. 149–169. In Noordegraaf et al. (2013).

Duranti, L. (2012, March). Interpares3 - team Canada final report. Technical report, University of British Columbia.

Edmondson, R. (2002, February). *Memory of the World: General Guidelines to Safe-guard Documentary Heritage*. Paris: UNESCO.

Ernst, W. (2010). Underway to the dual system. Classical archives and/or digital memory. *Netpioneers 1.0. Contextualizing Early Net-based Art*, pp. 81–99. Berlin: Sternberg Press.

Hattwick, I., I. Franco, and M. M. Wanderley (2017). The vibropixels: A scalable wireless tactile display system. In S. Yamamoto (Ed.), *International Conference on Human Interface and the Management of Information (HCI)*, Volume 10273, pp. 517–528. Cham: Springer.

Hedstrom, M. (2002, 12–13 April). It's about time: Research challenges in digital archiving and long-term preservation. Final report on a workshop on research chal-lenges in digital archiving. Technical report, Library of Congress, Washington, DC.

Hummelen, I. (2005). Conservation strategies for modern and contemporary art: Recent developments in the Netherlands. *CR: Interdisciplinair vakblad voor conservering en restauratie* Volume 3, pp. 22–26. Hoboken, NJ.

Ignoto, P. (2018). *Development and Implementation of a Vibrotactile Click Track to Assist Contemporary Music Conducting.* Ph.D. thesis, McGill University, Montréal, Canada.

Laurenson, P. and V. van Saaze (2014). Collecting performance-based art: New challenges and shifting perspectives, In O. Remes, L. MacCullock, M. Leino (Eds.), *Performativity in the Gallery: Staging Interactive Encounters*, pp. 27–41. Bern, Switzerland: Peter Lang.

Lerch, A. (2012). *An Introduction to Audio Content Analysis: Applications in Signal Processing and Music Informatics.* Hoboken, NJ: Wiley and Sons.

Noordegraaf, J., C. Saba, B. L. Maitre, and V. Hediger (Eds.) (2013). *Preserving and Exhibiting Media Art.* Amsterdam: Amsterdam University Press.

Phelan, P. (1993). *Unmarked: The Politics of Performance.* London: Routledge.

Rinehart, R. (2007). The media art notation system: Documenting and preserving digital/media art. *Leonardo Journal 40*(2), 181–187.

Salter, C. (2015). *Alien Agency. Experimental Encounters with Art in the Making.* Cambridge, MA: MIT Press.

# 6 Questions and challenges in ubiquitous creativity

*Jøran Rudi*

Ubiquitous technology and ubimus are terms that describe a new paradigm in musicking, characterised by wide participation as well as emergence of new art genres and types of collaboration. This development has been essential in developing professional and semi-professional culture, and it has contributed to the discussion of art's identity as artefact and as process. It has also been important in refocusing the discussion about informal learning, and revitalised broader, ecological perspectives in learning and music studies. The notion of ubiquitousness has found support in established perspectives from technology and sound studies, and the new lens of ubiquitousness directed towards music and musical practices is now important in multi-disciplinary approaches to musicology, social studies, acoustics and computer science. Furthermore, affordances of the online reality and its underlying technologies also form a foundation for music and the arts, and these also come into clear view though the ubiquitous lens.

An essential aspect in ubimus is the potential for creativity outside of established systems or hierarchies, and this chapter aims to contribute a critical understanding of creativity and musical quality to the discussion. The chapter will draw on established theory from learning science, as well as case material from the author's development of digital tools and educational initiatives from the last 20+ years.

## 6.1 Characteristics of ubimus

The term ubimus '...*encompasses ubiquitous computing, mobile and networked music, eco-composition and cooperative composition.*' (Pimenta et al., 2009). A more recent definition (Keller et al., 2014b) concentrates more on social context and targets '*systems of (1) human agents and (2) material resources that (3) afford musical activities through (4) creative support tools.*' Both definitions spring from the changes in music technology and artistic practices that have developed since digitalisation took hold in the early 1990s. Since that time, prices on general computing power and specific music technology have fallen, and general technologies such as the Internet, social media and the *internet of things* (IoT) have played a major role in these changes, as has the relatively recent upswing in *invisible computing*, DIY and maker-culture. Electronic technology has become commonplace, and the powerful and flexible affordances resulting from binary representation have transformed the way we use and partake in music. This broadening of perspective includes everyday nonprofessional activity which take place in venues not traditionally thought of as arenas for music or art. This has consequences for discussion and research on creativity – what it is and how different types of creativity might be adequately described.

In technology studies, a frequent focus is how new technological situations spring from social circumstances, and in turn result in new social circumstances. A much-used example from Weibe Bijker's work on sociotechnical change is his research on how the invention of the bicycle gave increased mobility for women and the relatively new urban proletariat, and the changes that brought for their life quality (Bijker, 1995). Technology is not only a tool; it is also a competence and a skill, and the mentioned bicycle would not have been of much significance had it not become used. The same perspective could be used on electronic technology, and the observable shift in how technology is viewed has part of its base in the broad use of consumer technology. The perception that technology creates alienation has largely been replaced by technology optimism, and there are hardly any societal problems where digital technology is not seen as part of the solution – even in cases that on the outset do not seem to be candidates for this type of approach. As described in Rudi (2019b), in Norway it was even essential in dealing with war refugees from Syria that walked into the country from Russia and Sweden in 2015. On top of their wish list was access to electronic communication, and a proposal for developing an app for helping them find their way in a new country seemed timely.

The two definitions on ubimus mentioned above complement one another and form the comprehensive premise that the study of ubimus must include psychological, technical and social perspectives. The term ubimus often also refers to music as an everyday occurrence; something that is no longer exclusive in either creation, participation or listening, but rather expands the notion of creativity as something that happens when people experience music, regardless of background or location. Everyone can make music. Looking at music through this type of lens pushes everyday musicking and collaborative aspects to the fore, in combination with an interest in availability, and the dramatic changes in communication technologies for computer and smart phone use. It is possible to argue that the focus now is more on music as something that *happens* than as something that is *presented*, and often in arenas and social situations that do not presuppose the (more or less specialist) qualifications and conventions of the past. New genres and combinations of tools, methods and creative content abound, compared to the situation only 20 years ago.

## 6.2   Consequences of ubiquity in music

The broad inclusion of technology in nearly all levels of society has brought new listening skills. We have become accustomed to a wide range of sounds in consumer technology, music and art, and the overall signal density in our everyday environment has increased manyfold as compared to the pre-digital situation. Furthermore, because nearly any sound can be transformed into any other sound, and because sound from digital instruments and production technology is part of nearly all media productions, listeners have been significantly primed for abstractions. Sounds previously unheard are brought to the surface in sound art and music, and listening to these types of sounds as music allows listeners to find music also in their environment. Music as *organised sounds* with or 'without references to their sources,' as described by Edgard Varèse and Pierre Schaeffer respectively, has become broadly accepted, and this type of investigative listening further relates to soundscape listening as described by Schafer (1977) and elaborated by Barry Truax in his *Handbook for Acoustic Ecology* (1978). Audiences for more conventional music also accept this listening mode more easily, previously appreciated only within acousmatic and electronic music. Just today, as a timely example, I am reading a review of a new pop-album that praises the artist for 'including sounds of everyday life: An alarm clock, a spin top, a piece of tape. The listener is allowed to share an expanded sound environment, always rhythmical.'[1]

One can safely say that the musical toolbox has been expanded for all listeners. The omnipresence of digital sound has obscured the notion and possibly the perception of 'the original,' and an undocumented experiment several years ago showed that even highly trained listeners were unable to distinguish originals from digitally processed copies. The experiment was done at NOTAM (Norwegian Centre for Technology in Music and the Arts) somewhere around 2004. Music examples from several genres were compressed to different degrees with several different algorithms. The output, approximately 20 different files, were presented to a panel of approximately 10 highly trained listeners; specialists in acousmatic and electroacoustic music. They were given the task to rank the examples according to quality; which version they believed was the closest to the original. Surprisingly, there was no agreement or even clear tendencies in the test group – nearly none of the participants found the original, neither was there any significant agreement in ranking which files sounded the best.

Regarding availability, technology prices have come down, while computation speed and capacity has increased. Complex sound manipulation can happen quickly, and at low cost. This advancement in hardware has significantly impacted participation, and it is no longer necessary to work in academic or private high-cost studios in order to craft technology-based expressions. Another noticeable technological change is in software design and the introduction of *apps*, mainly tailored for portable devices such as cellphones and tablets. Early generations of computer software for signal processing, starting with the text-based input in the Music N-family, required significant user competence in order to produce meaningful results. Early software with graphical user interfaces (GUIs) also required users to know music theory and/or signal processing methods, as for example sequencers with keyboard input and Miller Puckette's *Max*, launched in the late 1980s. At the time, there was not much of a commercial market, and most innovative software was made at academic institutions. Signal processing softwares were most often designed so that many types of processing could be made within the same program.

The situation today is close to the opposite, much because computation power has become more mobile. This has generated new user groups, in much the same way as radio use changed dramatically when the transistor radio made it possible to take the listening out of the family living room, where the stationary radio set was placed. Radio shows branched out to fit the tastes of the new listener groups, and new repertoire hit the airwaves. Today's parallel in technology is found in the app culture and in the abundance of ready-made components that make electronic experimentation and work affordable and possible without having studied either music or technology.

The major trend in app culture is that most functions are hidden from the user behind a simple-to-use graphical user interface (GUI). Choices are made for the user, the technology should *just work* so that using it should be easy. This approach is significant for the ubiquitous presence of technology and is tailored for the mass market although professional softwares also contribute. Technology and content is distributed efficiently via the Internet, and international material and impulses are present in the local context in the same manner as local material and impulses.

There are also dysfunctional aspects: With the growth of semantic web where different sets of parameters are linked automatically, gradually more of our musical choices can (and most likely will) be taken for us. It is not difficult to imagine that the relatively innocent automatic generation of playlists can be developed into more comprehensive vehicles for influencing musical tastes and actions. Zuboff (2019) presents a very interesting account on how semantic web is penetrating everyday life, and how our behaviour increasingly feeds algorithms that both suggest and control our behavioural patterns. The effect is that the private domain is increasingly being used for commercial exploitation, and that technology becomes more omnipresent and ubiquitous at the same time.

News has never travelled as fast as it does today with the Internet and in particular social media. Peers of different genres find each other easily, and physical distance has become less of an obstacle for collaboration. The Internet band Res Rocket Surfer was pioneering this field with its simple MIDI loops as early as in 1994, and another pioneering project was the Internet concert produced by The Warsaw Autumn Festival in 1998, in collaboration with the Sibelius Academy in Helsinki and NOTAM in Oslo.[2]

The internet steeps humanity in technology, and just searching for information has become synonymous with Google, the third most valuable company on the planet in 2019. The two most valuable companies do e-commerce and produce computers. The outer mechanics of this information age are easily described: availability and ease of use has made technology popular.

Internet distribution has also strengthened the commodity-aspect of music, as music has become virtually free. Although Anderson (2006) points out that Internet distribution makes all types of music available, there is ample evidence that the income from streaming services for the average musician is very small, and that they can rely less on sales of record music than before.[3]

The growth of the commodity-aspect has also reduced the perception that music contains something *essential*, in the sense that it requires concentration and skill from both performer and listener. This is in effect a question of quality, and the discussion about quality is not new. In an interview from the late 1980s, Norwegian composer Arne Nordheim fielded a witty critique about how the ease of technology could result in superficiality: "One thought - one finger," thus pointing to the value of the process of elaborating artistic ideas through skill. Composer Kåre Kolberg's thoughtful comment from 2013 was that "everyone now has access to a computer and a text editing program, but this does not mean that they all become authors."[4] Approximately 40 years earlier computer music pioneer Knut Wiggen saw that the new technology needed a parallel development in the arts for them not to become obsolete relics, and that the democratisation and welfare state (in Sweden) could best be supported if focus on conventional music skills was replaced by a concentration on new technology and composition techniques. As his answer to these challenges, he designed and built a hybrid computer music studio at the Swedish Radio,[5] and developed a new software for composing with numbers directly, omitting the score-based paradigm of the interval-based music and the demand for virtuosity in performance.[6]

Much of these ideas have been realised today in ubiquitous technology; making and performing music today requires less of the traditional competence, and music technology for listening and participation has become a general resource.

All music can be said to spring from a context, and the social aspects of different types of musicking determine much of the musical interaction. Behaviour in a concert hall differs from behaviour in a club setting, and large arenas command a different behaviour than small arenas. Music becomes a vehicle for different attitudes – the relationship between noise and traditional electroacoustic music can for example be likened to that of punk and conventional rock music during mid-late 1970s. Other aspects than well-crafted musicianship became important, because the new music was a voice of rebellion. The broad use of technology is often described as democratisation, and with the emphasis on user experience and ease of use one can easily add *rehumanisation*, as opposed to the previous understanding that technology led to *dehumanisation*. It can however be argued that the *automagic* experience from technology where processes and parameter choices are hidden from the user increases familiarity at the same time as it decreases the user's sense of control.

With this broad view, one can see that music technology is integrated into nearly all genres of music, and no longer reserved for a musical elite with access to specialised studios. Conventional electroacoustic and acousmatic music now represents only one of multiple electronic genres of music and sound art, and the listening mode of reduced listening is no longer dominant. On the contrary, the references to the sound's origin are often essential for grasping the works and appreciating their musical and extra-musical points. The world-renowned sound artist Jana Winderen, for example, is explicit in her focus on sounds from the ocean, and the allure of her works depends on revealing and bringing forth signs of life from the deep. That this contains an element of concern for environmental processes goes without saying. Accepting her sounds as musically worthwhile depends on their spectral qualities and her skills as a musician and composer, but the significance depends on the context of her material.

## 6.3   Ubimus in schools and music education

Ubimus comprises many different types of technology, many types of musical and artistic practices, and many types of creativity and learning. The term might be seen as an interpretative lens; however, if we look back on the technological basis and the immediate results, the essence of ubimus can (arguably) be described as broad participation and informal structures and practices for dissemination and learning. Ubimus depends on digital technologies, making it natural to discuss ubimus in schools from an information and computing technology (ICT) perspective.

### 6.3.1   Incorporation of ICT in schools

In Norway, many schools equip students with laptops or tablets, and electronic resources are well integrated in the teaching of various subjects. Several studies confirm that use of ICT in music education increases engagement and make students willing to work harder than in other classes (Cooper, 2009, Webster, 2007). Furthermore, analysis of the results from PISA tests (Bamford, 2011)[7] shows that systematic education in creative disciplines positively impacts results also in mathematics and language.[8] Chemi (2014) shows that creative activity structures the brain so that it learns better. One can say that creative activity increases the effect of meaning-making processes. Since the 1980s, the computer has invigorated electroacoustic music and become the basis for several new technology-based music genres. Despite this position in modern media production, dedicated educational music software for elementary and secondary schools hardly exists, and the software that is being used is often harvested arbitrarily from the Internet, and not designed and constructed for pupils and young students.

The ministry of education in Norway has had a positive view on including digital technology in music education since the early 1990s. In the education plan *L97* (1996) for Norwegian elementary schools, the general goals for children's music education were described as "playing, dancing, composing and listening." From sixth grade, students should learn how to use recording equipment in listening and evaluating their own music, and from seventh to tenth grade, the goal was to have the students use ICT and digital instruments in their work with music composition. These goals, however, were not described in any detail connecting the learning goals and working methods, types of music or how different types of software could be necessary. This was at an early point in the digital development, before software and other digital tools became abundant; nonetheless the intention of integrating technology was clearly positive.

In 2006, the new and much more detailed education plan for levels 1–10, *Kunnskapsløftet*[9] (Utdanningsdirektoratet, 2005) was launched as a deep reform of the educational system. Here, the overall goal for music education had been rephrased as "playing, composing and listening." For elementary school 4–6 grade, the pupils were expected to learn how to use digital music instruments and digital tools in musical creation, recording and processing of sound and music into personal compositions. At the end of tenth grade students were expected to have developed broad music technological competence for use in listening, playing and composing, and for manipulating sound and creating personal compositions. Again, a positive attitude was evident, but with the same lack of specification on pedagogical material, methods, different types of software and music.

The situation with clear teaching goals, but little concrete advice in this new field has left music teachers across the country without much help in finding appropriate software and tools, and unsurprisingly there is no consensus among the teachers about which softwares to use. As part of the NOTAM survey *Digital tools in music education – a national survey* from 2015, letters were sent to music teachers in all elementary schools in Norway, and about 7% of the schools answered. Eighty-six percent of the respondents knew about digital tools for music, and a little less, approximately 71% used them. Sixty percent of the respondents claimed to have average or better competence in music technology, and more than 80% expressed a need for training, advice and guidance in their teaching with technology. More than 50% said that they found it difficult to evaluate student work with technology, and more than 70% wished for a better integration of technology in music classes. There was clearly no organised coordination between the schools, and teachers used in all 49 different softwares in their teaching, ranging from passive playback of files from YouTube, via notation, sound editing, sequencing and grid-based sample placement as well as pure play with sound by way of interfaces that had nothing to do with sound or music. Of the 49 software packages, *Garageband* (DAW), *Audacity* (sound editor), *Soundation* (sequencer) and *Incredibox* (grid placement of readymade samples) were the most popular. The most popular was Garageband, followed closely by Audacity, and with four times as many users as Soundation and Incredibox.

From the numbers of software packages used, and the big differences between the top four, it is clearly no consensus about which tools are best suited in music education. However with such solid indication that music technology was desirable in education, and that more knowledge and guidance was needed, our interpretation of the data is that a larger and more coordinated effort in music technology would be beneficial. This leads us to the questions of learning goals and software design.

### 6.3.2  Examples of software and workflow design

When the new digital technology was being introduced to the wider music communities, computer skills were not particularly well distributed. For example, less than half of the students in Norway had access to a home computer during the early 1990s. Educational software was in its infancy, and what little there was had little appeal when compared to computer games, which was the genre of computer programs with which children had the most experience. Examples of software development since the early 1990s show how developers have attempted to design software and workflow in order to support broad participation and informal learning.

Computer music pioneer Morton Subotnick's software *Creating Music* (1995)[10] is an early example on software development for music education. The software was organised around notes, melodies and rhythms, and the users would for example move birds around on telephone wires for creating melodies, and cracking eggs in order to make rhythms. A piano roll-representation was also included. Sounds were included on the CD-ROM, and the users could choose between different orchestral instruments, but not replace them with their own sounds or change the sounds through any type of sound processing. No musical training was required to use the software, and a video of pre-school children shows how the software can be used.[11] This was an early example of what is now called *gamification*.

In 2000 French music centre IRCAM released their educational software *10 Jeux d'ecoute*. There is not much material to be found online about this publication, but The E-zine *Sonhors* has published a short description that outlines ten listening exercises, shaped as audio games.[12] Screenshots from the interface can be seen at the website of French Amazon.[13] The games would take the users through a series of core topics, such as classification of sounds, identification of sonic events, sound in space and so forth, and correct answers were needed in order to progress to the next level. The software did not encourage free exploration in the same way as Creating Music, but it attempted to train a type of attention to sound qualities most often associated with the electroacoustic music of that time.

A third example is *DSP* (1996) from Norwegian centre NOTAM.[14] This software was designed to be exploratory and game-like, with a user interface that looked like rusty metal and could have been taken from a computer game. The home screen was a mixer, and all results were placed into this mixer, in order to encourage a compositional focus (Rudi, 1997). Users could generate their own sounds through common synthesis algorithms, or import sounds from the disk on their computer. Sounds could be processed with both unconventional and conventional algorithms such as those found in most music productions. The game was published on a CD-ROM with help files and tutorial texts on sound, acoustics and listening, as well as a brief history of electroacoustic music. Users could also experiment with reverberation in a small program that allowed them to change the room size, sound source and microphone placement. The sound source could be any soundfile from the disk. DSP aimed for free composition of what Landy (2007) has described as sound-based music, and working within the paradigm of fixed intervals was intentionally difficult, as was working with regular rhythms. Thus, DSP can be viewed as a predecessor to 10 Jeux d'ecoute, however with a focus on creative activity, where learning would happen as users explored the program. *DSP* was a direct answer to the plans set out by the Ministry of Education in Norway, where teaching goals in elementary schools included use of technology for both composing and performing.

Apple's Garageband software was launched in 2004, a few years after Creating Music, DSP and 10 Jeux d'ecoute. The program has since the bare bones first version been developed into what now appears as a full-scale DAW. When starting a new session in Garageband, the home screen appears with tracks and instruments that can be performed from them. The user selects instruments (sound samples) from a menu, and sets the time signature, tempo and key. The program is bundled with sound files of different instruments from a large library of pre-made loops, and the sound material is more what one would find in pop music than score-based art music. The user composes by keying in sounds from the computer or playing via MIDI, and teachers find Garageband easy to use in the classroom (Vratulis and Morton, 2011).

A successful combination of sample playback and social media is *Incredibox*. The user will drag samples cut to correct length onto one of a number of tracks (represented as human performers) that will then play back the combination of samples in pre-set patterns within a pop-paradigm. "[Incredibox] has an 'intuitive,' engaging and easy-to-use interface for musical creation, and it employs interaction metaphors free from traditional musical references." (Lima et al., 2018). Most musical choices about sounds and arrangements are made for the user, securing a coherent outcome every time. The results can be saved, uploaded to the Incredibox server and published on the web. The user is given a link to the song for further publication under his/her own profiles.

The use of digital tools and apps is rapidly becoming the international norm in music education, and sequencer software such as Garageband is found to successfully support student work with little or no assistance from teachers (Wise et al., 2011). There has however also been concerns that types of software might lead to shallow fundamental knowledge of sound and music by limiting the users' creative span to the affordances of the tools (Folkestad et al., 1998, Truax, 1986) and the bias software has towards pop music has been critiqued for reinforcing existing paradigms of interval-based music (Beckstead, 2001), rather than exploring new forms of sonic expressions. This type of critique questions which types of learning and creation the technologies support.

### 6.3.3   *Learning and creativity*

Composing music is traditionally thought of as a solitary activity, for which cognitivist and constructivist models can be useful in describing the processes involved. Ubiquitous technology has however changed the way music is often made, and as Siemens (2004) points out, also how we live, learn and interact. He finds that "learning needs and theories that describe learning principles and processes, should be reflective of underlying social environments," and coins the term 'social connectivism' to describe his model. Savage (2005) points out that "the relationship between music and ICT is not one of servant and master, but rather a subtle, reciprocal and perhaps empathetic one (...)" and that technologies "could lead pupils and teachers to engage with and organise sounds in new ways, challenging the very nature of music itself at a fundamental level." Both Siemens and Savage point to music making and learning as socially embedded processes, which necessarily also involve informal learning out of formal contexts. There is a new balance between formal and informal learning, and as Dillon (2004) points out, the teacher has taken on more of a role as facilitator for processes of searching, listening and choosing, followed by reflecting and composing. This corresponds well with my experiences from more than 20 years of producing workshops with the DSP program, where learning has increasingly departed from students' tastes and experiences, making technology increasingly a community of practice.

A broad definition of musical creativity can be found in (Odena, 2014, 203), as "the development of a musical product that is novel for the individual and useful for the situated musical practice." (Keller et al., 2014a, 4) highlight three aspects of creativity: potentials, resources and products, complementing Odena's definition from a more ubiquitous perspective. Gall and Breeze (2005) have presented an elaboration on the 'possibility thinking'-perspective by focusing on the semiotic aspects of sound; where the sounds are coming from and what they mean. Their work matches with Wolf's findings (2013) that structured listening training and the teaching of key concepts in the genre of electroacoustic music enhanced appreciation, and that students gain better factual and conceptual knowledge after having been part of a structured educational effort in listening.

A detailed hierarchy of different types of creativity was originally proposed by Runco (2004), and expanded by Kaufman and Beghetto (2009) into four different types of creativity, starting with *mini c* (personal creative potential), via *little-c* (personal creative performance) and *pro-c* (creative performance that does not necessarily imply widespread recognition) to *big c* (socially acknowledged creative performance). These types are general descriptions, and (Keller et al., 2014a, 19) underline the ubimus focus on little-c as a natural consequence of attention given to creativity outside of professional contexts.

Working with software and other digital tools, and producing sound by way of a GUI, does not necessarily mean that users have learned much about music or composition, or that they have been creative in any way. In order to develop more detailed methods for analysing technology use and collaboration in learning music composition and performance, it is beneficial to study the contexts' social conventions, the processes in the learning situations, and the musical results – which potentials exist and how they have been used. An example attempting this approach is found in Pierroux and Rudi (2020), where we seek to better understand how software affordances and constraints affect types of learning by describing and comparing the compositional processes in Garageband and DSP. We discuss how users are restricted by technological affordances, social conventions and to a large degree also by the types of music they are familiar with.

One example of the impact new technology can have on types of creation is the competition for children "Breaking the Sound Barrier." During the first years of the competition, the submissions showed a huge variety of technical approaches and aesthetics, but as commercial sequencers made their way into the toolbox, a large majority of submissions started to sound very much alike, although still maintaining the character of 'little-c' works. The new, global technology had changed the way the children worked with music, and the previous local flavour was appropriated and reassembled by mechanisms of commercial globalisation.

Dissolving traditional curricular design, and working with musical readymades mainly from pop music forms a relatively new set of restrictions. 'Drag and drop' compositional approaches allow less advanced students to enjoy and complete composition courses without understanding Western music theory and notation, however the creativity-enhancing aspects of these approaches can be questioned, as referred in Wise et al. (2011), but there has not been much research on what competences courses and workshops like these have resulted in, and what the creativity in the outcomes has consisted of. These are difficult questions that would benefit from being addressed from within the ubimus community, as they are essential in all treatments of the effects of the technological affluence that lies at the base for much of the ubimus research.

## 6.4   Summary and conclusions

The study of ubimus aims to encompass systems of: '(1) human agents and (2) material resources that (3) afford musical activities through (4) creative support tools' (Keller et al., 2014a). If such studies are made without closer scrutiny of the learning and creative processes involved in the musical practices, important aspects of musical activities and creativity might remain unnoticed. If we accept Milton Babbitt's point from 1958, where he argues for (contemporary) music as an art that *demands* something from the composer, performer and listener, it becomes clear that skill is involved in both composition and listening.

Quality of music is a difficult subject to breach, as it depends much on personal inclination and knowledge of different musical contexts. Performances in art galleries, for example, emphasise other musical aspects than performances in concert halls, as evident in the discourse on sound art vs. music. Quality of interaction, however is observable through analysis of video recordings, which could impact closer investigations of how different potentials impact creativity. What type of creativity can be observed in workshops where untrained students work with for example Incredibox vs. workshops with a more open software such as DSP? If students are given responsibility for learning something they don't have a particularly well-developed language about, it becomes difficult to make sure that the core knowledge is understood and appreciated. That students have learned to operate a GUI does not make it certain that musical learning has taken place, and the choices they make can easily be more self-affirming than helping them develop new skills. Playing with the technology does not guarantee that any type of creativity has taken place.

One attempt of exploring the balance between prescripting and postscripting in software is the flexible permissions system built into the software *Composing with Sounds* (Pearse et al., 2019), an outcome of a European project anchored at De Montfort University. The software is built around a screen mixer paradigm much like the previously discussed *DSP*, but with non-destructive signal processing, many new sound processing methods, and a significantly updated interface. Here, teachers can open and close parts of the software for the students, and structure lessons according to topic, method, genre and so on. How does structured teaching in *Composing with Sounds* affect creativity in comparison with students' free exploration of the same software?

For ubimus perspectives to have influence on the development on a curricular level, research needs to show exactly what the ubimus contributions are on learning and creativity. A significant advance of the ubimus perspective could be made through investigations on how affordances and limitations of various digital tools shape different musical outcomes, with a focus on how different technologies impact and frame different types of learning. Combining a ubimus perspective with a stronger attention to concrete development of tools and educational efforts will be important in securing a more holistic understanding of creativity in music education, exploiting the digital competences of the student while at the same time letting the teacher direct the focus of the efforts.

## Notes

1 Review of the pop artist Anja Garbarek, In the digital music magazine Ballade (2019).

2 The concert WHO - HOW - WOH was produced with musicians in each of the three cities, and all the data was transmitted via the Internet, with an average ten second delay between each city pair. Several types of data was used, and the concert was an interesting research project in addition to being a well-received part of the Warsaw festival. More info here: http://joranrudi.no/who-how-woh/

3 In his book *Culture crash*, Timburg (2015) presents a well-documented and vivid account of how the conditions for the many genres of the creative class has changed dramatically with new Internet technologies.

4 Kåre Kolberg in an interview with the author (March 10, 2013).

5 The studio was called Elektronmusikstudion (EMS). More information about the current activities and profile at their website http://elektronmusikstudion.se.

6 Knut Wiggen laid out this perspective in several publications, and his book *De två musikkulturerna*, published by Swedish broadcasting corporation in 1972 provides a comprehensive overview. This book however is in Swedish, and readers are referred to Rudi (2018, 2019a, 2020) for further discussion of his approaches to music and technology.

7 Program for International Student Assessment (PISA) is an initiative from OECD. More information on their webpage http://www.oecd.org/pisa.

8 As an instance of this, see Chapter 8 for a comprehensive discussion of computational thinking in music, an approach which is supported by a mix of creative and technical concerns.

9 https://www.udir.no/kl06/MUS1-01/Hele/Hovedomraader.

10 http://www.creatingmusic.com.

11 https://www.youtube.com/watch?v=mqWB4M9AHYU.

12 http://sonhors.free.fr/kronik/10jeuxdecoute.htm.

13 https://www.amazon.fr/Hyptique-10-jeux-découte/dp/2914342012.

14 http://www.notam02.no/DSP/index-e.html.

## Bibliography

Anderson, C. (2006). *The Long Tail: Why the Future of Business Is Selling Less of More*. New York, NY: Hyperion.

Babbitt, M. (1958). Who cares if you listen? *High Fidelity 8*, 38–40, 126–127.

Ballade (2019). Edvard-pris til Ania Garbarek. http://www.ballade.no/sak/edvard-pris-til-anja-garbarek/.

Bamford, A. (2011). *Arts and Cultural Education in Norway*. Bodø: The Norwegian Centre for Arts and Cultural Education.

Beckstead, D. (2001). Will technology transform music education? *Music Educators Journal 87*(6), 44–49.

Bijker, W. (1995). *Of Bicycles, Bakelites, and Bulbs*. Cambridge, MA: MIT Press.

Chemi, T. (2014). The Art of Arts Integration. Aalborg: Aalborg universitetsforlag.

Cooper, L. (2009). The gender factor: Teaching composition in music technology lessons to boys and girls in year 9. In J. Finney and P. Burnard (Eds.), *Music Education with Digital Technology*, pp. 30–40. London: Continuum.

Dillon, T. (2004). 'It's in the mix baby': Exploring how meaning is created within music technology collaborations. In D. Miell and K. Littleton (Eds.), *Collaborative Creativity: Contemporary Perspectives*, pp. 144–157. London: Free Association Bo.

Folkestad, G., D. Hargreaves, and B. Lindström (1998). Compositional strategies in computer-based music-making. *British Journal of Music Education 15*(1), 83–97.

Gall, M. and N. Breeze (2005). Music composition lessons: The multimodal affordances of technology. *Educational Review 57*(4), 415–433.

Kaufman, J. C. and R. A. Beghetto (2009). Beyond big and little: The four c model of creativity. *Review of General Psychology 13*(1), 1–12.

Keller, D., V. Lazzarini, and M. Pimenta (2014a). Ubimus through the lens of creativity theories. In D. Keller, V. Lazzarini, and M. Pimenta (Eds.), *Ubiquitous Music*, pp. 3–23. Berlin: Springer.

Keller, D., V. Lazzarini, and M. Pimenta (2014b). *Ubiquitous Music*. Berlin: Springer.

Landy, L. (2007). *Understanding the Art of Sound Organisation*. Cambridge, MA: MIT Press.

Lima, M., D. Keller, and L. Flores (2018). Eco-composition and everyday creative musical practices: Theory and practice experience in ubiquitous music research at ufrgs application school with high school students in and out of the classroom. In *Proceedings of the 1st International Conference Music for and by Children*, pp. 139–151. Aveiro, Portugal.

Odena, O. (2014). Perspectives on musical creativity: Where next. In O. Odena (Ed.), *Musical Creativity: Insights from Music Education Research*, pp. 201–214. London: Routledge.

Pearse, S., L. Landy, D. Chapman, D. Holland, and M. Eniu (2019). Composing with sounds: Designing an object-oriented daw for the teaching of sound-based composition. In *Proceedings from Sound and Music Computing 2019*. http://smc2019.uma.es/articles/S4/S4_02_SMC2019_paper.pdf.

Pierroux, P. and J. Rudi (2020). Teaching composition with digital tools: A domain-specific perspective. In K. Knutson, T. Okada, and K. Crowley (Eds.), *Multidisciplinary Approaches to Art Learning and Creativity: Fostering Artistic Exploration in Formal and Informal Settings*. London: Routledge.

Pimenta, M., L. Flores, A. Capasso, P. Tinajero, and D. Keller (2009). Ubiquitous music: Concepts and metaphors. In *Proceedings of Brazilian Symposium on Computer Music*, pp. 139–150. Recife, Brazil.

Rudi, J. (1997). DSP for children. In *ICMC Proceedings*. http://www.joranrudi.no/mediefiler/DSP\%20for\%20Children\%20-\%20ICMC\%201997.pdf.

Rudi, J. (2018). Unpacking the musical and technical innovation of knut wiggen. *Organised Sound 23*(2), 195–207.

Rudi, J. (2019a). *Elektrisk lyd i Norge*. Oslo: Novus.

Rudi, J. (2019b). Representation, complexity and control – three aspects of technology-based sonic art. In T. Toft (Ed.), *Digital Dynamics*, pp. 161–178. London: Intellect/University of Chicago Press.

Rudi, J. (2020). The musical imagination of Knut Wiggen. In K. Hagan and M. Puckette (Eds.), *Between the Tracks*, pp. 83–111.. Cambridge, MA: MIT Press.

Runco, M. A. (2004). Creativity. *Annual Review of Psychology 55*(1), 657–687.

Savage, J. (2005). Working towards a theory for music technologies in the classroom: How pupils engage with and organise sounds with new technologies. *British Journal of Music Education 22*(2), 167–180.

Schafer, M. (1977). *The Tuning of The World*. New York, NY: Random House.

Siemens, G. (2004). Connectivism: A learning theory for the digital age. http://www.elearnspace.org/Articles/connectivism.htm.

Timburg, S. (2015). *Culture Crash*. New Haven, CT: Yale University Press.

Truax, B. (1978). *Handbook for Acoustic Ecology*. Vancouver: Arc Publications, Vancouver University.

Truax, B. (1986). Computer music language design and the composing process. In S. Emmerson (Ed.), *The Language of Electroacoustic Music*, pp. 155–173. London: MacMillan.

Utdanningsdirektoratet (2005). Kunnskapsløftet. https://www.udir.no/laring-og-trivsel/lareplanverket/finn-lareplan/lareplan/?kode=MUS1-01.

Veiteberg, J. (1996). Læreplanverket for den 10-årige grunnskolen, L97. https://www.nb.no/nbsok/nb/f4ce6bf9eadeb389172d939275c038bb.

Vratulis, V. and C. Morton (2011). A case study exploring the use of garageband and an electronic bulletin board in preservice music education. *British Journal of Music Education 11*(4), 398–419.

Webster, P. R. (2007). Computer-based technology and music teaching and learning: 2000–2005. In L. Bresler (Ed.), *International Handbook of Research in Arts Education*, pp. 1311–1328. Berlin: Springer.

Wiggen, K. (1972). *De två musikkulturerna*. Stockholm: Sveriges Radio.

Wise, S., J. Greenwood, and N. Davis (2011). Teachers' use of digital technology in secondary music education: Illustrations of changing classrooms. *British Journal of Music Education 28*(2), 117–134.

Wolf, J. (2013). The appreciation of electroacoustic music: The prototype of the pedagogical electroacoustic resource site. *Organised Sound 18*(2), 124–133.

Zuboff, S. (2019). *The Age of Surveillance Capitalism: The Fight for a Human Future at the New Frontier of Power*. London: Profile Books.

# 7 Ubiquitous music research in basic-education contexts

*Maria Helena de Lima, Luciano Vargas Flores, and Jean Carlos Figueiredo de Souza*

Applications and contributions of ubimus to the field of education are one of the many aspects of its research (Keller et al., 2014b). In this chapter, we focus on ubimus research in the field of formal education, specifically in basic-education context, by describing investigative and learning experiences carried out in the *Ubimus Research in Basic Education* project at the Rio Grande do Sul Federal University (UFRGS) Application School (CAp-UFRGS[1]). This project builds on the dialogical perspective proposed by Freire (1999), which centres on the experience of the teacher as a researcher of his/her own educational praxis, and on the students as collaborators, researchers, and actors of investigative actions in the school context, both in and out of the classroom. We highlight, during the whole research process, the participation of high-school students from CAp – enabled through *junior scientific induction* (ICJr)[2] sponsorship – as ubimus researchers themselves. Also, partnerships and collaborations with the g-ubimus researchers – representing various areas of knowledge – were important throughout the process. All that emphasises the multidisciplinary nature of the g-ubimus, as well as the interdisciplinary and transdisciplinary qualities of ubimus research.

This chapter addresses the following aspects of the investigative process in basic education, implemented by student-researchers under teacher's advice: the application of a cognitive-ecological approach; creation, composition, collaboration, and sharing activities using available technological infrastructure, and in settings not originally planned for artistic activity; and eco-compositional practice. The latter is of special interest to the development and application of proposals and initiatives related to musical creativity in school environments, as it enables an expanded view of space, time, and resources: where, when, and how creative activities can be accomplished.

Finally, we also report some contributions from students and former students of CAp, who took part in the project as fellow researchers in ubimus: their narratives, testimonials, reflections, and the repercussion and impact of ubimus in their visions about music, creativity, and in their connections with the world.

All the activities reported here, involving ubimus teaching and research, were carried out in the school context (encompassing its everyday formal and informal settings), at a public school, in an urban environment. Although the CAp application school represents a different reality from the majority of other Brazilian public schools as it is associated with a university, it still shares with them many of common challenges and opportunities found in these settings. In general, we should note that application schools in Brazil represent public spaces for the implementation of experiments in teaching, research, and community engagement on basic education. It is our belief that an aspect of the mission of application schools is precisely to produce knowledge and to divulge experiences in basic education, so that these can be potentially reflected and replicated in great extent. Our research project represents one of such efforts.

## 7.1   Ubimus and its applications in basic education

The ubimus research in basic education, as implemented in CAp-UFRGS, is methodologically grounded on the application of the dialogical approach, and on the perspective of collective knowledge construction (Freire, 1999), by regarding the teacher as researcher and instigator of actions that encourage students to participate and perform as researchers.

Since 2012, several ubimus teaching and research activities, involving the participation of basic-education students, have been conducted at CAp-UFRGS. Accomplished experiments in ubimus research and learning contributed to strengthen discussion and to expand potential fields of action in this emerging research area, within basic education, especially in relation to the subject of *everyday musical creativity* (or little-c music, see Chapter 2). In that sense, we note that one of the main research questions raised in ubimus is to understand appropriation, by musicians and novices, of ordinary tools which are available in their environment, to perform activities of music creation straight from their niches.[3] From that perspective, ubimus research in the basic-education context has aimed at developing proposals which will foster reasoning, and which enhance the foundation of works in music education that emphasise the importance of the creative and compositional process. Furthermore, that emphasise the repurposing of technological infrastructure and of existing resources in educational settings (inside and outside of the classroom), through cognitive-ecological creative practices.

## 7.2   Musical creativity: cognitive-ecological creative practices

One of the three perspectives applied to ubimus research is the ecological approach, also described as cognitive-ecological creative practices (also eco-cognitive, or eco-compositional) (Keller and Lazzarini, 2017). This branch of investigation seeks to apply ecological concepts to the interaction design field, and to educational practices (Lima et al., 2014).

Regarding eco-systemic perspectives, one can say that those, at first, considered creativity as the result of interactions between multiple variables, here including interactions between living and inorganic components, and focusing on *problem-solving* strategies (Harrington, 1990). In contrast, cognitive-ecological creative practices broaden the focus of creativity beyond problem solving, since they assume the perspective that not every creative occurrence involves solving problems, and that not every problem solution demands creativity (Runco, 2004). In this sense, creativity may be defined as the useful and effective response to evolutionary changes. This definition allows for including phenomena which cannot be characterised a priori as *problems*.

For Donald (2006), one of the aspects which characterises artistic labour is auto-reflection. That means, artistic activity does not solely involve material resources, it also demands behavioural changes regarding the understanding of the world. Accordingly, artistic effort at the same time modifies the environment in which it occurs and the agents that take part in such activity.

Another aspect that is not considered by views centred in problem solving, comprises the knowledge acquisition strategy. A teleological creative approach requires delimiting the problem in order to allow the search for solutions (Fantauzzacoffin and Rogers, 2013). Observations made in multiple ubimus experiments indicate that persons involved in creative musical activities often spend a great amount of the time in exploring resources and possibilities of action, which are considered epistemic activities (Keller et al., 2014a, Kirsh and Maglio, 1994). Thus, support for exploration in ubimus, following exchange and dialogue-based approaches – or dialogical approaches – seems to be a more effective educational strategy than encouraging the delimitation of a task, considering satisfaction of the demands of creative practices.

As an alternative to the teleological standpoint, ecological practices concentrate in getting the most out of resources which enable the creative activity (Keller et al., 2014a). Harrington (1990) suggests that there is a dynamics of the flow of cognitive and environmental material resources, which lifts creative processes. From this point, creative phenomena would not be just a consequence of personality factors but would turn up as emerging properties of the interaction between agents and the environment. Such a perspective is consistent with methods adopted in cognitive-ecological creative practices (Keller et al., 2014a).

Projects from g-ubimus are supporting a set of methods based on ecological cognition, aiming at assisting everyday musical creativity (Keller and Lima, 2016). Aliel et al. (2015) refer to some common features of ecological cognition based approaches: (1) Social interaction as central to creative processes (Keller and Capasso, 2006); (2) Everyday settings as the ideal venue for artistic practice (Keller et al., 2013); and (3) Incentive to exploratory activity by using local resources (Burtner, 2005), and through technological support.

Educational implications are multiple. The first item agrees with the dialogical proposals (Freire, 1999) already present in ubimus efforts in the educational field (Lima, 2013, 2018, Lima et al., 2012, 2014, 2017, 2018). It also stresses the need to reason over the development of collaborative technologies which allow forms of social interaction in line with ubimus perspectives, as the increase in information circulation, fostered by virtual social networks, points to severe problems when content control aims at commercial purposes. By considering the impact of the creative activity on the environment, the ecological approach emphasises individual responsibility in the creative act, seeking to avoid low-quality sub-products, or activities demanding high investments and with limited social benefit (Small, 1986).

The second aspect, diversification of creative work spaces, gives rise to new demands for technological support and suggests points in common with ethnomusicology research. Yet, an important difference between ecological methods in creativity and ethnomusicologic studies lies in the studied subject: whereas ethnomusicology focuses established cultural manifestations, ubimus research concentrates on the creative potential. This emphasis puts in evidence the need to develop methods applicable not only to existing musical practices (e.g., the manifestations of instrumental music), but also to forthcoming ones. An example of such developments is the musical exploration of the Internet of Things, or, in this particular case, the Internet of Musical Things (IoMusT, see Chapter 9). As this research area comes out of the ubimus domain, it may have important implications to music making and educational actions in domestic environments (Keller and Lazzarini, 2017).

As for the usage of local resources, current creative musical activities depend upon the existence of support infrastructure. Availability of IoMusT is a good example, since technologic-musical activities become constrained to the existence of internet access services, which in some cases may be limiting if we consider the scope of Basic Education spaces, and the great social diversity – sometimes inequity in reaching resources – as observed in the Brazilian context.

Ecological approaches, cognitive-ecological, eco-cognitive, or eco-compositional creative practices, when applied to the fields of interaction design and educational practice (Lima et al., 2014) constitute research challenges in ubimus. For the last years of research, we noticed an increase in the application of interdisciplinary and transdisciplinary approaches to ubimus research, in all levels. Also, the application of these approaches has been aiming to fulfil growing demands which emerge daily in this multidisciplinary field.

## 7.3   Interdisciplinarity and transdisciplinarity in ubimus research

Ubimus research, as a whole, has been approaching interdisciplinary practices over its years of existence. Our research project at CAp-UFRGS has been seeking both to apply and to focus on interdisciplinary research approaches, as well as over transdisciplinary opportunities. That means, both approaches permeate the whole research process, and they are also topics for studies and regular discussions/seminars organised with the group of scientific induction fellows. From the standpoint of the cognitive-ecological view in ubimus, and considering research also as an educating process in the realm of basic education, interdisciplinary and transdisciplinary research approaches may present themselves as options which fulfil, to a greater extent, the complexity of demands and paths taken throughout the process.

Work in education with an emphasis on research, and having basic-education students as research partners, is a challenge. The school environment, where students live most of the time, presents itself, in its diversity and complexity, as a space that is rich in learning and coexistence opportunities. At the same time, it is a challenging environment as a result of that same complexity. Thus, working with focus on creativity means deciding to go beyond the limitations imposed by disciplines.

Domingues (2012) points out that both interdisciplinarity and transdisciplinarity offer a more plastic viewpoint of education since they favour experimentation and disciplinary transgression. For Nicolescu (2000), interdisciplinary research relates to transferring methods from one discipline to the other, but still remains inscribed in disciplinary research. Transdisciplinarity, instead, as indicated by its prefix, "...deals with what is, at the same time, between disciplines, crossing different disciplines, and beyond any discipline, aiming understanding of the present world through knowledge unification" (Nicolescu, 2000, 11). Nicolescu stresses that transdisciplinary research is complementary, though radically distinct from interdisciplinary research, since its purpose is "...the understanding of the current world, something impossible to inscribe in disciplinary research" (Nicolescu, 2000, 13). Transdisciplinarity comprises the attempt to go beyond and through disciplines, in a transgressive move which breaks barriers and disciplinary rules, and which confronts disciplines. Its approach does not aim at the knowledge domain of several disciplines, but to open all disciplines to what they share and to what exceeds them (Nicolescu, 1999). For Klein (2004), the goal of transdisciplinarity is to offer comprehensive theoretical syntheses that are capable of unifying knowledge, in the vein of systems and complexity theory. It represents a new paradigm, not just an attitude, a method, or a view. Also, there is not an inevitable progression from multidisciplinarity, to interdisciplinarity, and arriving at transdisciplinarity (Jordan apud (Pombo et al., 2006: 94)).

Research and scientific induction approaches with youngsters in a school context tend to benefit from interdisciplinary and transdisciplinary views. For, according to Nicolescu (2000), *learning to know* means to be able to build bridges between a multitude of expertise, between that knowledge and their meanings for ordinary life, between that knowledge and our own individual references. Thus, a transdisciplinary approach can be an essential complement to the disciplinary process, since it leads to the emergence of individuals capable of adapting to the changing demands of professional life. They are thus embodied with permanent flexibility, always aimed at updating their inner potentials (Domingues, 2012). The adoption of an interdisciplinary and transdisciplinary approach to ubimus research, in the context of basic education at CAp, has the goal to seek an expanded and plastic viewpoint for musical research related to everyday musical creativity. From an inter- and transdisciplinary research perspective, we see musical production as a complex phenomenon, which involves social, scientific, technical, and educational aspects. Those can be studied as measurable and computable facts, and at the same time as a semantically complex phenomenon. By establishing strict relationships between knowledge areas, the vision of the students' musical knowledge is refined and grounded on experience.

### 7.4 Experiencing scientific induction in ubimus with high-school students from CAp

At UFRGS, research activities of scientific induction level are offered to high-school students through the junior scientific induction program (PIBIC, PIBIC-CNPq, and FAPERGS[4] scholarships), promoted by UFRGS research administration and implemented exclusively at CAp. Through this program, many students that are still in basic education have the opportunity to conduct specialised research, coordinated and advised by teachers/researchers from different areas and departments of UFRGS. Our ubimus research project at CAp is one of the actions that have been providing, to a great extent, opportunities for student participation in research and studies linked to this topic.

Several ICJr fellow students have been experiencing ubimus research, with results being systematically presented at the main research event of the university (*Salão de Pesquisa da UFRGS*) and in research events promoted by CAp itself. Results are also being published and presented in music education and music research events in Brazil and abroad, such as the International Society for Music Education (ISME) (Lima, 2018, Lima et al., 2014), Musichildren – Music for and by Children: Perspectives from Children Composers, Performers and Educators (Lima et al., 2018), and the National Association for Research and Post-Graduation in Music (ANPPOM) (Keller et al., 2014), and in education and music education publications, as the *Journal of Music, Technology and Education* (Lima et al., 2012, 2017), as well as the *Oxford Handbook of Community Music* (Brown et al., 2018).

Methodologically, students' research activities comprise both individual and collective moments. The latter include small-scale seminars involving the proposal of reading topics which interconnect (technology, technique and science; complexity, interdisciplinarity, transdisciplinarity; ethics, society; mind and music; music, composition, creativity), together with readings in topics related to ubimus research. The introduction of transversal themes, through collective reading and discussion, allows the students an opportunity for thought and for potential broadening of their views on research and on music.

Besides, during these collective moments, discussions take place concerning the specific research themes developed by each student-researcher. In these events, students have the opportunity to present and share their own research and the data they collected, results, individual questions and demands with their colleagues. They also have the chance to hear suggestions about their research, and about strategies for collective action and experiment planning, method choices, and for setting up protocols for experiment execution and data gathering and analysis.

During the individual research moments, each student focuses on their specific subject, dedicating time to take notes, do bibliographic reviews, and plan research strategies aiming the design of ubimus experiments. Throughout the whole research process, students are motivated to:

- do their own interventions and creative experiments, following the idea that we are not just recipients of sound, but also co-authors of our own soundscapes;
- explore the creative possibilities of sonic intervention in their daily lives/niches, including the available tools and technologies to realise their own musical compositions/creations (i.e., eco-composition);
- find relationships among activities, individual and collective experiments, and knowledge acquired in ubimus, with other knowledge areas; and
- share experiences by presenting their research in the seminars proposed by the school and the university.

### 7.4.1   Creative experiments in ubimus research

Between 2012 and 2018, ubimus student-researchers were encouraged to implement and take part in ubimus studies and experiments in the school context, in and out of the classroom, with colleagues and teachers. These experiments targeted everyday musical creativity, particularly eco-composition activities, where the focus of experimental sessions (and their evaluation) was not the tools and technology, but the whole experience of their use for creative ends (Lima et al., 2012).

Several aspects, raised from the studies conducted in that period, indicate educational possibilities to explore and develop within ubimus. The studies conducted involved the participation of high-school students and students from other levels of basic education, since the primary grades (see Section 7.5), besides teachers from CAp. These studies took place at different moments of the school routine. Two studies were conducted during curricular courses offered as elective disciplines to the high-school students of CAp. One of the experiments in eco-composition, which spanned a complete semester, is described in detail in Lima (2018), and Lima et al. (2018). To illustrate how we apply, in practice, our methodology based upon individual and collective activities, and how eco-composition may take part in ubimus research experiments, a brief description of this experiment follows.

Initially, music audition sessions featured listening and discussion of *Tacet 4'33"* (John Cage, 1952) and *Toco Y Me Voy* (Touch'n'go, Damián Keller, 1999). These works were used as triggers for discussion of concepts such as music, sound, silence, artistic creation, composition, sonic materials, and resources used for musical creation. Topics related to acoustic and physical phenomena of sound were also discussed during the meetings.

Other activities carried out by the participants included:

- Readings, hearings, video sessions, and discussions of concepts such as creation, composition, and ubiquitous music;
- Try-outs and analyses of tools for composition: CODES (Miletto et al., 2011), Kristal (Kreatives.org, 2020), Audacity (Audacity, 2020), etc.;
- Audio-sampling sessions using mobile phones;
- Sharing of the collected audio data within the groups;
- Choosing, converting, and editing audio; and
- Group asynchronous composition of the *Sounds of CAp* piece, its presentation to an audience, and assessment of the creative products.

After a period of familiarisation with sound-manipulation tools, students proceeded to collect daily sounds around the CAp premises. They performed soundwalks (while keeping in silence) through the various spaces of the school (Schafer, 1986). Next, they recorded audio samples using their mobile phones. These recordings continued to take place in the later stages and at other places within CAp. Students dealt with sound file conversion, editing, and sharing of the collected audio data. Editing sessions were usually performed in pairs on desktop computers available in the music room. After several weeks of activities, the group agreed that the final objective was to achieve a collective composition. The group did not aim at a *compositional patchwork* or a puzzle of isolated pieces. Their goal was to conceive a collective composition/creation. Hence, the materials were shared among all participants so that all editions could be analysed and modified by everyone. The choices of sonic manipulations also were discussed among the group members.

After the compositional process, the students were also involved in planning and preparing the venue setup for the public presentation of the piece. Their involvement was intense: the group selected and tested equipment distribution, placing speakers in the four corners of the room. They arranged a circle of chairs at the centre of the room. They reduced external light by covering the windows with sheets of paper. The intent was to have the audience immersed in the sound, minimising external distractions.

The presentation sessions attracted students from various levels of Basic Education (from 6 to 17 years old). At the end of each session, students talked about their impressions and were also invited to write or draw about it. A total of 41 participants from the audience left remarks after each listening session, through written records or drawings (these made by the younger kids). This material was shared among the group of research-students, so they could analyse it and discuss their interpretations.

The five research-students elaborated their research conclusions based on their personal observations and on the data collected all through the project activities. Discussions focused on three topics: tools, processes, and creative outcomes. Aside from systematic observations carried during the Sounds of CAp study, we collected informal statements from the research-students.

These testimonials provide interesting insights into their creative processes. Furthermore, the discussions fostered reflections on the students' experiences as creators and researchers.

While dealing with tools (devices, software, and supporting materials), research-students drew attention to the importance of user interfaces in minimising the need for tutorials. They noticed that much of the commercially available software still follows an instrumentally oriented view of music making (Tanaka, 2009), enforcing individual authorship and demanding domain specific knowledge (e.g., of instrumental music theory). From their perspective, these features hinder a more extensive usage by laypeople and prevent the adoption in distinct learning contexts. They believe that music creation programs need simpler and more "intuitive" interfaces, to foster the participation of untrained people and the educational applications of musical creative activities. The research-students also suggested that multi-platform tools would support activities across multiple devices – whether connected to the network or not. Another important feature pointed out was remote sharing between users, which supports collective asynchronous activities.

Regarding the creative process, several research-students concluded that, among current frameworks within ubiquitous music research, eco-composition encourages reflection on the potential of creative and critical attitudes in daily life. After analysing data from the questionnaires, the *in-loco* observations, and their personal annotations, the student-researchers noted that the majority of participants described the exploration of materials and the creation of sound products as being fun. They also observed, while sharing ideas and materials during the creative process, that there is a game-like quality associated with the exploratory use of technological tools.

Another aspect raised by student-researchers, was that none of the participants expressed any need for training on (pre-existing or traditional) musical knowledge while doing their creative explorations. The experiments highlighted the differences between the design of user interfaces for musicians and the demands of everyday musical tasks. The participants observed that the use of metaphors associated with everyday activities may help the development of applications targeting a general, non-specialist, public. Hence, people who never thought of making music could eventually get access to creative music making.

From the analysis of data gathered during the public presentation of the Sounds of CAp composition, students observed that, despite being always immersed in a sonic ambient in their everyday life, most people usually do not notice their surrounding soundscape. But as the days go by, we are not aware of the subtle sonic effects of our actions on our surroundings. The recordings collected by the students throughout the semester highlighted their responsibility as active agents of multiple transformations in our environment.

Finally, research-students noticed that the adoption of a systematic research project helped them to expand their understanding of connections between their research topics and existing knowledge, also helping them to be prepared for their future academic experiences. According to a 14 y.o. student-researcher, "humans have always tried to understand the world, their surroundings and themselves. Scientific research, as well as its methods, constitutes a tool to aid in building this understanding. We do research because we want to understand what surrounds us, and we want to understand ourselves". More specifically on music research, a 16 y.o. student-researcher stated that "despite we recognise that we are surrounded, affected and influenced by sounds at all times, we don't give enough attention to research related to music. Maybe because it is an area engaged with subjective, artistic, aesthetic and even emotional aspects, the presence of music as a field in the scientific domain is still somewhat limited. Its value is diminished". Other insightful observations, by research-students from the Ubimus Research at CAp project, are the subject of Section 7.5

### 7.4.2   *G-ubimus partnerships*

Many partnership actions have been implemented with members of the g-ubimus joined to the ubimus research project at CAp. Such partnerships take place through occasional actions (meetings, talks), implemented projects, experiments and information exchange, as well as through publication of results from these actions in common.

Some of the occasional events counted on the participation of members from LCM (the Computer Music Lab at UFRGS) (LCM, 2019). ICJr fellowship students from the Ubimus Research Project at CAp visited the LCM, and were able to share their thematic research, exchange information, ideas and references with researchers from the g-ubimus. One of the activities realised with the LCM at the time was a sound synthesis workshop. During the IV Ubimus Workshop, organised in 2013 by the LCM and the Institute of Informatics in cooperation with CAp-UFRGS, high-school students who took part in ubimus activities at CAp had the opportunity to meet g-ubimus members and to exchange ideas and information.

One of the initiatives which gathered several g-ubimus members with student-researchers from the CAp Ubimus Research Project, is an interdisciplinary project named CODES – COoperative Musical Prototype DESign (Miletto et al., 2011). This project is a platform that allows ordinary web users, non-musicians, to carry out collaborative musical experiments. CODES project intended to design interaction and interface so to build a useful and usable system, even for lay people in music, through a graphical interface with an alternative, simplified musical representation. During 2014–2015, CAp was a partner of the Rio Grande do Sul Federal Institute (IFRS) Porto Alegre Campus and LCM-UFRGS in the CODES project. As part of this, research fellows from the ubimus project at CAp collaborated with developers from IFRS. The research-students contributed with great amounts of data, collected from educational experiments at the CAp school using CODES. They also shared their impressions, analyses and ideas based upon studies of their own, and contributing to the implementation of the system.

Several actions, discussions and information interchanges also took place with members from NAP – the Amazon Centre for Music Research, from the Federal University of Acre (UFAC) and the Federal Institute of Acre (IFAC), in northwestern Brazil. This dialogue is continuing through student implemented projects, and via experiments implemented with tools developed by NAP, e.g., the mixDroid and the SoundSphere (Bessa et al., 2015, Farias et al., 2014). Furthermore, such collaboration has also extended to the exchange of ideas on data gathering tools used during experiments at CAp in the basic-education context.

Finally, also experiments on the creation of musical prototypes using Arduino-based tools have been implemented by the CAp Ubimus Research Project, in partnership with the CTA (Academic Technology Centre), linked to CAp and the Institute of Physics from UFRGS. Work made with Arduino is grounded on the concept, within ubimus, of music creation by means of accessible, available, and low-cost technology (see also Chapter 3 for an overview on DIY hardware).

## 7.5 Ubimus research with high-school student-researchers: the student perspective

As previously stated, one of the key efforts of the Ubimus Research Project at CAp is the participation of high-school students, fostered by Junior Scientific induction programs. From the beginning of the project, we have seen a growing interest from high-school students for research related to the field of music and its connections with technology.

Between 2017 and 2019, a data compilation process was done by an undergraduate research fellow linked to the project, as part of ubimus research at CAp. Its goal was to map (quantitatively and qualitatively) the impact of the experience in junior scientific induction among fellow and former fellow students, who took part in the ubimus research at CAp since 2012–2019. One activity from this research consists of surveying those students, using questionnaires and interviews. Questionnaires aimed at aspects concerning the students' former experience with research in junior scientific induction context, their perspective of the research process, their opinion about research in Ubimus and about its relation with educational contexts. They also focused on gathering personal impressions from the research-students, in relation to the time spent participating in the research, and about possible *paradigm shifts* they perceived during the process concerning previously-assumed concepts. This section presents data collected through these applied questionnaires between the first semester of 2018 and the first semester of 2019, from a sample of ten fellowship and former fellowship students.

On previous experiences in scientific induction, 70% of the students stated they already had participated in scientific induction programs during primary education. Note that curricular scientific induction is implemented by CAp through all levels of primary education, and from the lower secondary stages onward as elective courses. As for ICJr-funded projects, these programmes are offered in association with research projects coordinated and developed by teachers from the application school and from other departments of UFRGS. Regarding the scientific induction experience, the following comments were made by the students, concerning the importance of participating in the program:

> Scientific induction completely opened my mind to the world. Learning to apply method, to write and research, helps in understanding the world and how it works. It helps me to understand things and to perceive that which we normally don't perceive. And of course, scientific induction during high school is helping me now that I'm in college, and I believe I am one step ahead of my colleagues who didn't have the same opportunity. It is amazing to see the difference between the students who were already researchers and those who were not. Building up hypotheses goes much faster and well-grounded, logical thinking is faster and reaches further. Research transformed my life this way.

> Practicing scientific research since the school years adds knowledge, critical/analytical viewpoint, responsibility, and autonomy to the researcher, who deals with situations which the majority will only face in college. The practice of observing phenomena, proposing experiments, reading scientific papers, and having contact with a more academic context contributes useful abilities to the young researcher, which will be carried throughout their lives.

Concerning prior music knowledge, brought from before the research experience (e.g., taking music classes), the majority, 90% of the students, declared having some degree of musical knowledge and of previous experiences, mainly through the curricular music course from the own CAp, and one subject reported having taken music classes since the age of 3. Of these, 66.7% considered the previous musical knowledge was useful (for researching in ubimus) and relevant to some extent. Nevertheless, 33.3% of the students stated the opposite – that formal musical knowledge was irrelevant, or of little help concerning the research practice. Comments from two survey participants reveal these two opinions:

> It helped. Having some experience in music, even just a little, helped me to understand how things work [in music]. What was necessary for a music application to be considered good, how its user interface should be designed to allow even the lay, as well as the musician, to use that application satisfactorily, among other things.

> The music course, in my case, was useful as an opportunity for me to express myself musically in a location, in my view, not much suited for

creativity, and also gave me the chance to study using my body and mind in a way not as physically stressful as in physical education. But, since my research field (free ubiquitous musical creation in a school environment) is more pointed towards studying music as a form of science, knowing how to play certain instruments and understanding musical scores did not provide me with significant support for my studies.

When questioned whether formal musical knowledge is essential to musical creative work, 50% of the students answered "no", 20% answered "a little bit", 20% said "yes", and 10% answered "maybe".

On the research process, 50% of students reported having gradually expanded their understanding of the focus of research, mainly due to new knowledge being acquired and to their comprehension of the research process getting progressively more clear. The remaining 50% reported being well aware of the research focus since its beginning. The following is a report from one of the participants about the evolution of his/her research process:

> The research itself improved, since during its process the search for data was getting more refined, because the focus was getting clearer. It's like building a clay sculpture, for example, you visualise how it is going to be after you extract it from the block of clay, but you will only know how it is really going to be during the moulding process.

As regards to what may have contributed for this result, the readings suggested during the research project, as well as the theoretical seminars for theme discussion and guidance, were seen as essential. The results showed that 80% of the students considered that bibliographic references aided their work, as well as helped them to think in an interdisciplinary way:

> Being able to make use of references indicated by specialists in the field of your study is invaluable, not just to acquire a basis of information in which to trust, for creating the initial hypotheses related to the research, but also to get confident in your own ability to research. References reading is also crucial for building personal criteria and standards for future autonomous reference research.

> ...helped me to develop interdisciplinary thoughts.

> Even if some readings don't add to answering questions made during the research, they helped with a possible path for us to get to the answers, with ways of thinking, ways of planning, and others.

Nevertheless, 20% of students thought that readings helped, but not much:

> Few of the readings really helped me to focus on my objective. But they were useful.

The greater part of students considered the research in Ubimus as having connections with the educational context (80% "yes", 10% "maybe"). One student (10%) declared not to consider that there is some relation between ubimus research and educational context, saying: "I never noticed that". Accounts from two students follow, who believe positively that there are relationships:

> In my view, ubimus research relates to the educational context, as it studies precisely the field of ubiquitous musicianship, a solid example of multidisciplinarity which comprises several – if not most – of the disciplines studied nowadays.

> From the fact that it is a research in Ubimus, it already has relations with educational context because, from the moment you research some subject, you learn from that, and you develop the aptitude to teach about that subject, since you have the knowledge that is believed to be required for that task.

Most (90%) of participants affirmed (10% mentioned "maybe") that everyday technology may contribute to music making, but one of them advised:

> I can tell from my own experience, that musical exploring may indeed be extended by means of technological devices, but these carry always several limitations and flaws with them. Such flaws may end inhibiting the user's creativity, by enabling frustrating experiences and asking for solutions at a moment when it should allow creative freedom without restrictions.

> One of the concepts in ubimus is that we can create music with anything, anyplace. But if that is not enough, the most ordinary technology nowadays, the smartphone, enables you to do that easily.

> I don't believe that formal knowledge in music is mandatory to music creation work, but it may ease the effort and show things that maybe some layperson would not notice. I saw that when I was with my research colleagues who had more musical knowledge than me, but this also did not cause me not to produce a good work. And once again, technologies are facilitators, with the right tools you can expand your mind, and with music it's not different. Besides, they allow people who never thought to be possible to make music, to make it. Just that already adds to creative musical experiences which, if these technologies did not exist, we would never see.

All the students confirmed that doing research in music at scientific induction is relevant, and also believe that it is possible to do science within music:

> The research proved one of the questions of my own development. Through it I understood that it was possible to do science with anything, basically.

> Music is something I love, it's something I wish to work with someday, being as a teacher or even in research, for instance, in ubiquitous music.

Very much relevant, even because, while the focus is in music, all the studied parameters may be generalised to other areas. For example, in my research I approached some aspects about the inclusion of people with hearing or viewing disabilities, that means, applications were about music, but the analyses were about life in general.

When questioned as to whether taking part and conducting research in the field of ubimus changed somehow their concept of science, 20% stated "little", 30% said "no", 40% stated "yes", and 10% stated "maybe". Students' testimonies on this survey question:

My definitions of science remain the same, comparing with when I still hadn't begun my research in ubimus.

I'm not sure, I know I learned a lot, but my conception of science wasn't really extensive, due to little [previous] experience.

Actually it was the first time that science was in fact presented to me. Just hearing this or that matter is science doesn't make you enter the realm of science, neither helps you understand why it is science and what makes it be that. Taking part in the project enabled me that approach.

Ninety percent of the students answered "yes", and 10% "little", when questioned if taking part and conducting research in the field of ubimus changed somehow their concept of music. It may be noticed that, during the ubimus research process, some changes did occur:

In my mind music was a composition with instruments plus voice. Understanding the processes that lead the music towards me, and knowing these processes can be altered, remodelled, collaborated...That is great! Changes the way you understand what earlier was just a song listened to on your MP3 [player] on the way home.

Before I started my research, I can say I saw music only as a form of enjoyment and art, but now I can connect it to the way humanity expresses its creativity and explores the sense of hearing as much as intellectually than as recreation.

I discovered how wide the field of music is and may become.

In general, through data obtained during the period of the surveys, we perceived the impact of the scientific induction experience, more specifically the experience of ubimus research, was important to the students' instruction, even at high school. We hope the collected data contributes towards highlighting the significance and demand for implementations of research and teaching works in music education, since basic education. These should stimulate reflection, and be conducted by teachers and students as researchers, grounded on everyday musical creativity.

We also stress the importance of a collective and dialogical aspect of knowledge building, of an attention to everyday environments, and an incentive towards exploratory activity by means of localised resources, this including technological support available in educational spaces and context (in and out of the classroom).

## 7.6   Conclusions

One of the goals of ubimus research in the basic education context is the reflection, through dialogical practice together with the students, about educational applications related to everyday musical creativity, including composition, eco-composition, and the possible uses of everyday technology to these ends, and that includes making use of and thinking about technology.

Through junior scientific induction in ubimus, students had the opportunity, already as part of their basic education programme, to be protagonists in individual thematic research, as well as to work in a collaborative way with their research peers. As part of this, they also were able to engage directly with the work of graduate and postgraduate researchers from partner institutions, who conduct studies on music and its artistic, social, scientific, and technological interfaces.

The inter- and transdisciplinary, complex and dialogical approach adopted by the ubimus research in basic-education context at CAp, has been enabling actions, discussions, and investigations. These are related to creative processes of musical production (make, share, and think about music) associated with everyday technology infrastructure; production of music and sound technology; music as an acoustic and physical phenomenon; music making as a social activity, exercised, shared, done in various locations and moments (not only at "official" spaces for music making). This approach also enables students to see music as a complex investigation field – social, scientific, technical, educational – that can be studied as a physical phenomenon, measurable, computable, but that also constitutes a complex social and semantic phenomenon.

Regarding outcomes and processes involving creativity, related to ubimus research and applications in the field of basic education (specifically to the research in ubimus at CAp), it is important to point out that research actions are focused on processes which relate to time, context (the ecosystem), and with social and knowledge relations that take place during the activities. The product constitutes the natural result of all these transversal aspects interconnected. Therefore, when creativity is thought of as a natural outcome of all exposed variables: time, medium, tools, materials, interactions, the importance of the product, as result of a creative process of problem solution demands, is diminished.

From this eco-systemic perspective of creativity as a result of the aforementioned variables, it may also be inferred that, in the context of ubimus research at CAp, this focus applies simultaneously to processes of the conducted eco-compositional experiences, and to research processes from involved partakers (teachers and students). Furthermore, we believe the adopted inter-

and transdisciplinary research approaches expand the set of applications of the cognitive-ecological view.

In line with the nature of g-ubimus and with work, research and discussion proposed by the group, we can say that ubimus research, and as such Ubimus itself, stands not just as one more – isolated – knowledge area, but instead as a field of diverse approaches, open to multiple associations, potentially inter- and transdisciplinary, and ready to dialogue with daily life and the knowledge it devises. This dialogical attitude relates directly with Freire's (Freire, 1999) dialogical approach, which stresses and recognises the importance of reference; of the context; of knowledge; of the daily life of agents involved in the educational process; of collective (students, teachers, school, communities, home) knowledge building; as well as of the connections, experiences, and reflections shared during the processes which involve research.

We believe that establishing a dynamic, adaptive and dialogical system, as in the ecological view in ubimus, contrasts with visions that consider creativity as a purely mental and individual process. We have noticed, through the actions taken in research and teaching of ubimus in basic-education context at CAp, that by means of implementing dialogical iterative cycles of resources interchange, everyday creative activities stimulate collective assessment and reflection, and exchange of knowledge. Therefore, also stimulate participants to develop a critical view about their creative processes and the shared musical outcomes, and possibly extend that creative critical view to their daily lives.

Research developed by ICJr fellows within ubimus research, from an inter- and transdisciplinary perspective, seeks to engage aspects related and transversal to diverse knowledge areas: technology, human, and language (computing, physics, mathematics, sociology, philosophy, education, psychology, music). Since the beginning of the project, we saw a growing demand from high-school students to take part in studies related to music and its connections with technology. Through the process of research and teaching, and experiments carried by the ubimus project at CAp-UFRGS, we realised the existence and potential contribution of our field to deepening discussions and expanding possible areas of action, as well as their intersections with basic education, particularly with regards to everyday musical creativity.

## Acknowledgements

Authors would like to thank the UFRGS research administration and CNPq for enabling students, who are still in basic education, to take part in research with aid from scientific induction and junior scientific induction programmes.

## Notes

1 Basic Education level school, affiliated to the Federal University of Rio Grande do Sul – Brazil.
2 The scientific induction program, *programa de inicia cão científica*, is one of the pillars of the support by the federal and state research councils to the public

university system in Brasil, sponsoring small-scale undergraduate research projects. The ICJr program extends this to second-level education.

3 The ecological niche concept was introduced by ecological perspectives in music research (Keller, 2000, 2012, Keller et al., 2014). It encompasses the impact of local resources in creative activities, and the actions of individuals generating new resources, producing adaptations in their surroundings.

4 *Programa institucional de bolsas de inicia cão científica*, scientific induction programs from Brazilian Research Council (CNPq) and Rio Grande do Sul Research Council (FAPERGS).

## Bibliography

Aliel, L., D. Keller, and R. Costa (2015). Comprovisação: Abordagens desde a heurística estética em ecocomposição (Comprovisation: An approach from aesthetic heuristics in eco-composition). In *Proceedings of the Brazilian Symposium on Computer Music (SBCM 2015)*, Campinas, SP, Brazil, pp. 169–180.

Audacity (2020). http://www.audacityteam.org.

Bessa, W. R. B., D. Keller, F. M. Farias, E. Ferreira, F. Pinheiro Da Silva, and V. S. Pereira (2015). Soundsphere v. 1.0: Documentação e análise dos primeiros testes. In *Anais do Simpósio Internacional de Música na Amazônia (IV SIMA)*, Porto Velho, RO, Brazil.

Brown, A. R., D. Keller, and M. H. Lima (2018). How ubiquitous technologies support ubiquitous music. In B.-L. Bartleet and L. Higgins (Eds.), *The Oxford Handbook of Community Music*, pp. 131–151. New York, NY: Oxford University Press.

Burtner, M. (2005). Ecoacoustic and shamanic technologies for multimedia composition and performance. *Organised Sound 10*(1), 3–19.

Domingues, I. (2012). Multi, inter and transdisciplinarity – where are we and where are we going? *Pesquisa em Educação Ambiental 7*(2), 11–26.

Donald, M. (2006). Art and cognitive evolution. In M. Turner (Ed.), *The Artful Mind*, pp. 3–20. New York, NY: Oxford University Press.

Fantauzzacoffin, J. and J. D. Rogers (2013). Considering patterns of creative work process in creativity support. In *Proceedings of the ACM CHI Conference on Human Factors in Computing Systems (CHI'13)*, Paris.

Farias, F. M., D. Keller, F. Pinheiro Da Silva, M. S. Pimenta, V. Lazzarini, M. H. Lima, L. Costalonga, and M. Johann (2014). Suporte para a criatividade musical cotidiana: mixdroid segunda geração (everyday musical creativity support). In *Proceedings of the V Workshop on Ubiquitous Music (V UbiMus)*, Vitória, ES, Brazil.

Freire, P. (1999). *Pedagogia da Esperança: Um Reencontro com a Pedagogia do Oprimido (Pedagogy of Hope)*. Rio de Janeiro, RJ: Paz e Terra.

Harrington, D. M. (1990). The ecology of human creativity: A psychological perspective. In M. Runco and R. Albert (Eds.), *Theories of Creativity*, pp. 143–170. Thousand Oaks, CA: Sage Publications.

Keller, D. (2000). Compositional processes from an ecological perspective. *Leonardo Music Journal 10*, 55–60.

Keller, D. (2012). Sonic ecologies. In A. R. Brown (Ed.), *Sound Musicianship: Understanding the Crafts of Music*, pp. 213–227. Newcastle upon Tyne: Cambridge Scholars Publishing.

Keller, D. and A. Capasso (2006). New concepts and techniques in eco-composition. *Organised Sound 11*(1), 55–62.

Keller, D., E. Ferreira, F. Pinheiro Da Silva, M. H. Lima, M. S. Pimenta, and V. Lazzarini (2013). Criatividade musical cotidiana: Um estudo exploratório com sons vocais percussivos (everyday musical creativity). In *Anais do Congresso da Associação Nacional de Pesquisa e Pós-Graduação em Música (ANPPOM 2013)*. Natal, Brazil.

Keller, D. and V. Lazzarini (2017). Ecologically grounded creative practices in ubiquitous music. *Organised Sound 22*(1), 61–72.

Keller, D., V. Lazzarini, and M. S. Pimenta (2014a). Ubimus through the lens of creativity theories. In D. Keller, V. Lazzarini, and M. S. Pimenta (Eds.), *Ubiquitous Music*, pp. 3–23. Berlin and Heidelberg: Springer International Publishing.

Keller, D., V. Lazzarini, and M. S. Pimenta (2014b). *Ubiquitous Music*. Berlin and Heidelberg: Springer International Publishing.

Keller, D. and M. H. Lima (2016). Supporting everyday creativity in ubiquitous music making. In P. Kostagiolas, K. Martzoukou, and C. Lavranos (Eds.), *Trends in Music Information Seeking, Behavior, and Retrieval for Creativity*. Vancouver, BC: IGI Global Press.

Keller, D., M. H. Lima, and J. Fornari (2014). Painel: Desafios da pesquisa em música ubíqua (Round table: Challenges in ubiquitous music research). In *Anais do XXIV Congresso da Associação Nacional de Pesquisa e Pós-Graduação em Música (ANPPOM 2014)*. São Paulo, Brazil.

Keller, D., J. Timoney, L. Costalonga, A. Capasso, P. Tinajero, V. Lazzarini, M. S. Pimenta, M. H. Lima, and M. Johann (2014). Ecologically grounded multimodal design: The palafito 1.0 study. In *Proceedings of the International Computer Music Conference (ICMC 2014)*. Athens, Greece.

Kirsh, D. and P. P. Maglio (1994). On distinguishing epistemic from pragmatic action. *Cognitive Science 18*(4), 513–549.

Klein, J. T. (2004). Interdisciplinarity and complexity: An evolving relationship. *E:CO 6*(1–2), 2–10.

Kreatives.org (2020). Kristal audio engine. http://www.kreatives.org/kristal/.

LCM (2019). Lcm – ufrgs – home. http://www.inf.ufrgs.br/lcm/.

Lima, M. H. (2013). *Diásporas Mentais e Mentes Diaspóricas: Emergências, Novas Tecnologias, Educação (Mind Diasporas and Diasporic Minds)*. Doctoral Thesis (Education), Porto Alegre, RS, Brazil: Universidade Federal do Rio Grande do Sul.

Lima, M. H. (2018). Theory and practice in ubiquitous music research at a basic education context with high school students in and out of the classroom. In *Proceedings of ISME 2018 – MISTEC – Music in the School and Teacher Education Commission*, New York University, Prague, Czech Republic.

Lima, M. H., D. Keller, and L. V. Flores (2018). Eco-composition and everyday creative musical practices: Theory and practice experience in ubiquitous music research at ufrgs application school with high school students in and out of the classroom. In *Music for and by Children: Online Proceedings of the International Conference Musichildren'17*, Aveiro, Portugal, pp. 139–151.

Lima, M. H., D. Keller, L. V. Flores, and E. Ferreira (2017). Ubiquitous music research: Everyday musical phenomena and their multidisciplinary implications for creativity and education. *Journal of Music, Technology and Education 10*(1), 73–92.

Lima, M. H., D. Keller, N. Otero, M. S. Pimenta, V. Lazzarini, M. Johann, and L. Costalonga (2014). Eco-compositional techniques in ubiquitous music practices in educational settings: Sonic sketching. In *Proceedings of the SEMPRE*

*(MET2014):* Researching Music, Education, Technology: Critical Insights, pp. 123–127. London, UK.

Lima, M. H., D. Keller, M. S. Pimenta, and V. Lazzarini (2014). The everywhere music: Research on ubiquitous music, ict, music, education. In *Proceedings of the 31st World Conference on Music Education (ISME 2014)*, Porto Alegre, RS, Brazil.

Lima, M. H., D. Keller, M. S. Pimenta, V. Lazzarini, and E. M. Miletto (2012). Creativity-centred design for ubiquitous musical activities: Two case studies. *Journal of Music, Technology and Education 5*(2), 195–222.

Miletto, E. M., M. S. Pimenta, F. Bouchet, J.-P. Sansonnet, and D. Keller (2011). Principles for music creation by novices in networked music environments. *Journal of New Music Research 40*(3), 205–216.

Nicolescu, B. (1999). *O Manifesto da Transdisciplinaridade (Transdisciplinarity Manifesto)*. São Paulo: TRIOM.

Nicolescu, B. (2000). Um novo tipo de conhecimento: transdisciplinaridade (a new kind of knowledge). In B. Nicolescu et al. (Eds.), *Educação e Transdisciplinaridade*, pp. 9–25. Brasília: UNESCO. http://unesdoc.unesco.org/ark: /48223/pf0000127511.

Pombo, Guimarães, and Levy (2006). *Interdisciplinaridade. Antologia (Interdisciplinarity. Anthology)*. Porto: Campo das Letras, Col. Campo das Ciências.

Runco, M. A. (2004). Creativity. *Annual Review of Psychology 55*(1), 657–687.

Schafer, R. M. (1986). *The Thinking Ear: Complete Writings on Music Education*. Toronto: Arcana Editions.

Small, C. (1986). Performance as ritual: Sketch for an enquiry into the true nature of a symphony concert. *The Sociological Review 34*(S1), 6–32.

Tanaka, A. (2009). Sensor-based musical instruments and interactive music. In R. T. Dean (Ed.), *Handbook of Computer Music*, pp. 233–257. New York, NY: Oxford University Press.

# 8 Computational thinking in ubiquitous music ecologies

*Nuno Otero, Marc Jansen, Victor Lazzarini, and Damián Keller*

Ubimus music contexts are diverse and might include distinct types of tools and technologies. Digital tools are an important part of this picture and we need to allow people to explore and exploit these tools in their creative music making practices. However, important questions emerge:

- How do we scaffold the learning about the tools features and creative potential?
- How do we encourage people to explore the conceptual issues behind music making and facilitate understanding about the on-going processes that influence/shape the activity?
- How should the knowledge about ubimus music making be packaged so that it fosters comprehension about music and music making?

In this chapter we explore the potential of facilitating the exploration and understanding of digital tools for music making through a computer science perspective. By doing so we intend to show that creating bridges between core concepts of computer science and music making is possible, accessible and probably beneficial for learners and music makers.

Critical thinking and problem solving are crucial skills for 21st-century societal challenges in a world infused of digital technologies. Computer and learning scientists have been proposing that these skills can be fostered through educational programs involving explaining how computer scientists approach problem solving: computational thinking (CT). CT fosters the learning of methods like abstraction, generalisation and algorithmic design, that are essential to provide problem solving competences and allow learners to successfully engage with a wide range of problems. These competences might facilitate the emergence of strategic ways to problem solving and contribute to the recognition of commonalities in different problems with the consequent potential for re-use of past successful solutions.

We argue that the usefulness of the referred to competences go well beyond the domains of software engineering, engineering in general or mathematics. For example, there are numerous cases of what we can call music metaphors that can be used to develop elements of CT as mathematical concepts, and, of course, the other way around. To illustrate, at a high level, we can use the study of pitch, through its continuum as well as through discrete collections, to exemplify and manipulate principles such as linear and logarithmic relationships. Equally, it is possible to work on building musical scales that linearise the pitch dimension and demonstrate how we can go from an underlying logarithmic-perception quantity (frequency) to a linear one (pitch classes/scales). At a more detailed/advanced level, one can use delay lines in music to explore not only time relationships, but also the frequency and spectrum.

However, music making might also involve intense social interaction, self-reflection and – in some cases – the use of tacit knowledge for on-the-fly decision making. Hence, it may demand approaches not supported by the use of explicit knowledge, traditionally linked to problem solving. Ubimus practices and the corresponding social interactions might require particular types of support strategies, including external representations. For instance, instrumental music notational practices are difficult to apply within the context of open-form artworks. When the aesthetic decisions depend on the behaviour of the stakeholders, computer-based dynamic representations may be more suitable than the standard fixed representations. These perspectives are well represented in practices gathered under the label of *comprovisational* techniques.

This chapter is organised as follows. We first introduce some fundamental principles of CT. reviewing some important steps of the development of the field. As part of this, we will employ a number of simple examples in a music programming language to demonstrate the key concepts exposed. Next, we will turn to music and apply the ideas introduced in the earlier section to a select set of musical elements, taking the ubimus approach of not being prescriptive in terms of the musical practices discussed. This will reveal a significant number of touching points between the principles of CT and various aspects of music. This is followed by a discussion of CT from the perspective of knowledge transfer in music composition. The chapter is completed with an examination of the contributions to the learning of music, within a ubimus context, which are enabled by a CT approach.

## 8.1   Computational thinking

The term computational thinking is closely associated with the efforts to convey a systematic and well-structured way of solving problems. A number of tools and techniques used in computer science are usually used for this purpose. Extensive research has already been done to confirm the effectiveness and sustainability of this approach. In order to get to the bottom of the more precise definition of the term, this chapter examines the fundamentals of theoretical computer science in order to work out which informatics components are necessary for solving problems. The basic perspective of theoretical computer science and corresponding concepts are examined in order to describe the theoretical building blocks in a systematic way and to describe an approach for teaching and learning about CT.

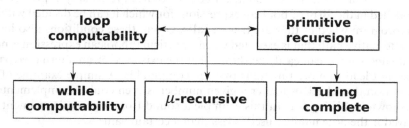

*Figure 8.1* Relation of the different computability classes.

In order to define which types of problems can be solved by CT, it is worth looking at Alan Turing's definition of computability (Turing, 1936). While Gödel (1931) had already proved that there are theories in every axiom system which cannot be proved and therefore cannot be computed, Turing proposed a formal definition of computational theorems by defining Turing-computable functions, also known as Turing-complete functions. These functions are such ones that can be solved with a Turing machine. According to Church's theorem (Kleene, 1943), the set of naive calculable functions corresponds to the set of Turing calculable functions. Therefore, one could say that any problem that can be solved in this way can be solved with a Turing machine. Building on this, a perspective to the existing definition of CT may be to take a look at the mechanisms used by Turing machines and other computational approaches to solve these kinds of problems. Especially the theory of $\mu$-recursive functions, for-, while- and goto-calculability are in the foreground. Figure 8.1 illustrates the relationships between the different computability classes.

The analysis of these basic theories of computable functions shows that there are a number of concepts necessary to solve problems with the help of computers:

- Conditions: as with Turing machines in the form of the transition function.
- Loops: as in for- and while-calculable functions.
- Goto / subroutines - like goto-calculable functions
- Recursion - as in $\mu$-recursive functions

The following subsections give a brief overview of the possible applications of CT in relation to the composition of music. The examples are given in the Csound language (Lazzarini et al., 2016), and make use of the MIDI conventions (Lazzarini, 2017), where the steps of the 12-tone equal-tempered are given integer values, with middle C being equivalent to MIDI note number 60 (see also Section 8.2). A user-defined piano Csound instrument is also referred to, but not provided.[1]

### 8.1.1   *Conditions*

In principle, *conditions* make it possible to distinguish between cases. Usually also called *if-this-then-that* (IFTTT), conditions allow different states of a (or part of a) problem to be treated differently. States are usually expressed or modelled in the form of boolean expressions for which it can be decided within the program whether they are true or false. Often, these conditions also have an alternative path that is executed when a particular boolean expression is not evaluated true. It can easily be shown that the existence of an alternative part does not lead to more functions that are computable. A simple example of a condition that checks whether a given number is even could be implemented as shown in Listing 8.1. In this example a sound from a piano instrument is played if the note number used is less than a certain value.

*Listing 8.1:* Simple condition

```
if  (iNote  <  72)  then
    schedule("piano",  0,  1,  iNote)
endif
```

In this case, the call to schedule(i, s, d, nn) takes an instrument name $i$, a start time $s$, a duration $d$, and a note number $nn$. Therefore any note number iNote below 72 is played, but nothing that is at that pitch or above.

Interestingly, the approach of expressing complete programs as a set of IFTTT instructions is again very prominent, e.g. in the area of Internet of Things (IoT, also specifically here the Internet of Musical Things, IoMusT, see Chapter 9) and/or blockchain-based technologies. Both examples offer very current questions in which a multitude of scenarios can be implemented on the basis of simple IFTTT conditions. This underlines the importance and strength of this type of modelling.

### 8.1.2  Loops

Loops are a means to repeat a certain task. In computer theory, two different types of loops are usually used:

- Count-controlled loops, in which a certain task is executed a defined number of times
- Condition-controlled loops, in which the task is executed as long as a certain condition is fulfilled

It is easy to show that count-controlled loops can also be expressed as condition-controlled loops, but not vice versa. Therefore, it could be said that the concept of condition-controlled loops is more powerful than the concept of count-controlled loops. However, count-controlled loops are often easier to understand because counting is a very simple task, while conditions provide a more complicated model.

An easy to implement example based on a count-controlled loop is given by playing a scale starting from a given note. In Listing 8.2, we schedule a sequence of notes in an ascending chromatic scale starting from middle C.

*Listing 8.2:* Count-controlled loop

```
iCount = 0
while icount < 12 do
  iNote = iCount + 60
  schedule("piano", iCount+1, 1, iNote)
  icount += 1
od
```

### 8.1.3   Goto / functions / methods / subroutines

Another class of computable functions (equivalent to the state-controlled loops) are *goto computable functions*. Goto constructs basically allow to jump to certain parts of a program, while Turing machines have to work sequentially through their memory. Although, as already mentioned, the class of goto computable functions corresponds to the class of functions that can be calculated with conditional loops, the concept is remarkable because it offers a first possibility to implement subroutines, which can be further extended to functions, methods and other types of subroutines. Thus this construct provides a very powerful tool for the abstraction of individual tasks, so subroutines are usually used to allow reuse of the implemented functionality. In Csound, these can be constructed as *user-defined opcodes* (UDOs).

Taking the example shown in Listing 8.1 and expanding it, we can create a function that will play a piano chord (triad) depending on what note number and chord type is passed. To use it, we have to invoke it by passing the necessary parameters, the note number and chord type (0 for minor, any other number for major). This is shown in Listing 8.3

*Listing 8.3:* Simple function

```
opcode PlayChord, 0, ii
  iNote, iChord xin
  schedule("piano", 0, 1, iNote)
  schedule("piano", 0, 1, iNote+7)
  if(iChord != 0) then
    schedule("piano", 0, 1, iNote+4)
  else
    schedule("piano", 0, 1, iNote+3)
  endif
endop

PlayChord(60, 1) // plays C major chord
PlayChord(62, 0) // plays D minor chord
```

### 8.1.4   Recursion

Finally, after the discussion that conditions and loops are the basic control structures of computational functions, recursion can be introduced. Although recursion is initially a mathematical mechanism used for functions that call themselves, it could also be understood as a control structure, since it influences the order of commands executed by a program. It is also a very powerful mechanism to describe some mathematical functions, such as the famous *Fibonacci sequence.*

It has been shown that the class of primitive recursive functions corresponds to the class of functions that can be calculated by count-controlled loops (Cutland, 1980), which means in particular that any primitive recursive function can also be expressed as a count-controlled loop. Using the example of a scale generation in Listing 8.2, we can re-implement the same functionality using recursion. In this case, the function employed takes two parameters, the end and beginning values of the count, as shown in Listing 8.4.

*Listing 8.4:* Recursion

```
opcode RecurScale,0,ii
  iN, iCount xin
  if (iCount < iN) then
    iNote = 60 + iCount
    schedule("piano", iCount, 1, iNote)
    RecurScale(iN, iCount+1)
  endif
endop

// plays 12 notes of the chromatic scale
    from middle C
RecurScale(12, 0)
```

Here, an interesting task from a CT perspective might be to change the representation of simple functions from their recursive representation to a solution based on a count controlled loop and vice versa, in order to promote the understanding of both concepts. It is also known that the class of $\mu$-recursive functions corresponds to the class of functions that can be calculated by condition-controlled loops. Recursion is in fact a process that is involved in different aspects of music, as we will see in Section 8.2.

As mentioned at the beginning of this chapter, the concepts presented here can be seen as building blocks to find a complementary way to solve problems from a computer science point of view. In contrast to more traditional views on CT, which take a social and behavioural viewpoint, our approach, therefore, results from a theoretical computer science perspective. The concepts discussed here are the basic tools with which computer scientists can think in order to formulate problems and explore solutions. One of the key ideas behind CT is that this specific way of problem solving can be presented to learners at an early stage and as such has the potential to improve their thinking skills in various areas.

## 8.2   Computational thinking in music: general concepts

Musical parameters that may be manipulated in the simplest of compositions provide opportunities for the introduction of metaphors that have relevance to fundamental aspects of CT. In fact, as metaphors are a common way to discuss musical matters, we may say that they take the function of a metalanguage in this scenario. For example, we lack a natural means to describe the different levels of an instrument's pitch. Instead, we use a spatial metaphor, *high* or *low*, and we often accompany that with matching gestures. More elaborate metaphors follow, targeting musical structures and the processes employed to organise musical materials. While this is an accepted and mostly unnoticed part of musical training, a CT-based approach that tackles these issues as reusable solutions could turn on its head the extant know-how and could provide insights into the physical, mathematical and musical problems that have not been addressed in music theory. In this section, we will outline some aspects of music which have relevance not only to the ideas introduced in Section 8.1, which are not only related directly to the development of stored-program digital computers, but also to some aspects of analogue computing, explored in Chapter 12.

### 8.2.1   *Manipulating pitch*

Building on the principles developed so far, we could start by paring down traditional forms of music-making to separate parameters, which could be manipulated with an intent to highlight their potential for use as part of a CT approach. The parametrisation of this type has been made by composers at various stages in the history of Western music,[2] and has become an important methodology for composers in the 20th and 21st century, especially where electronic sound sources (both digital and analogue) are present. A fundamental parameter to many types of music making is the aforementioned pitch. In successive approximations, we can describe it first as high or low, as we did above, then more closely with various attributes: monotone (that is, with very little variation), in tune (conforming to some sort of expected norm), well-defined (as opposed to noisy, clangorous), vibrato (with fine periodic variations), glissando (continuously ascending or descending), clustered (an aggregate of closely-spaced simultaneous elements).

It might be worth at this point, to define pitch more precisely. Pitch is a psychoacoustic attribute of our auditory perception (Howard and Angus, 2009). It arises when a number of conditions are present, and it is correlated to the fundamental frequency of an acoustic wave. In very simple conditions, it is linked to how many times a waveform pattern repeats within a given period of time. Under these conditions, we can connect directly the high-low metaphor with a physical counterpart: high is fast, low is slow. Interestingly, in traditional instrumental music making these notions of speed have been limited to ancillary aspects of pitch manipulation, such as vibrato or the use of beating in microtonal distances.

At this fundamental level of structure, manipulating pitch allows us to link time, iteration, and periodic structures together, which may have some relevance to CT. For instance, we can start with a nondescript short thud or clang with an undefined pitch. Play it once, to demonstrate what it is, then work out what repeating it may reveal. Slow iterations will of course form a steady rhythmic pattern, a beat. At this stage, we can show the effect of shortening the period. Above 20 times a second, a low tone emerges. As we shorten the iteration period, we will hear a rising pitch. We can use this technique to play a simple sequence of tones by manipulating the duration of periods. This illustration forms part of a classic electronic music piece by K. Stockhausen, *Kontakte*, which relates different temporal levels through continuous transformations (Manning, 2004). Looking back at what we have achieved in this process, we see that we have used pitch in two ways: continuously (creating an upwards glide) and discretely, when we played a simple melodic sequence. This opens up a window into the discrete representations of continuously varying phenomena. Moreover, this allows us to discuss musical scales as an example of such discretisation. In fact, from this perspective, we can also explore logarithmic and linear relationships which are brought to the fore by the translation of frequency ratios into musical intervals. Figure 8.2 shows the pitches in the 12-tone equal-tempered scale (12TET) as discrete MIDI note numbers, from 0 to 127.

Musical intervals can be defined as the distance between two pitches. Within a scale, pitches are linearly ordered. That is, several steps make up an interval, which can be enlarged or reduced by adding or subtracting steps. At the same time, intervals are related to ratios of (fundamental) frequencies that are equivalent to the pitch of the tones being Compared.[3] This way, the distance is given in the logarithmic scale, and intervals may be manipulated via multiplication or division. Examples of this can be given as algorithms to manipulate melodies: starting with a given pitch sequence, we can transpose it by either adding scale steps to each one of its tones, or by multiplying each fundamental frequency by

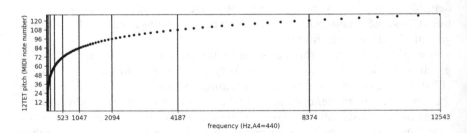

*Figure 8.2* 12-tone equal-tempered (12TET) pitch versus frequencies. The intervals in the 12TET scale are linearly spaced, whereas their translation into frequencies employs a logarithmic function. Vertical lines indicate the frequencies of the note C in successive octaves.

a given value. Other forms of manipulation, such as inversion, follow similar procedures.

In fact, these simple operations can be also seen as recursively-applied functions. A melody can be generated through the application of a NextNote(current, interval) function, which takes the current note and finds the following one according to a given interval. A stepwise melodic line in a major key can be constructed using the recursive code shown in Listing 8.5. The condition in this code checks that the value of iCount modulus 7 (the number of steps in a scale) is not the third or seventh step (counting from 0). If this is the case, an interval of a single semitone is applied, otherwise, a two-semitone interval is used.

*Listing 8.5:* Scale sequence

```
opcode NextNote,0,iii
  iNote, iStep, iCount xin
    schedule("piano", iCount, 1, iNote)
    iNote += iStep
  if (iCount%7 !=2 || iCount%7 != 6) then
    NextNote(iNote, 2, iCount+1)
  else
    NextNote(iNote, 1, iCount+2)
  endif
endop
```

We should observe that in this example we did not set any limits to the recursion, therefore the melodic line will continue upwards indefinitely, but it is easy enough to place this constraint to the code. Other examples of recursion in music can be found in melodic/harmonic sequences, where a given pattern is repeated in the transposed form, as for instance seen in Baroque music (but not limited to it, two examples are found in Vivaldi's *Four Seasons* and in Gloria Gaynor's *I Will Survive*). Such sequences, which are typical of tonal-functional music can be constructed by a similar recursive approach as in Listing 8.5, for instance with the use of transposition functions and tonal-based conditions. Another example is in the construction of tuning systems, such as the Pythagorean method, where a recursive application of the pure fifth interval (3:2) is used to tune the full set of seven scale steps. Hofstadter (1979) provides a comprehensive discussion of recursive relationships in mathematics, music, and visual art, that is highly relevant to the CT ideas discussed here.

Recursion is also very important in music theory. Tone networks or *tonnetze* (Cohn, 1998, Gollin, 1998), which can be used to model tonal-functional chord progressions, are constructed recursively by interval application, in a manner similar to the Pythagorean scale example. The 7,4-tonnetz, for example, can be constructed by employing two recursive applications of the NexNote() function, with the interval parameters set to 7 and 5. Figure 8.3 shows such a tone network with the two dimensions positioned diagonally for easier reference. In this arrangement, upstanding triangles represent major chords and

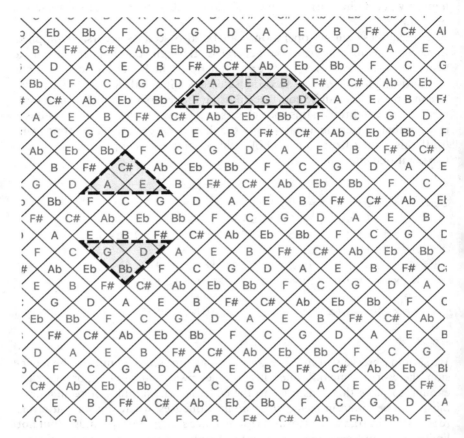

*Figure 8.3* The 7,4 tonnetz, recursively created by applying the `NextNote(x,7)` and `NextNote(x,4)` in diagonally-arranged directions. Upward-oriented triangles represent major triads, and downward ones minor triads. A major key region is a trapezoid centred on a major chord.

inverted triangles characterise minor chords. A major key centre is a trapezoid figure set around a major chord (the tonic), with two overlapping triangles on each side (the subdominant on the left, and the dominant on the right).

These aspects of music theory are very amenable to be treated via geometric methods. In fact, the tonnetz itself, if set in 12TET tuning and with octave equivalence[4] can be topologically modelled by a torus (Tymoczko, 2011) (Figure 8.4). We can easily demonstrate this by deforming the plane in Figure 8.3 into a cylinder, by glueing its left and right edges together. This is possible because the notes, or pitch classes, at these edges are the same. This cylinder can be further deformed into a torus by glueing the top and bottom edges in a similar fashion. Tonal-functional harmonic movement can be modelled by

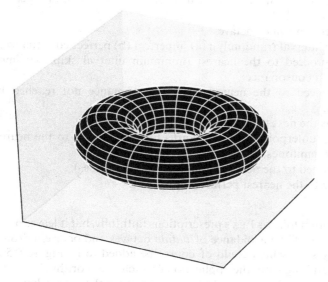

*Figure 8.4* A graphic representation of a torus.

navigating the surface of this manifold, in small, *parsimonious* (Douthett and Steinbach, 1998), movements.

Algorithmic means of manipulating pitch have played an important part in Western-music composition, which we can trace back to treatises such as Fux's *Gradus ad Parnassum* (Fux, 1943). There, the treatment of two-part modal counterpoint is given a fairly strict algorithmic treatment. Starting with a given *cantus firmus* and a with an initial interval between the parts, rules are provided to generate a second part (the *counterpoint*). There are multiple algorithms that produce two-part pieces according to the stylistic principles of early polyphony (Adiloglu and Alpaslan, 2007, Komosinski and Szachewicz, 2015). It is the case that solutions are often not unique and more than one version fulfils the constraints of the style. More complex topics such as solution trees may be explored within this context, especially in the types (called species) of counterpoint involving more varied rhythmic activity.

We can provide an example of a simple algorithm for first-species (note against note) counterpoint, in accordance to Fux's rules. Allowed intervals between the two parts are perfect consonances (0, 7, 12 semitones), imperfect consonances (3, 4, 8, 9 semitones). The motion between two consecutive intervals is significant: we characterise *direct motion* when two parts move in the same direction (upwards or downwards). The cantus firmus is given in one of the diatonic modes and the counterpoint intervals are required to stay within this mode (excluding the next-to-last interval, which may require a raised semitone). The maximum interval between the parts should be set to 15 semitones. With these basic conditions, we can define this algorithm as follows:

1   If the counterpoint is above cantus firmus, start with any perfect consonance;
    else select unison or octave.
2   Choose interval (randomly): (a) imperfect (b) perfect consonance;
3   If (a) proceed to the nearest (minimum interval skip, parsimoniously) imperfect consonance;
    else proceed to the nearest perfect consonance not reached by direct motion.
4   If this is the next to last note, goto 5; else goto 2;
5   If the counterpoint is above cantus firmus, proceed to the nearest major sixth (9 semitones);
    else proceed to the nearest minor third (3 semitones).
6   Proceed to the nearest perfect consonance.
7   End.

This algorithm follows Fux's prescriptions faithfully, but it leaves out the more subtle details of the avoidance of *batuta* octaves and octave/unison intervals reached by skip, which could of course be added to it. Figure 8.5 shows an example resulting from the application of such an algorithm.

The algorithm does not include a provision for the cases where a dead-end is reached, at for instance step 3. One modification may include some sort of back-tracing if no viable forward option exists. This produces a slightly more complex but more robust algorithm. Alternatively, we could simply begin at 1 again; this could be characterised as a *brute force* approach, which nevertheless might still be practical in such a simple algorithm for a short (10–12 note) cantus firmus. Both methods allow us to build *decision trees*, to identify all possible paths from a given starting interval, including full and incomplete solutions. These procedures are useful for theoretical investigations and for creative approaches to musical analysis, such as analysis by modelling (Keller and Ferneyhough, 2004).

Although we restrained our discussion to the manipulation of pitch and to the reproduction of existing models of musical construction, the potential for supporting creativity-oriented interaction design can be expanded significantly. In fact, if we consider this as a first-order computational-thinking approach, we can work out how to apply similar processes to higher orders of musical construction, such as timbre interaction. The combination of generative techniques with the support strategies currently being developed in ubimus

*Figure 8.5* Counterpoint example following Fux's algorithm, cantus firmus in the lower voice (Fux, 1943, 29).

projects could lead to musical metaphors that balance technical knowledge with ease of use. This may have significant implications to ubimus interaction design.

### 8.2.2 *Manipulating time*

When we think about time relationships in music, we can speak of several levels of focus: the duration of individual sonic entities (events, notes, gestures), the pace of feature changes (e.g. how fast harmonies, timbres, and other compound elements change over time), the temporal grid over which these occur (when dealing with regular or periodic organisations of time), the length of the structures which serve to segment the sonic continuum, and on a larger scale, the impact of music making on the ecosystems. Not only these happen at different timescales, but part of these elements can also be manipulated through algorithmic processes to harness their potential for CT explorations.

To illustrate this, we focus on short-timescale aspects of musical time, which are usually equated to simple units such as beats or rhythmic cells. Two complementary approaches can be taken, each one of them involving an inbuilt generative process. The first one of these, which is the most common in the Western-music tradition is to define a time block usually known as a *metre*, then proceed to apply periodic subdivisions. These subdivisions represent a pulse which establishes a recurring, underlying pattern that sustains the shorter segments. The conceptual basis of this approach implies a tree-like structure where longer durations can be split into same-sized shorter durations, in simple cases binarily or ternarily. Given the hierarchical structure of this process, all metre-based time frames can be subdivided in arbitrary segments. These segments, in turn, can also be subdivided generating highly complex and potentially infinite compartmentalised temporal structures (cf. *Bone Alphabet* for percussion (1991) by B. Ferneyhough).

Another approach is to start from a basic pulse, which will generally define the shortest temporal unit (that can be embellished with simple one-level subdivisions at specific times). From this unit, we can make longer cells by aggregation, creating various rhythmic structures through an *additive* process. Unlike metric rhythm, we do not need to apply hierarchical tree-like structures. Instead, time is often treated in terms of (usually long) cycles that are repeated periodically, or in terms of short patterns or rhythmic cells that can be freely combined. The addition or subtraction of elements tends to generate irregular temporal segments that can be handled through various techniques, such as mirroring, contraction, expansion. These operations are facilitated by the use of a small-scale temporal reference, rather than applying fixed larger structures as it is the case in metre-based time (cf. Messiaen (1946)).

The two approaches, which we could call metric and ametric (or additive), can of course be seen as complementary. It is possible to obtain metric temporal structures using additive processes, as it is feasible to generate non-periodic rhythms through metre-based procedures. However, trying to engage with one using the resources tailored for the other leads to unsatisfactory or unintuitive notations. An example of this is observed in the use of metric notation to accommodate an ametric approach in Stravinsky's *Rite of Spring* (among other works). Furthermore, the examples above highlight the limitations of some of the applications of CT in musical tasks. Take, for instance, the use of Lego Music (Baraé et al., 2017). Using lego bricks as surrogates for proportional time representations – where space is equivalent to duration – may provide an interesting avenue to be explored. This approach also seems to be promising for ametric temporal organisations. But when applied to hierarchical metre-based temporal manipulations, as soon as we reach basic two-level or three-level embeddings, the representation fails miserably. As a thought experiment, try building the last four measures of Ferneyhough's example using standard bricks.

### 8.2.3  *Delays as computational thinking devices*

Turning to electronic music, we can find a number of other interesting aspects of time manipulation, which also have connections with some fundamentals of CT. A typical example is that of the use of time delays, through delay lines (Lazzarini, 2017). In digital implementations, these are effectively memory locations that are used to store and recall snippets of recorded audio. The concept of loops is intimately linked to this, from a macro perspective, as well as a lower-level programming point of view. A repeated audio snippet is the embodiment of a loop in musical terms, as we can describe it as a sequence of events, or as an audio waveform, depending on the model we are applying, that gets executed repeatedly.

A recursive time delay loop is also a good example of some of the ideas we have been exploring so far. In this case, not only the sequence is repeated, but it gets re-injected into the delay line and mixed to its input, creating delayed copies which can be also characterised as echoes. Historically, this was also the method employed in the construction of *canons*, where delayed copy or copies of the melodic sequence would be added as a counterpoint to the original line.[5] We can also characterise this, using a signal processing approach, as a linear time-invariant (LTI) system (Oppenheim et al., 1999). It is linear, as the original sequence is not modified, it is time-invariant as the existing time relationships are not subject to change. Figure 8.6 shows three configurations of delay lines: for looping, where the memory is filled, the input is switched off and the sound snippet recirculates recursively (the output is fed back into the input; for a two-voice canon, where a single delayed copy is needed; and for a two-voice infinite canon, or *round*, where the delayed copy starts mid-way through the melodic sequence, so the delay is *tapped* at mid-point.

Another way to describe this is through the concept of *convolution*. The convolution of a sequence by another involves three steps: shift, scale, and sum. For example, consider two sequences: 1,2,3,4 and 1,1,2. We first apply a shift of the first by each position of the second, obtaining three sequences,

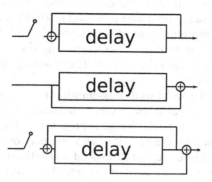

*Figure 8.6* Three configurations of delay lines: for a sound loop (top); for a two-voice canon (middle); and for a two-voice round (bottom).

1,2,3,4, 0,1,2,3,4, and 0,0,1,2,3,4. Then we scale each by the corresponding value of the second sequence: 1,2,3,4, 0,1,2,3,4, and 0,0,2,4,6,8. Finally we add these sequences together: 1,3,7,11,10,8. A simple two-voice canon can be described as the convolution of the original melody by a sequence that is 1,0,...,0,1, with the zeros filling in the respective time delay between the two entries. The summing is represented by the mixing of the two voices, and the scaling is unity, since both voices are normally played at the same intensity. Other examples can be given. A single echo of a sound can be similarly described, but with the scaling factor in the second sequence proportional with any reduction in the intensity of the sound that may occur. The second sequence in this type of operation is often called the *impulse response*.

These examples have employed fixed delay times, but other interesting ideas can be developed by relaxing this constraint. A time-varying system would be characterised by a varying time delay, where the time difference between the original and the delayed copy is not fixed. That type of system can also be discussed from a CT point of view. Some interesting aspects arise from it, which have to do with the interdependence of time and frequency. When a snippet of sound is captured by a delay line and repeated, we are actually playing back the contents of the computer memory at the original speed in which they were recorded. However if we dynamically vary the time delay, which means changing the size of the memory employed, the playback speed will also have to change to accommodate this. Thus, if the time delay gets shorter, a smaller memory space is used and the playback will read through it at a faster rate. If it gets longer, it will have to slow down.

We know instinctively that if play a recording at a higher speed than the original, we will transpose the pitch upwards. Likewise, if we playback the recording at a lower rate, the pitch will go down. So these manipulations of time delay reveal a link between frequency and time that is very interesting to consider. As the delay increases, we will have a downward pitch change, and as it decreases we have an inversion of this effect. Another analogy that can be made is between delay time and distance: a sound coming from a certain position will take a given amount of time to reach the listener. Decreasing or increasing the delay will be equivalent to making this sound source move in space, towards or away from the subject. The resulting change in pitch is also called the *Doppler* effect.

This analogy could also let us discuss another important mathematical and physical concept, that of differentiation. Examining closer these pitch effects, we can determine that the pitch change is proportional to the playback speed, and this is determined by the *rate of change* in delay over time. The Doppler effect analogy links this to the fact that speed is also the rate of distance change with respect to time. This tells us that the actual amount of frequency change is proportional to the rate of change in delay time: if the delay is decreasing steadily, a fixed transposed effect results. If we want to create a continuous sliding pitch then we need to modify this rate of change over time. At this stage, it is possible to put this in terms of differentiation and speak of pitch transposition as proportional to the time derivative of delay.

Creative electronic music exercises using modulation of delay time producing frequency modulation effects can be used to play around with these concepts. Furthermore, in Chapter 12 we saw that mathematical tools, such as differential equations and integration, can be manipulated in very interesting ways via the principles of analogue computing within a creative environment of music programming. Therefore it is possible to think of extensions to the usual ideas embodied in CT, as discussed in Section 8.1, which would also embrace such principles.

## 8.3    Computational thinking and music composition: challenges related to knowledge transfer

Promoting the understanding of CT poses particular challenges because it is not only a subject matter per se but it is intended to be a thinking tool that allows a distinct way to frame and tackle problems emerging from different disciplines/domains. In other words, it is close to what has been termed as a transdisciplinary effort.

Fostering the comprehension of the issues underlying music composition is also a complex challenge not only concerning the subject itself but also due to the preconceptions people have regarding their own musical abilities and ways that music making can occur, be understood and enjoyed. The proposals of ubimus that are being followed in this book push the boundaries of what traditionally has been conceived as music creation and open the possibility for a wider range of music making contexts. Additionally, the links we are proposing in this chapter between CT and music composition intend to promote people's interest in the connections between the two domains. However, in practical terms how can this occur? The examples given in previous sections of this chapter should give us clear indications of these connections. In this section we want to address an issue that can be considered crucial to the potential success of cross fertilisation between domains: knowledge transfer.

### 8.3.1   Knowledge transfer in CT and ubimus ecologies

The problem of ensuring efficient transfer of knowledge between domains and situations is indeed an old question with distinct theories and conceptual approaches being proposed. Bransford and Schwartz (1999) argue for the need to reframe how knowledge transfer should be conceptualised and assessed. Their *preparation for future learning* (PFL) approach emphasises the need to consider learning situations that enable learners to gather knowledge and competences that equips them to deal with new situations by actively enquiring about them. In other words, instead of just considering replication of knowledge structures from one domain and/or situation to another, PFL fosters inquiry and prepares learners for an active role in looking for analogies, transfer of knowledge and additional learning resources. This approach also demands a new way of evaluating learning and knowledge transfer: instead of just considering if knowledge was applied to a new situation and/or domain, PFL argues for the need to look at the way learners are able to frame the new situation and/or domain. We consider this to be important for our present discussion due to the very nature of the two domains we are addressing: CT and ubimus ecologies. CT aims at transdisciplinary understanding and framing. Ubimus ecologies propose and show the fluidity of music making practices.

In line with such ideas, a successful knowledge transfer approach for CT and music composition metaphors will need to include the following aspects:

A   *Encourage the use of analogies so that the music makers and music learners are stimulated to explore potential connections between subject matters.* In the previous section of this chapter a set of music metaphors have been explored in relation to computer science concepts. As such, the explanations already provided show some indications for the construction of the analogies that will act as bridges between domains (see, for example, the coverage of the time, iteration, and the unveiling of periodic structures in music). Nevertheless, more research is needed to actually flesh out the appropriate analogies since, at the moment, our conceptual analysis just established the links without concretizing into specific instantiations. We would expect that research addressing this topic will need to create the analogies and then analyse if and how music makers and learners appropriate and assimilate these into their music making activities and understanding.

B   *Avoid excessive focus on the contextualisation of the activity and underlying problems so that music makers and learners are not submerged in detail and fail to abstract.* Music making and learning are entrancing activities that demand full attention to the unfolding actions. For example, being fully immersed in music making might lead to difficulties recalling later important aspects of the playing or composing or even keep track of the on-going dance between the overall defining themes of the piece and the details that are created. Furthermore, these difficulties can also hinder reflections about the connections between domains which is of crucial importance to our particular proposal of CT and music making.

C   *Provide the necessary tools that facilitate abstraction in relation to the core concepts of computation and music composition.* This is in close connection with (a) and (b) since cross-domain facilitating analogies will be instantiated as particular external representations and tools. These external representations and tools will need to support the elicitation and externalisation of knowledge gained in the music making activity that will, in turn, foster the understanding of the relevant concepts and cross-domain exploration. Nevertheless, as further explored below when considering the challenges of designing and using multiple representations, the issue is far from settled.

Two other crucial aspects concern (a) how to teach the different concepts and (b) which tools seem suitable to support this process.

### 8.3.2   *Ubimus and CT: some ideas on teaching and design of supporting tools*

Our main aim is to encourage learners and musicians with different levels of expertise to explore the connections between CT and music making. In our perspective, the teaching of CT benefits from being closely tied to the learning activity of modelling distinct phenomena. Encouraging students to construct models of different phenomena is a well-established educational activity (see for example, Milrad et al. (2003) and Pinkwart (2005)). Models can be of very distinct types, from qualitative to quantitative, using graphical/pictorial symbolisms and/or formal notations. In ubimus, models of music making activity and learning need to account for the diverse nature of the resources that can be used and the richness of the social context.

From a psychological perspective, there is an ongoing debate regarding the way the distinct types of models can and should be integrated, not only in relation to the age group of the learner or music player but also to the actual stage of problem comprehension and ability to represent in a meaningful way the state of affairs. From a CT point of view, considering the different notions involving CT we need to assume that at some point learners will need to specify the model in such a way that it is amenable to computing. From a ubimus perspective, however, modelling music making processes will need to be a flexible process that respects cycles of creativity, social interactions, and a diversity of representing tools that allow music expressiveness. The challenge will be to facilitate processes that allow learners and music makers to dynamically link representations from both domains and encourage reflections about these connections. This encouragement of reflection will, in turn, foster understanding and promote the creation of new connections. Nevertheless, we believe, the challenge of integrating domains might require some degree of formalisation and such will need to be in line with the cognitive skills of the learners and music makers. Relevant questions that can be posed are then:

- What are the appropriate levels of formalisation for the models considering the age group, cognitive skills and previous knowledge of the learners?
- How to ensure that the increasing levels of formal sophistication are clearly followed through by learners and music makers (in other words, do the learners and music makers understand the connections between the distinct formalisms)?

The aspect concerning learners' understanding of the distinct levels of formalisms sophistication also connects with the notion of using multiple external representations to foster the learning of CT and promote ubimus activities. The transdisciplinary nature of the two themes clearly suggests the use of a varied range of external representations (some connected with computational concepts and some connected with the particular domain of music making and ubimus). But as previous research pointed out being able to establish the connections between distinct external representations is far from trivial (Ainsworth, 1999, Ainsworth and Labeke, 2004). Research needs to account for how different external representations combine, looking for synergies and clearly justify cost/benefits of using them. Nevertheless, multiple external representations can support deeper understanding by promoting processes such as abstraction, extension or generalisation of knowledge especially if efficient highlighting of the links between different representations is in place.

1 How to capture the learners' skills regarding the transfer of knowledge?
2 How to capture and understand the learners' representational skills in different educational contexts?
3 What methods are particularly suited to account for (a) and (b) at distinct stages of human development?

## 8.4 Computational thinking and the fostering of learning of music-making practices

CT in ubimus does not only entail the use of computers to generate musical data, it can also be applied to conceptual issues to attain a better understanding of musical phenomena, leading to appropriate design solutions. For instance, Jansen et al. (2018) enrol abstraction, design patterns and frameworks as forms of computational thinking. These issues have been well explored within the literature of creative music making and have gained practical weight through the applications proposed within ubimus research.

### 8.4.1 Abstractions

The use of abstractions through object-oriented techniques was very popular in computer-based music making during the 1980s and 1990s (Pope, 1991). In an influential article, Argentinian composer Horacio Vaggione (2001) argued for the adoption of object-oriented techniques in acousmatic music-making, pointing to the need for support to deal with complex issues that are difficult to verbalise or conceptualise and that are refractive to formalisation.

After almost 20 years of their writing, his words still sound fresh:

> Composers are concerned with the creation of musical situations emerging concretely out of a critical interaction with their materials, including their algorithms. This task *cannot be exhausted by a linear (a priori, non-interactive) problem-solving approach.* Interaction is here matching an important feature of musical composition processes, giving room for the emergence of irreducible situations through non-linear interaction. Irreducibility is perhaps a key word in this context, as we are dealing with music's categories and ends. Music is not dependent on logical constructs unverified by physical experience. Composers, especially those using computers, have learned - sometimes painfully - that the formal rigor of a generative function does not guarantee by itself the musical coherence of a result.
>
> (Vaggione, 2001, 54, our italics)

Despite the many formalist examples in Section 8.2, "music cannot be reduced to a formalised discipline: even if music actually uses knowledge and tools coming from formalised disciplines, formalisation does not play a foundational role in regard to musical processes" (Vaggione, 2001, 54). Thus, while fostering the use of computers for creative purposes, Vaggione points out that practices geared towards the advancement of musical knowledge cannot be found exclusively upon teleological processes. While some forms of music making, such as rule-based instrumental counterpoint writing of the kind discussed in Section 8.2.1, are amenable to teleological methods, most 21st century musical practices resist explicit formalisation. Problem-solving demands full knowledge of the resources to be applied to the solution of the problem at hand. Furthermore, it requires a clear understanding of what constitutes *a solution* for the given problem. Those two conditions are not generally met in creative music making.

Music making that enlarges the extant musical knowledge presents scenarios that are not amenable to the teleological perspective. For instance, some musical resources only become available through the act of composing. Take as an example the exploration of a new synthesis algorithm. Its range of sonic possibilities, the parametric configurations that yield musically useful content and the (usually large) range of behaviours that are artistically useless can only be known after the fact, i.e., after extensively exploring the possibilities of the tool. Thus, the sonic resources and their effectiveness can only be appraised after extensive usage.

Complementarily, what is original or creative in music is strongly dependent on the social context where the musical action takes place. We can say that musical knowledge is a strictly social construct. It only makes sense when it is linked to a community – no matter how small this community may be. Consequently, collective music-making entails not just sharing musical resources, it also demands that the stakeholders *understand* what is being shared. This idea has many implications for the effective support of creative musical activities and has fuelled very interesting findings within ubimus research targeting, for instance, meaningful engagement (Brown et al., 2014). At the core of this issue lies the problem of knowledge transfer (see Section 8.3).

## 8.4.2  Design patterns

Flores et al. (2010) discuss four design patterns that have been applied in ubimus developments: natural interaction, event sequencing, process control and sound mixing. Natural interaction attempts to reproduce everyday behaviours usually involved in handling a sound-producing object. All musical gestures regarded as being *natural* may be explored: striking, scrubbing, shaking, plucking, bowing, blowing, etc. In event sequencing, users interact by editing sequences of musical events. This can be applied to any interpretation individual notes, audio samples, manipulations of parameters, and other types of musical material.

Process control targets parameter handling through generative algorithms. Flores et al. (2010) mention repurposing of non-specific devices with limited keyboards and visual displays, which are not ergonomically suited to be played as instruments, as promising devices for ubimus deployments.[6] According to the authors, the sound-mixing pattern entails selecting and triggering multiple sounds. The musical product consists of layered sounds. Furthermore, sound mixing can be described as the realtime version of event sequencing. After implementing several simple prototypes to demonstrate each of the design patterns, the authors presented examples of usage to 28 participants. Natural interaction and sound mixing were correctly identified by 78% of the subjects. Process control and event sequencing got scores slightly above chance (60% and 57%, respectively).

Other research groups have also adopted similar patterns to support decisions at the early stages of design. Recent advances underline the need to consider the potential for creative outcomes as a key aspect of ubimus design.

## 8.4.3  Distributed resources

Ubimus methods employ technological and environmental resources for creative music making that may not be amenable to acoustic-instrumental views on creativity.[7] Consider the use of massively distributed resources – such as the Internet of Musical Things (see Chapter 9) – which may entail the deployment of creativity support metaphors that target probable behaviours rather than deterministic outcomes. This particular demand is rooted in the limitations of the transmission protocols, on the heterogeneity of the devices and on the large physical distances involved in some deployments. Given this context, the relationship one-physical-action, one-sonic-outcome of the acoustic-instrumental approach becomes meaningless. What are the consequences for the ubimus perspectives that engage with forms of CT to achieve creative outcomes by untrained subjects?

One of the implications is that abstractions may become increasingly important as tools for accessible design (see creative surrogates – Keller et al. (2015)). Another implication is that music making may have to be released from the straightjacket of synchronisation (see Bhagwati (2013) for a related approach). Notational practices have reinforced the idea that musical thought needs to target results that can be represented on discrete temporal grids (as featured in the two examples provided in Section 8.2). But the practice of music making on computational networks and the trends that involve intense asynchronous collaborations relegate synchronised musical renditions to a marginal manifestation. CT that involves massive parallelism may be more natural to ubimus than the hierarchical organisations based on common-practice notation.

### 8.4.4   *Frameworks for creativity*

Regarding the use of frameworks in ubimus projects, a tight bond between the models and the data gathering and analytical processes tends to increase the weight of the framework. Ideally, a model should be falsifiable and replicable. It should also be possible to establish a range of potential applications. Probably the most important requirement for creative activity is that bad choices should be easy to avoid. Creative endeavours deal with elusive objects, precluding clear-cut boundaries, therefore falsifiability and replicability are hard to come by. As argued by Vaggione and other experienced practitioners, creative music making yields products and processes that cannot be defined a priori. If we extend this observation to the epistemology of creativity, it becomes clear that the validity of a compositional theory cannot be circumscribed to the extant musical repertoire.

Creativity-oriented tools should support new ways of doing and thinking. When musical models are turned into prescriptive tools, the artistic results may be satisfactory. But more often than not, they yield uninteresting results. As exemplified in the discussions included in this book, ubimus tools provide effective support for creative music making by laypeople. Hence, the requirements of composer-centric creativity, the disappearance of performers, and the analytical expertise of the listeners have been displaced by extremely taxing demands on creativity-oriented interaction. A question that this chapter attempts to answer is how musical CT can move beyond the mechanical calculation of parameters to strategies widely applicable for creative ends.

## 8.5   Conclusions

In this chapter we attempted to introduce connections between computational thinking and music, within the wider context of ubimus. We presented a number of possibilities of fostering the understanding of music making in order to develop links with key concepts of CT and mathematics, promoting music as a catalyst for intellectual discoveries. Following a brief introduction to the subject of CT, with examples directed to music computing, we looked at some fundamental elements of musical manipulation, involving the structuring of pitch and time. To do this, we leveraged several key concepts of CT, and provided various applications of these in the creation of scales, melody, harmony, counterpoint, as well as in the exploration of rhythm and sound transformation. This allowed us to delineate the various points of connections between CT and music at a very basic, foundational, level. We can conclude that their affinities run deep and that this approach can be very fruitful in promoting intellectual development.

However, we also wanted to consider challenges related to the possibilities of making such conceptual connections between the different domains accessible to learners and music makers in general. Doing so, we believe, is necessary in order to increase the understanding regarding ways to encourage abstract thinking and to foster ways for people to express the connections between the domains. Interestingly, elsewhere in this book, in Chapter 7, Lima and co-authors explicitly mentioned the potential people see in being encouraged to reflect on music and science, broadening their views and incorporating new knowledge that might trigger creative practices. Nevertheless, such goal of connecting domains presents challenges and we considered these through the lenses of knowledge transfer conceptual approaches.

The last section of this chapter discusses and integrates the issues mentioned before in other sections but adds a crucial perspective: the impact on frameworks for creativity in Ubimus contexts. Highlighting the connections between domains like CT and music need some level of abstraction. However, the task of abstracting and reflecting about connecting points, analogies and metaphors cannot hinder the unfolding activities and creative practices. We argue that for Ubimus music making contexts this point is crucial as well as not just focusing on end-goals but also on the actual processes that lead to them. Ubimus proposals also emphasise the need for learners and music makers to understand what is being shared when engaged with creative music activities. Such understanding involves enabling learners and music makers to externalise knowledge in ways that elicit common ground. In order to support all these aspects supporting tools need to be created.

Future research will need to investigate if learners and music makers are indeed interested in learning about CT and music. Probably the approaches to motivate different learners and music makers to engage with this content might need to be distinct depending on background knowledge and levels of expertise with the domains. Additionally, we will need to flesh out exactly which tools need to be used to support learning and understanding.

## Notes

1 See the Csound FLOSS Manual (Heintz, 2019) for various examples of such instruments, and the sound synthesis techniques used to create them. Readers are referred to (Lazzarini et al., 2016) for further details on the Csound language.

2 By Western music, we mean the practices linked to instrumental music making strongly anchored on common music notation and later incorporated within electroacoustic music techniques.

3 In general pitch is an emergent percept that may be hard to define, but for the sake of this particular example, we are making the simplification of equating fundamental frequency and pitch.

4 In this case, we disregard the octave in which a note occurs, and make every occurrence of a note in all octaves an instance of the same *pitch class*.

5 See also Hofstadter (1979) for a discussion of the relationships between these types of musical structuring and computation.

6 It should be noted that this paper was written at the time of the first ubimus publications, hence it lacks the conceptual grounding provided by the later works.

7 According to Keller and Costa (2018), the acoustic-instrumental approach targets simplified forms of sonic parameter manipulations involving, for instance, the usage of discrete pitches (preferably following the standard temperament), time parsed into discrete durations (ideally represented as notes within a meter-based representation) and the adoption of a fixed set of timbres (usually based on acoustic-instrumental models).

## Bibliography

Adiloglu, K. and F. Alpaslan (2007, 04). A machine learning approach to two-voice counterpoint composition. *Knowledge-Based Systems 20*, 300–309.

Ainsworth, S. (1999, September). The functions of multiple representations. *Computers and Education 33*(2-3), 131–152.

Ainsworth, S. E. and N. V. Labeke (2004, June). Multiple forms of dynamic representation. *Learning and Instruction 14*(3), 241–255.

Baraé, A., L. A. Ludovico, and D. Malchiodi (2017). Fostering computational thinking in primary school through a lego-based music notation. *Procedia Computer Science 112*, 1334–1344.

Bhagwati, S. (2013). Towards interactive onscreen notations for comprovisation in large ensembles. In P. de Assis, W. Brooks, and K. Coessens (Eds.), *Sound & Score: Essays on Sound, Score and Notation*, pp. 143–177. Brussels: Leuven University Press.

Bransford, J. D. and D. L. Schwartz (1999). Rethinking transfer: A simple proposal with multiple implications. *Review of Research in Education 24*, 61–100.

Brown, A. R., D. Stewart, A. Hansen, and A. Stewart (2014). Making meaningful musical experiences accessible using the ipad. In D. Keller, V. Lazzarini, and M. S. Pimenta (Eds.), *Ubiquitous Music*, Computational Music Science, pp. 65–81. Heidelberg and Berlin: Springer International Publishing.

Cohn, R. (1998). Introduction to neo-Riemannian theory: A survey and a historical perspective. *Journal of Music Theory 42*(2), 167–180.

Cutland, N. (1980). *Computability*. Cambridge: Cambridge University Press.

Douthett, J. and P. Steinbach (1998). Parsimonious graphs: A study in parsimony, contextual transformations, and modes of limited transposition. *Journal of Music Theory 42*(2), 241–263.

Flores, L. V., M. S. Pimenta, E. R. Miranda, E. A. A. Radanovitsck, and D. Keller (2010). Patterns for the design of musical interaction with everyday mobile devices. In *Proceedings of the IX Symposium on Human Factors in Computing Systems*, IHC '10, Belo Horizonte, MG: SBC, pp. 121–128. Belo Horizonte, MG: SBC.

Fux, J. J. (1943). *The Study of Counterpoint, Steps to Parnassus*. London: J.M. Dent and Sons.

Gödel, K. (1931). Über formal unentscheidbare sätze der principia mathematica und verwandter systeme i. *Monatshefte für Mathematik und Physik 38*(1), 173–198.

Gollin, E. (1998). Some aspects of three-dimensional "tonnetze". *Journal of Music Theory 42*(2), 195–206.

Heintz, J. (2019). The csound floss manual. http://write.flossmanuals.net/csound/preface/.

Hofstadter, D. R. (1979). *Godel, Escher, Bach: An Eternal Golden Braid*. New York, NY, USA: Basic Books, Inc.

Howard, D. and J. Angus (2009). *Acoustics and Psychoacoustics*. London, UK: Focal Press.

Jansen, M., D. Kohen-Vacs, N. Otero, and M. Milrad (2018). A complementary view for better understanding the term computational thinking. In *International Conference on Computational Thinking Education*, Hong Kong, pp. 1–7.

Keller, D. and R. Costa (2018). Special issue música hodie: Contributions of sound and music computing to current musical and artistic knowledge. *Música Hodie 18*(1), 03–15.

Keller, D. and B. Ferneyhough (2004). Analysis by modeling: Xenakis's st/10-1 080262. *Journal of New Music Research 33*(2), 161–171.

Keller, D., N. Otero, V. Lazzarini, M. S. Pimenta, M. H. Lima, M. Johann, and L. L. Costalonga (2015). Interaction aesthetics and ubiquitous music. In N. Zagalo and P. Blanco (Eds.), *Creativity in the Digital Age*, Series on Cultural Computing, pp. 91–105. London: Springer.

Kleene, S. C. (1943). Recursive predicates and quantifiers. *Transactions of the American Mathematical Society 53*(1), 41–73.

Komosinski, M. and P. Szachewicz (2015). Automatic species counterpoint composition by means of the dominance relation. *Journal of Mathematics and Music 9*(1), 75–94.

Lazzarini, V. (2017). *Computer Music Instruments: Foundations, Design and Development*. Berlin: Springer.

Lazzarini, V., J. ffitch, S. Yi, J. Heintz, Ø. Brandtsegg, and I. McCurdy (2016). *Csound: A Sound and Music Computing System*. Berlin: Springer.

Manning, P. (2004). *Electronic and Computer Music*. Oxford: Oxford University Press.

Messiaen, O. (1946). *Mode de valeurs et d'intensités*. Paris: Durand.

Milrad, M., J. M. Spector, and P. I. Davidsen (2003). Model facilitated learning. In S. Naidu (Ed.), *eLearning: Technology and the development of teaching and learning.* pp. 13–27. London, UK: Kogan Page Publishers.

Oppenheim, A. V., R. W. Schafer, and J. R. Buck (1999). *Discrete-time Signal Processing* (2nd Ed.). Upper Saddle River, NJ: Prentice-Hall, Inc.

Pinkwart, N. (2005). Collaborative modeling in graph based environments. dissertation.de.

Pope, S. T. (1991). *The Well-Tempered Object: Musical Applications of Object-Oriented Software Technology*. Cambridge, MA: MIT Press.

Turing, A. M. (1936). On computable numbers, with an application to the Entscheidungsproblem. *Proceedings of the London Mathematical Society 2*(42), 230–265.

Tymoczko, D. (2011). *The Geometry of Music*. New York, NY: Oxford University Press.

Vaggione, H. (2001, 03). Some ontological remarks about music composition processes. *Computer Music Journal 25*, 54–61.

# 9 Ubiquitous music and the internet of musical things

*Luca Turchet, Georg Essl, and Carlo Fisichione*

The Internet of Musical Things (IoMusT) is an emerging field that originates from the integration of many lines of existing research including ubimus (Keller et al., 2014), Internet of Things (Borgia, 2014), new interfaces for musical expression (Jensenius and Lyons, 2017), networked music performance systems (Rottondi et al., 2016), music information retrieval (Burgoyne et al., 2016), human-computer interaction (Rowland et al., 2015), and participatory art (Hödl et al., 2017).

Ubimus refers to music or musical activities that are supported by ubiquitous computing concepts and technology (Satyanarayanan, 2001, Weiser, 1991). The ubimus field proposes to study how social interaction with mobile and distributed technologies can converge to form novel creativity support tools and music artistic practices. Keller and Lazzarini discussed a vision of IoMusT in the context of theoretical frameworks for ubimus, where IoMusT is part of a ubimus ecosystem (Keller and Lazzarini, 2017). In a different vein, Hazzard et al. used the term IoMusT within the context of musical instruments augmented with QR codes pointing users towards online data about the instrument (such as its social history) (Hazzard et al., 2014).

A definition of IoMusT has been proposed as

> the collection of ecosystems, networks, Musical Things, protocols and associated music-related information representations that enable services and applications related to musical content and activities, in physical and/or digital environments. Music-related information refers to data sensed and/or processed by a Musical Thing, and/or communicated to a human or another Musical Thing for musical purposes. A Musical Thing (MusT) is a device capable of sensing, acquiring, actuating, exchanging, or processing data for musical purposes.
>
> (Turchet et al., 2018)

The IoMusT technological infrastructure enables an ecosystem of interoperable devices that connect musicians with each other, as well as with audiences. This multiplies the interaction possibilities between different stakeholders such as performers, composers, conductors, studio producers, live sound engineers, and audience members, both in co-located and remote settings. The hardware and software platforms around which an IoMusT ecosystem is formed may support ubiquitous musical activities that take place outside of traditional venues such as concert halls and that may involve the audience in the creative process.

In this chapter we aim to explore the relation between the field of ubimus and IoMusT, especially in the light of the latest research works in these two intersecting fields. We first present different types of *musical things*, namely smart instruments, mobile devices, and wearables, which enable ubiquitous musical activities. Secondly, we present current trends in research on communication technologies, which can support networked ubimus interactions between different human actors. Finally, we discuss some of the challenges currently present in the IoMusT field whose solutions are expected to positively impact the ubimus field.

## 9.1   Musical things for ubiquitous musical activities

This section surveys recent technological advances related to devices capable of supporting musical activities in ubiquitous contexts.

### 9.1.1   Smart musical instruments

Recent advances within the field of new interfaces for musical expression (Jensenius and Lyons, 2017) have led to the proposal of the *smart musical instruments* or *smart instruments* (Turchet, 2019), a class of musical instruments characterised by embedded sensors, actuators, wireless connectivity, and on-board processing. Smart instruments are the result of the integration of various technologies that were conceived and developed for different purposes. These include sensor- and actuator-based *augmented instruments* (McPherson, 2015, Miranda and Wanderley, 2006, Overholt et al., 2011), Internet of Things (Borgia, 2014), embedded acoustic and electronic instruments (Berdahl, 2014, MacConnell et al., 2013), networked music performance systems (Rottondi et al., 2016), as well as methods for sensor fusion (Pardue et al., 2015), audio pattern recognition (Dannenberg and Hu, 2003), semantic audio (Slaney, 2002), and machine learning (Fiebrink and Caramiaux, 2016).

To date, only a few musical instruments that encompass the features of smart instruments exist in both industry and academy. One such example is the Sensus Smart Guitar developed by Elk (Turchet et al., 2017). It consists of a hollow body guitar augmented with several sensors embedded in various parts of the instrument, on-board processing, a system of multiple actuators attached to the soundboard, and interoperable wireless communication (using protocols for wireless transmission and reception such as Wi-Fi and Bluetooth, and for exchange of musical data such as MIDI and OSC). The internal sound engine affords a large variety of sound effects and sound generators, as well as it is programmable via dedicated apps on desktop PCs, smartphones, and tablets.

Another example of the smart instrument from the industry is the Smart Acoustic Guitar by HyVibe, which shares with the Sensus Smart Guitar low-latency on-board processing, Bluetooth connectivity, and a sound delivery system based on multiple actuators. Nevertheless, it does not possess an advanced sensor interface for gesture tracking, full interoperability features, a large range of sound effects and generators, or capabilities of programming.

An instance of smart instruments developed within the context of academic research is the Smart Cajón reported in (Turchet et al., 2018a). This instrument consists of a conventional acoustic cajón smartified with sensors, Wi-Fi connectivity, motors for vibro-tactile feedback, the Bela board for low-latency audio and sensors processing (McPherson et al., 2016), which runs a sound engine composed by a sampler and various audio effects. A peculiarity of the embedded intelligence is the use of sensor fusion and semantic audio techniques to estimate the location of the players' hits on the instrument's front and side panels, and to map this information to different sound samples simulating various percussive instruments (Turchet et al., 2018b).

Gregorio and Kim (2018) developed a drum-based digital musical instrument that shares several features with the smart instruments vision proposed in Turchet (2019): sensors and actuators enhancements, embedded sound processing, wireless connectivity for the reception of OSC messages. Turchet developed a Smart Mandolin (Turchet, 2018) starting from a design of an augmented instrument previously developed, the Hyper-Mandolin (Turchet, 2017). The instrument is based on a classic Neapolitan mandolin. The smartifying technology consists of a sensor interface capable of tracking several gestures of the player, a computational unit, and an integrated loudspeaker.

The features of smart instruments enable novel forms of interaction between musicians and their instruments (Turchet, 2018), between musicians and audience members (Turchet and Barthet, 2019b, Turchet et al., 2019), or between musicians (Turchet and Barthet, 2019c). Such technologically mediated interactions may occur in both co-located and remote settings. Ubiquitous musical activities are supported by the interactions enabled by smart instruments. Indeed the self-contained nature of smart instruments provides benefits such as ease of setup, portability, reduction of required space, and freedom of movement, which a multitude of equipment otherwise needed to recreate a similar setup can't offer (e.g., by combining a soundcard, cables, microphones, loudspeaker, MIDI controllers, laptop). Smart instruments do not require to plug various cables, turn on and off different pieces of equipment, as well as connect and use them. Musicians can simply turn on an instrument ready to use and easy to carry when travelling. In addition, the connectivity options embedded in a smart instrument allow for the transmission and reception of content communicated via remote networks. Such a connectivity supports collaborative music making wherever such network infrastructure is available (both with other musicians and audience members) (Turchet and Barthet,

2019c), along with a ubiquitous use of resources such as cloud computing or online repositories (Turchet et al., 2019), or ubiquitous musical interactions with social networks (Turchet et al., 2017).

### 9.1.2 Mobile devices and musical applications

Mobile devices are central to users' access and participation in ubiquitous activities. In fact, mobile devices were among the entities envisioned by Mark Weiser when he formulated the notion of ubiquitous computing (Weiser, 1991). While mobile devices such as smart phones and tablets were not primarily designed as musical interfaces, the extreme range of distribution and access currently makes them the most ubiquitous of musical things. Substantial research activities have advanced the potential for the use of these generic devices for musical purposes (Essl and Lee, 2017). For our purposes, these research efforts fall into two broad categories: (i) how can a commodity mobile device be programmed, augmented, and used as a musical thing?, and (ii) how do mobile music interfaces in a networked eco-systems facilitate new forms of performance?

Often these concerns are researched together since musical interfacing and connected performance frequently go hand in hand. Furthermore this intersection itself leads to research question that addresses the easiness of access and participation in networked performances. To this end, (Essl, 2011) developed the use of ZeroConf network discovery to organise networked mobile performances based on high-level performance-centric needs such as the roles of the participants in the performance. The commercial API Ableton Link looks to solve needs of standardised interconnectivity, network synchronisation within the Ableton music ecosystem, and supports the cross-linking of mobile apps.[1] The support of geo-location was central to the networked mobile music project by Allison and co-workers (Allison and Dell, 2012). The interface design of mobile devices for musical purposes is central to appropriating them as musical things . Substantial research has tackled this question either through individual designs (see e.g., Ocarina (Wang, 2014)), through developing platforms for flexible interface prototyping (see e.g., urMus (Essl and Müller, 2010)), or through direct HCI research that investigates musical interface capabilities (Yang, 2015, Yang and Essl, 2015).

Ubiquity has led to a broadening of the role of participants in the performance. The audience in particular has drawn substantial interest as a role that can be conceived in new ways. On the simplest level, networked access enables a new kind of remote audienceship breaking the barrier of physical co-location. Already early on in artistic projects using mobile devices, there was substantial interest in overcoming the general passivity of the audience and enable various degrees of audience involvement and participation.

Audience involvement corresponds to a musical performance where the audience is not participating in the creation of the musical performance itself but is empowered to respond to it (e.g., by clapping). On the contrary, audience participation requires some forms of participation of the audience in the performance outcome. Many apps by Smule (Wang et al., 2009) contain various forms of networked-distributed audience involvement. One particular form of such involvement is what Wang and co-authors call World Stage (Wang et al., 2015) where a distributed audience can provide feedback (such as likes) after listening to performances asynchronously. A mild form of audience participation goes back to Golan Levin's seminal Dialtones performance in 2001 where mobile devices were used as a distributed speaker array that can be individually addressed, an approach that is still being the subject of research and performance today (Shaw et al., 2015). This work has blossomed into a wide-ranging field of research into the support of audience participation (Oh and Wang, 2011).

The distribution of software that provides participation interfaces for mobile devices is a central issue for the facilitation of audience participation pieces. Hindle proposed the use of captive web portals to distribute web-based interfaces (Hindle, 2013). Captive portals use forced http redirects to deliver web pages without the need for the user to address that page. Web technologies in general help push capabilities into a scaling distributed and increasingly ubiquitous sphere. Interfaces and music generation are becoming accessible from anywhere by the increase in refinement of the capabilities of the Web Audio API. This allows the acceleration and simplification of the realisation of audience participation music performances (Lee et al., 2016). As an example, Soundworks provides a framework to support web-based collaborative mobile performances (Robaszkiewicz and Schnell, 2015).

While web-based systems are well-suited for ubiquitous access, native technologies still see substantial attention due to their greater computational efficiencies. Lee and co-workers (Lee et al., 2014) investigated network protocols for discovery and distribution in a concert hall network. Cloud computing infrastructure and methods can also be used to support the distribution of information to mobile devices. Pusher services offer massively scalable distribution of data through the cloud. Hence, large numbers of participating audience members can receive performance data (Carvalho Junior et al., 2016). A cloud-based database approach is behind the MassMobile environment (Weitzner et al., 2013) in order to support large-scale audience participation including mobile devices. Networked performances based on the software Pure Data, which include the mobile music instruments utilising the Libpd environment (Brinkmann et al., 2011), are supported by the multi-platform environment A.bel (Clément et al., 2016). A pathway to notions such as ubiquitous composition is demonstrated by distributed web-based composition interfaces for guided mobile music instruments (Hamilton et al., 2011). Vote-based systems include the Mood Conductor (Fazekas et al., 2014) which invites audiences to conduct performers through dynamic votes of musical moods, and Open Symphony (Wu et al., 2017) which conveys audience members a collective role in determining the musical structure of a live piece.

Various projects consider specific performance settings. For example, the Echobo project (Lee and Freeman, 2013) realises a hybrid mobile and classical musical instrument performance that illustrates taxonomies of audience participation, design principles for mobile audience participation more broadly. Another example of performance enables the audience to control the stereo output of a lead guitarist via their mobile devices as part of a live rock concert (Hödl et al., 2012).

Despite many recent developments some of the most ubiquitous mobile music performances were envisioned early in the history of this field (Behrendt, 2005). LIGNA's *Wählt die Signale* (German for *Call the Signal*) allowed audience members to call into 144 mobile device number attached to mobile phones arranged as a speaker array and delivered over a Radio broadcast of a musical piece hence allowing ubiquitous audience input to a piece reaching about 4,000 participants. Pieces like this hint at the potential of ubiquitous mobile music, which sits at the intersection of ubiquitous technology (mobile devices, networking), ubiquitous access (massive distribution and ownership of mobile devices), music playing, and participatory live art.

### 9.1.3 Wearables

Recent years have seen an increase of devices in the market, which can be worn on the body as accessories, such as smart watches or smart bracelets. Such devices are able to sense body activity (such as movements, heart rate, body temperature, galvanic skin response) as well as wirelessly communicate the sensed data to external equipment. This communication is typically achieved through point-to-point connections via Body Area Networks (Patel and Wang, 2010) or Personal Area Network (Johansson et al., 2001) enabled through a portable hub such as a mobile device. A peculiar characteristic of these devices is their unobtrusiveness: they are designed to be worn during everyday activity and to passively collect data without regular intervention by the user. To date, scarce research has been conducted on the use of wearable devices in musical contexts, which could lead to ubiquitous musical activities. An example towards this direction is the work by Migicovsky et al. where the accelerometers embedded in smart watches are utilised to track gestures of the user and are mapped to the parameters of a sound engine by leveraging a smartphone as a bridge (Migicovsky et al., 2014).

In a different vein, a new family of wearable devices that can complement, support, or enable networked ubiquitous musical activities has been recently proposed, the *musical haptic wearables* for performers (Turchet and Barthet, 2019a) and for audience members (Turchet and Barthet, 2019b). These devices may encompass haptic stimulation, tracking of gestures and physiological parameters, and wireless connectivity features. Musical haptic wearables were conceived to enhance creative communication between musicians as well as between musicians and audience members by leveraging the sense of touch, in both co-located and remote settings. They were also devised to enrich musical experiences of audiences of music performances by integrating haptic stimulations, as well as provide new capabilities for creative participation thanks to embedded sensor interfaces.

Regarding musical haptic wearables for performers, the work reported in (Turchet and Barthet, 2019a) describes the use of three chest-, foot- and arm-worn haptic wearables respectively for co-performer, performer-conductor, and performer-sound engineer interactions. Results of experimental validation of such devices provided evidence that musical haptic wearables can be an effective medium of communication between performers. Another example of musical haptic wearable is Vibropixel, which has been used to assist a conductor with a tactile representation of metronome clicks (Ignoto et al., 2017).

As far as musical haptic wearables for audience members are concerned, the study reported in (Turchet et al., 2019) investigated the role of haptic stimuli in affecting the perception of live music enriched with simultaneous haptic stimuli. The authors conducted concert-experiments involving a smart mandolin interconnected with jackets for the audience that was enhanced with actuators capable of providing vibro-tactile sensations in response to the performed music. Results showed that the audio-haptic experience was not homogeneous across participants, who could be grouped as those appreciative of the vibrations and those less appreciative of them. The causes for a lack of appreciation of the haptic experience were mainly identified as the sensation of unpleasantness caused by the vibrations in certain parts of the body and the lack of the comprehension of the relation between what was felt and what was heard. Such results suggest that the design of musical haptic wearables for audiences should consider the need of mechanisms of personalisation, systems able to minimise the latency between the sound and the vibrations, and a time of adaptation to the vibrations.

Recent years have also witnessed the emergence of garments enhanced with fabric-based sensors, the so-called electronic textiles (e-textiles) (Weng et al., 2016). This technology may also be involved for ubiquitous musical activities. Lately, e-textiles have made inroads into music performance settings. A noticeable example is the work reported in (Skach et al., 2018), which presents a system that allows musicians to manipulate sounds through gestural interactions captured by textile wearable sensors. The sensors embedded in the e-textiles are used to control, in realtime, audio processing algorithms working with content interactively downloaded from the Internet thanks to wireless connectivity over a 4G network.

## 9.2   Connectivity for networked ubiquitous musical activities

The IoMusT has as background communication technology wireless sensor networks (WSNs) (Dargie and Poellabauer, 2010), Internet of Things (IoT) (Borgia, 2014), and Tactile Internet (Fettweis, 2014, Maier et al., 2016). At the state-of-the-art of communication technology and theory, what is missing is the realtime dimension (in particular, the synchronisation and low-latency aspects). In the following, we give an overview of the existing communication technology with a focus on the capability of supporting the realtime transmission of music information.

A WSN is a network of electronic devices (called nodes) that can be potentially embedded in any physical object and can wirelessly communicate for monitoring, communication, and automation purposes. The term Internet of Things has later emerged to emphasise that the nodes could be reached via the Internet Protocol. Given its potential societal impact, IoT has been the object of intense research, both in academia and industry (e.g., (Willig, 2008)). Within communication networking engineering, this has resulted in the emergence of new communication protocols, especially for low data rate and low power consumption, such as IEEE 802.15.4 (LAN/MAN Standards Committee, 2003) and Zigbee.[2] Presently, researchers are investigating the integration of IoT with the cellular wireless communication systems. This will result, in the future, in the so-called wireless networks of 5th generation (5G networks), which will connect the devices of IoT via cellular wireless base stations, the same that we use today for our cellular phones. The state-of-the art of IoT and 5G is the narrow-band IoT (Landström et al., 2016).

Unfortunately, despite the research described above, the wireless networking of musical things that require ultra-low latency and high reliability in the communication cannot be served by most of the existing IoT wireless communication protocols. These protocols will provide communication latencies in the order of tens of milliseconds, which is generally insufficient for the wireless interconnection of musical things such as smart instruments. To transmit music streams from a smart instrument to a listener/performer located on another side of the communication networks, we need communication latencies in the order of milliseconds (Rottondi et al., 2015, 2016), while the probability of successful message receptions will have to be in the order of $10^{-10}$ to avoid perceivable deteriorations of the signal (Fettweis, 2014). These stringent requirements not only are for IoMusT but are also common to a large plethora of future technologies, such as virtual reality, telepresence, telesurgery, autonomous car driving, or smart power transmission grids.

The large class of technologies mentioned above, as well as the communication requirements of IoMusT, is motivating the future development of the emerging paradigm of the *Tactile Internet* (Aijaz et al., 2017, Fettweis, 2014). Tactile Internet research proposes to substantially augment an Internet network so that the communication delay between a transmitter and a receiver would be so low that even information associated to human touch, vision, and audition could be transmitted back and forth in realtime with regard to the human senses. Not only Tactile Internet is expected to ensure low latencies with very low probability of missing messages, but also to ensure both low and high data rates. This will enable seamless remote interaction experiences among players geographically distant or located at positions physically far from each other.

To make the Tactile Internet a reality, there are still major unsolved technical questions especially concerning the wireless access networks, namely the initial network that will connect with wireless communications an instrument to the Internet. Within such wireless part, we will probably be able to obtain low latencies by wireless transmissions over the mmWaves frequencies. These are wireless frequencies within the range of 10 to 300 GHz (Landström et al., 2016, Shokri-Ghadikolaei et al., 2015, 2016). MmWaves communications will offer data rates of giga bits per seconds over relatively short distances. Within the realm of musical instruments, such a wireless technology appears particularly interesting due to the very small size of the antennas and therefore of the transceivers. Thus the electronic platform supporting such communications would be easily embedded in musical instruments (as proposed in the Smart Instruments paradigm (Turchet, 2019)). Moreover, the high data rates will enable the transmission of multimodal content in high resolution.

In the Tactile Internet, while the wireless transmission medium is the most critical from the point of view of ensuring low latencies over relatively limited geographic areas of the order of maximum some Km, the wired media is the one posing ultimate limitations for the geographic distance over which the communications will be possible (Fettweis, 2014). After the messages are transmitted over the wireless medium, they are forwarded over some wired medium such as copper cables, or more likely, optical fibres. If we make the ideal assumption that only optical fibres be used, the speed of light is the fastest speed at which messages can be theoretically transmitted. Therefore, point-to-point communications with latencies of around 1 ms would be realisable among players that are spread within an area encircled at most in 100–300 km.

## 9.3   Discussion and conclusions

Ubimus and IoMusT are the two independent fields of research that have many features in common, including part of their technological base. Definitions for the former have been put forward in Chapter 1, and in this chapter we have introduced in detail the major components of the latter. The IoMusT paradigm includes, among other things, a ubimus dimension, which is fundamental to it. However, it also considers other musical activities beyond the scope of ubimus, which may coexist with it. The envisioned musical things, as well as the IoMusT connectivity infrastructure have the potential to support a wide range of interactions: non-ubiquitous (e.g., between musicians and audiences, such as those happening in conventional settings like concert halls); ubiquitous (e.g., between co-located musicians, such as those happening in non-conventional musical settings, such as streets); synchronous (e.g., between performers playing together); and asynchronous (e.g., between performers and producers, such as those happening in studios for music production). Besides the non-ubiquitous ones, such interactions may be viewed from a pure IoMusT perspective, or be also considered within the scope of ubimus research.

The IoMusT paradigm shares with other professional ubimus-related work (such as crossadaptive performance, Chapter 11) the focus on interactions where the actors are live sound engineers, conductors, composers, or studio producers. The aspects of the IoMusT discussed in this chapter also rely strongly on the use of professional audio equipment and advanced architectures (e.g., the Elk operating system[3]). This has also been a feature of some ubimus research (see, for instance, Zawacki and Johann (2014)), alongside work covering DIY concerns and activities (Lazzarini et al., 2015, Morreale et al., 2017) (see Chapter 3).

Another dimension of the IoMusT as presented here is its multi-sensory nature. This is shared with some works in ubimus (see for instance McGlynn et al. (2012, 2013), and Chapter 5), as its research agenda is not particularly limited solely to sonic or musical concerns (Keller and Lazzarini, 2017). In the IoMusT, the concept of musical content may encompass the use of musical things capable of providing their users with visual or haptic stimuli in addition to the sonic ones. Examples are musical haptic wearables (Turchet and Barthet, 2019a) or virtual reality applications for collaborative networked music creations (Men and Bryan-Kinns, 2018). Common to both fields is the fact that ubiquitous musical activities may be networked. In the IoMusT vision the emphasis is on networked musical interactions between human actors or between human actors and their machines. Nevertheless, in ubimus the musical activities may not be based on networks.

As discussed in Section 9.1.1 the features of smart instruments are well suited for ubiquitous musical activities. To this regard it is worth noting that different indicators such as the 2017, 2018, and 2019 Global Report of the National Association of Music Merchants, recent panel discussions at music fairs,[4] as well as recent academic publications (Turchet and Barthet, 2019c, Turchet et al., 2018a, 2019) suggest that contemporary musicians' needs are changing. Musicians' need for enhanced ways of connectivity supporting interactions with the audience and other musicians is increasingly growing, along with a solid desire of wireless, portable, upgradeable, and cloud-based solutions. Such trends may be key drivers in musicians' adoption of smart instruments, and as a consequence, they may lead to an increment of ubiquitous musical activities. However, few smart instruments are present on the market and little research has been conducted in academic contexts so far.

Along the same lines, little research has also been conducted on the use of wearables (both wearable devices and e-textiles) in musical contexts as shown by the few examples reported in Section 9.1.3. Nevertheless, smartphones are today the musical things that more than others are capable of enabling ubiquitous musical activities, given the fact that they are so widespread. Differently from smart instruments or other specific musical things, smartphones are (and are expected to continue to be) one of the objects we mostly interact with on a daily basis.

Since networking technologies are accelerating at a steady pace, one expects that smartphones will have a more prominent role in musical activities that are networked, collaborative, and ubiquitous. Ubimus has employed mobile devices (amongst other platforms), which may include interfaces not primarily designed for musical purposes. A main challenge for smartphones and tablet remains organising them specifically as musical things, and creating software infrastructure that supports scaling. Furthermore, with the increasing availability of software support for ubiquitous music and the ease of use of networking, the attention shifts towards social and artistic aspects of the creative activities, as articulated by Behrendt (2017).

Several open challenges in networks research affect the IoMusT. Of particular interest for the ubimus field are challenges related to low-latency, high-reliability, and synchronisation in IoMusT communications, as well as to interoperability and standardisation. The transmission of low-latency high-quality audio (and in general multimodal) streams over networks, both wireless and wired, is one of the most demanding engineering challenges. Indeed, the transmission of messages over wireless or wired networks is always subjected to some forms of randomness (e.g., due to the random interference in wireless channels, or the random background traffic on wired networks), which produce random delays between the transmitter and the receiver that are in general difficult to control. The design of communication networks capable of supporting true realtime music services needs to be addressed by developing fundamentally new methods for low latency and stable message reception rates. The future Tactile Internet (Fettweis, 2014, Maier et al., 2016) is expected to solve these issues. On the other hand, the success of IoMusT relies heavily on standardisation activities. The definition of standards for formats, protocols, and interfaces is crucial for the achievement of interoperability between musical things. To date, however, standardisation activities concerning the Internet of Things technologies for musical applications are largely unrealised.

The solution of all IoMusT-related challenges mentioned above are expected to positively impact also the ubimus field by facilitating and improving networked ubiquitous musical activities.

## Acknowledgements

The authors are grateful to Dr. Mathieu Barthet for the fruitful discussions concerning some ideas of this paper.

## Notes

1 https://www.ableton.com/en/link/.
2 www.zigbee.org.
3 www.elk.audio.
4 See e.g., Slush Music http://www.slush.org.

## Bibliography

Aijaz, A., M. Dohler, A. Aghvami, V. Friderikos, and M. Frodigh (2017). Realizing the tactile internet: Haptic communications over next generation 5g cellular networks. *IEEE Wireless Communications* 24(2), 82–89.

Allison, J. and C. Dell (2012). Aural: A mobile interactive system for geo-locative audio synthesis. In *Proceedings of the Conference on New Interfaces for Musical Expression*. Ann Arbor, Michigan, USA.

Behrendt, F. (2005). *Handymusik. Klangkunst und "mobile devices"*. Epos. Available online at: www.epos.uos.de/music/templates/buch.php?id=57.

Behrendt, F. (2017). Author commentary: Mobile music technology: From innovation to ubiquitous use. In A. Jensenius and M. Lyons (Eds.), *A NIME Reader*, pp. 261–262. Cham, Switzerland: Springer Verlag.

Berdahl, E. (2014). How to make embedded acoustic instruments. In *Proceedings of the Conference on New Interfaces for Musical Expression*, pp. 140–143. London, UK.

Borgia, E. (2014). The Internet of Things vision: Key features, applications and open issues. *Computer Communications 54*, 1–31.

Brinkmann, P., P. Kirn, R. Lawler, C. McCormick, M. Roth, and H. Steiner (2011). Embedding pure data with libpd. In *Proceedings of the Pure Data Convention*, Volume 291. Weimar, Germany.

Burgoyne, J., I. Fujinaga, and J. Downie (2016). Music information retrieval. In S. Schreibman, R. Siemens, and J. Unsworth (Eds.), *A New Companion to Digital Humanities*, pp. 213–228. Hoboken, NJ: Wiley.

Carvalho Junior, A., S. Lee, and G. Essl (2016). Understanding cloud support for the audience participation concert performance of crowd in c[loud]. In *Proceedings of the Conference on New Interfaces for Musical Expression*, pp. 176–181. Brighton,UK.

Clément, A. R., F. Ribeiro, and R. Penha (2016). Bridging the gap between performers and the audience using networked smartphones: The a.bel system. In *Proceedings of the International Conference on Live Interfaces*. Brighton, UK.

Dannenberg, R. and N. Hu (2003). Pattern discovery techniques for music audio. *Journal of New Music Research 32*(2), 153–163.

Dargie, W. and C. Poellabauer (2010). *Fundamentals of Wireless Sensor Networks: Theory and Practice*. John Wiley & Sons.

Essl, G. (2011). Automated Ad Hoc Networking for Mobile and Hybrid Music Performance. In *Proceedings of the International Computer Music Conference*. Huddersfield, UK.

Essl, G. and S. W. Lee (2017). Mobile devices as musical instruments-state of the art and future prospects. In *Proceedings of the International Symposium on Computer Music Multidisciplinary Research*, pp. 525–539. Cham: Springer.

Essl, G. and A. Müller (2010). Designing mobile musical instruments and environments with urmus. In *Proceedings of the Conference on New Interfaces for Musical Expression*. Sydney, Australia.

Fazekas, G., M. Barthet, and M. Sandler (2014). Novel methods in facilitating audience and performer interaction using the mood conductor framework. In M. Aramaki, O. Derrien, R. Kronland-Martinet, and S. Ystad (Eds.), *Sound, Music, and Motion*, pp. 122–147. Berlin: Springer.

Fettweis, G. (2014). The Tactile Internet: applications and challenges. *IEEE Vehicular Technology Magazine 9*(1), 64–70.

Fiebrink, R. and B. Caramiaux (2016). The machine learning algorithm as creative musical tool. In R. Dean and A. McLean (Eds.), *Oxford Handbook of Algorithmic Music*. New York: Oxford University Press.

Gregorio, J. and Y. Kim (2018). Augmentation of acoustic drums using electromagnetic actuation and wireless control. *Journal of the Audio Engineering Society 66*(4), 202–210.

Hamilton, R., J. Smith, and G. Wang (2011). Social composition: Musical data systems for expressive mobile music. *Leonardo Music Journal 21*, 57–64.

Hazzard, A., S. Benford, A. Chamberlain, C. Greenhalgh, and H. Kwon (2014). Musical intersections across the digital and physical. In *Digital Music Research Network Abstracts (DMRN+9)*. London.

Hindle, A. (2013). Swarmed: Captive portals, mobile devices, and audience participation in multi-user music performance. In *Proceedings of the Conference on New Interfaces for Musical Expression*, pp. 174–179. Daejeon.

Hödl, O., G. Fitzpatrick, and F. Kayali (2017). Design implications for technology-mediated audience participation in live music. In *Proceedings of the Sound and Music Computing Conference*, pp. 28–34. Espoo, Finland.

Hödl, O., F. Kayali, and G. Fitzpatrick (2012). Designing interactive audience participation using smart phones in a musical performance. In *Proceedings of the International Computer Music Conference*. Ljubljana, Slovenia.

Ignoto, P., I. Hattwick, and M. Wanderley (2017). Development of a vibrotactile metronome to assist in conducting contemporary classical music. In *International Conference on Applied Human Factors and Ergonomics*, pp. 248–258. Springer.

Jensenius, A. and M. Lyons (2017). *A NIME Reader: Fifteen Years of New Interfaces for Musical Expression*. Cham, Switzerland: Springer.

Johansson, P., M. Kazantzidis, R. Kapoor, and M. Gerla (2001). Bluetooth: An enabler for personal area networking. *IEEE Network 15*(5), 28–37.

Keller, D. and V. Lazzarini (2017). Ecologically grounded creative practices in ubiquitous music. *Organised Sound 22*(1), 61–72.

Keller, D., V. Lazzarini, and M. Pimenta (2014). *Ubiquitous Music*. Berlin: Springer.

LAN/MAN Standards Committee (2003). Part 15.4: wireless medium access control (MAC) and physical layer (PHY) specifications for low-rate wireless personal area networks (LR-WPANs). IEEE Computer Society.

Landström, S., J. Bergström, E. Westerberg, and D. Hammarwall (2016). Nb-iot: A sustainable technology for connecting billions of devices. *Ericsson Technology Review 93*(3), 1–12.

Lazzarini, V., J. Timoney, and S. Byrne (2015). Embedded sound synthesis. In *Proceedings of the Linux Audio Conference*. Mainz, Germany.

Lee, S., A. Carvalho Junior, and G. Essl (2016). Understanding cloud support for the audience participation concert performance of crowd in c[loud]. In *Proceedings of the Conference on New Interfaces for Musical Expression*, pp. 176–181. Brisbane, Australia.

Lee, S., G. Essl, and Z. M. Mao (2014). Distributing mobile music applications for audience participation using mobile ad-hoc network (MANET). In *Proceedings of the Conference on New Interfaces for Musical Expression*, pp. 533–536. London, UK.

Lee, S. and J. Freeman (2013). Echobo: Audience participation using the mobile music instrument. In *Proceedings of the Conference on New Interfaces for Musical Expression*, pp. 450–455. Daejeon.

MacConnell, D., S. Trail, G. Tzanetakis, P. Driessen, W. Page, and N. Wellington (2013). Reconfigurable autonomous novel guitar effects (RANGE). In *Proceedings of the International Conference on Sound and Music Computing*. Stockholm, Sweden.

Maier, M., M. Chowdhury, B. Rimal, and D. Van (2016). The tactile internet: Vision, recent progress, and open challenges. *IEEE Communications Magazine 54*(5), 138–145.

McGlynn, P., V. Lazzarini, and G. Delap (2012). Recontextualizing the multi-touch surface. In *Proceedings of the New Instruments for Musical Expression Conference*, University of Michigan, Ann Arbor, pp. 8 pp.

McGlynn, P., V. Lazzarini, and G. Delap (2013). Análise de dados multitoque para expressividade em performance musical. *Sonic Ideas 5*(10), 74–79.

McPherson, A. (2015). Buttons, handles, and keys: Advances in continuous-control keyboard instruments. *Computer Music Journal 39*(2), 28–46.

McPherson, A., R. Jack, and G. Moro (2016). Action-sound latency: Are our tools fast enough? In *Proceedings of the Conference on New Interfaces for Musical Expression*. Brisbane, Australia.

Men, L. and N. Bryan-Kinns (2018). Lemo: Supporting collaborative music making in virtual reality. In *IEEE VR Workshop on Sonic Interactions for Virtual Environments*. Reutlingen.

Migicovsky, A., J. Scheinerman, and G. Essl (2014). Moveosc - smart watches in mobile music performance. In *In Joint Proceedings of the International Computer Music Conference and the Sound and Music Computing Conference*, pp. 692–696. Athens, Greece.

Miranda, E. and M. Wanderley (2006). *New Digital Musical Instruments: Control and Interaction Beyond the Keyboard*, Volume 21. Madison: AR Editions, Inc.

Morreale, F., G. Moro, A. Chamberlain, S. Benford, and A. McPherson (2017). Building a maker community around an open hardware platform. In *Proceedings of the Conference on Human Factors in Computing Systems*, pp. 6948–6959. DENVER: ACM.

Oh, J. and G. Wang (2011). Audience-participation techniques based on social mobile computing. In *Proceedings of the International Computer Music Conference*. Huddersfield, UK.

Overholt, D., E. Berdahl, and R. Hamilton (2011). Advancements in actuated musical instruments. *Organised Sound 16*(02), 154–165.

Pardue, L., C. Harte, and A. McPherson (2015). A low-cost real-time tracking system for violin. *Journal of New Music Research 44*(4), 305–323.

Patel, M. and J. Wang (2010). Applications, challenges, and prospective in emerging body area networking technologies. *IEEE Wireless communications 17*(1), 80–88.

Robaszkiewicz, S. and N. Schnell (2015). Soundworks – a playground for artists and developers to create collaborative mobile web performances. In *Proceedings of the Web Audio Conference*. Paris.

Rottondi, C., M. Buccoli, M. Zanoni, D. Garao, G. Verticale, and A. Sarti (2015). Feature-based analysis of the effects of packet delay on networked musical interactions. *Journal of the Audio Engineering Society 63*(11), 864–875.

Rottondi, C., C. Chafe, C. Allocchio, and A. Sarti (2016). An overview on networked music performance technologies. *IEEE Access 4*, 8823–8843.

Rowland, C., E. Goodman, M. Charlier, A. Light, and A. Lui (2015). *Designing Connected Products: UX for the Consumer Internet of Things*. Sebastopol, CA: O'Reilly Media, Inc.

Satyanarayanan, M. (2001). Pervasive computing: Vision and challenges. *IEEE Personal Communications 8*(4), 10–17. Sebastopol, California, USA.

Shaw, T., S. Piquemal, and J. Bowers (2015). Fields: An exploration into the use of mobile devices as a medium for sound diffusion. In E. Berdahl and J. Allison (Eds.), *Proceedings of the Conference on New Interfaces for Musical Expression*, pp. 281–284. Baton Rouge, Louisiana, USA.

Shokri-Ghadikolaei, H., C. Fischione, G. Fodor, P. Popovski, and M. Zorzi (2015). Millimeter wave cellular networks: A MAC layer perspective. *IEEE Transactions on Communications 63*(10), 3437–3458.

Shokri-Ghadikolaei, H., C. Fischione, P. Popovski, and M. Zorzi (2016). Design aspects of short-range millimeter-wave networks: A MAC layer perspective. *IEEE Network 30*(3), 88–96.

Skach, S., A. Xambó, L. Turchet, A. Stolfi, R. Stewart, and M. Barthet (2018). Embodied interactions with e-textiles and the internet of sounds for performing arts. In *Proceedings of the International Conference on Tangible, Embedded, and Embodied Interaction*, pp. 80–87. ACM.

Slaney, M. (2002). Semantic-audio retrieval. In *IEEE International Conference on Acoustics, Speech, and Signal Processing*, Volume 4, pp. 4108–4111. Orlando, FL, USA.

Turchet, L. (2017). The Hyper-Mandolin. In *Proceedings of Audio Mostly Conference*, pp. 1:1–1:8. London, UK.

Turchet, L. (2018). Smart Mandolin: autobiographical design, implementation, use cases, and lessons learned. In *Proceedings of Audio Mostly Conference*, pp. 13:1–13:7. Wrexham, UK.

Turchet, L. (2019). Smart musical instruments: Vision, design principles, and future directions. *IEEE Access 7*, 8944–8963.

Turchet, L. and M. Barthet (2019a). Co-design of Musical Haptic Wearables for electronic music performer's communication. *IEEE Transactions on Human-Machine Systems 49*(2), 183–193.

Turchet, L. and M. Barthet (2019b). Haptification of performer's control gestures in live electronic music performance. In *Proceedings of Audio Mostly Conference*, pp. 244–247. Nottingham, UK.

Turchet, L. and M. Barthet (2019c). An ubiquitous smart guitar system for collaborative musical practice. *Journal of New Music Research 48*(4), 352–365.

Turchet, L., M. Benincaso, and C. Fischione (2017). Examples of use cases with smart instruments. In *Proceedings of Audio Mostly Conference*, pp. 47:1–47:5. London, UK.

Turchet, L., C. Fischione, G. Essl, D. Keller, and M. Barthet (2018). Internet of musical things: Vision and challenges. *IEEE Access 6*, 61994–62017.

Turchet, L., A. McPherson, and M. Barthet (2018a). Co-design of a Smart Cajón. *Journal of the Audio Engineering Society 66*(4), 220–230.

Turchet, L., A. McPherson, and M. Barthet (2018b). Real-time hit classification in a Smart Cajón. *Frontiers in ICT 5*(16), 1–14.

Turchet, L., J. Pauwels, C. Fischione, and G. Fazekas (2019). Cloud-smart musical instrument interactions: Querying a large music collection with a smart guitar. *ACM Transactions on the Internet of Things 1*(3), 1–29.

Turchet, L., T. West, and M. M. Wanderley (2019). Smart Mandolin and Musical Haptic Gilet: Effects of vibro-tactile stimuli during live music performance. In *Proceedings of Audio Mostly Conference*, pp 168–175. Nottingham, UK.

Wang, G. (2014). Ocarina: Designing the iphone's magic flute. *Computer Music Journal 38*(2), 8–21.

Wang, G. et al. (2009). Smule = sonic media: An intersection of the mobile, musical, and social. In *Proceedings of the International Computer Music Conference*. Montreal, Canada.

Wang, G., S. Salazar, J. Oh, and R. Hamilton (2015). World stage: Crowdsourcing paradigm for expressive social mobile music. *Journal of New Music Research 44*(2), 112–128.

Weiser, M. (1991). The computer for the 21st century. *Scientific American 265*(3), 94–105.

Weitzner, N., J. Freeman, Y. Chen, and S. Garrett (2013). Massmobile: Towards a flexible framework for large-scale participatory collaborations in live performances. *Organised Sound 18*(1), 30–42.

Weng, W., P. Chen, S. He, X. Sun, and H. Peng (2016). Smart electronic textiles. *Angewandte Chemie International Edition 55*(21), 6140–6169.

Willig, A. (2008). Recent and emerging topics in wireless industrial communication. *IEEE Transactions on Industrial Informatics 4*(2), 102–124.

Wu, Y., L. Zhang, N. Bryan-Kinns, and M. Barthet (2017). Open symphony: Creative participation for audiences of live music performances. *IEEE MultiMedia 24*(1), 48–62.

Yang, Q. (2015). *Not All Gestures Are Created Equal: Gesture and Visual Feedback in Interaction Spaces*. Ph.D. thesis, University of Michigan.

Yang, Q. and G. Essl (2015). Representation-plurality in multi-touch mobile visual programming for music. In *Proceedings of the Conference on New Interfaces for Musical Expression*. Baton Rouge, Louisiana, USA.

Zawacki, L. and M. Johann (2014). Analogue audio recording using remote servers. In D. Keller, V. Lazzarini, and M. Pimenta (Eds.), *Ubiquitous Music*, pp. 83–107. Berlin: Springer.

# 10 The browser as a platform for ubiquitous music

*Steven Yi and Stéphane Letz*

## 10.1 Introduction

Web browsers today provide a virtualised system and set of technologies to support ubiquitous access to rich media applications. Browsers offering implementations of W3C standards for open web technologies can deliver and execute programs across a variety of device types including desktop and mobile devices. These standards provide Application Programming Interfaces (APIs) that allow web developers the ability to access numerous facilities commonly used to build Ubiquitous Music applications.

In 2013, Wyse and Subramanian (2013) published an extensive look at the Web Browser as a Computer Music Platform, taking into account the history of browser-based music applications and the state of the art at that time. Since 2013, numerous advancements in the web platform have opened up new possibilities for developing low-latency music applications. In particular, the introduction and adoption of WebAssembly by all of the major browser vendors has opened up new approaches in designing and developing ubimus applications for the browser.

In this chapter, we will focus on design issues involved with creating ubimus applications for the browser platform. We will look at strategies for sound and music computing using Web Audio; application packaging and deployment; and cross-platform application design. We will then provide case studies illustrating these strategies.

## 10.2 The technologies of the browser platform

The browser platform is a sandboxed-platform that runs web applications. The platform itself is most commonly used within native applications running on a native platform (Figure 10.1). Developers create applications for the platform which provides a number of APIs that interoperate with the native platform to access hardware (e.g., graphics, touchscreen, audio interfaces, etc.) and other services. This native application may be a web browser application (such as Chrome or Firefox), a program that fetches and loads web applications over the network, or it may also be custom software, one that the ubimus developer

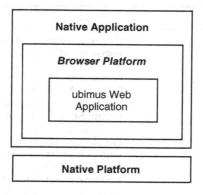

*Figure 10.1* Relationship of ubimus web application, browser platform, native application, and native platform.

creates and delivers to the user which embeds the platform and web application code.

The browser platform today provides a full-featured technology stack that covers most use cases for client-side development. They support many different media file formats for playback; asynchronous and synchronous network requests; 2D and 3D graphics rendering; performant code execution through WebAssembly; I/O processing with audio and MIDI hardware; installation to the desktop through Progressive Web Applications; and more.

Table 10.1, based on Table 1 from Wyse and Subramanian (2013), provides an overview of W3C Web technologies relevant to ubimus application development, updated for developments since 2013. Some newer APIs (such as WebXR, USB, and Serial) are early on in the process of W3C proposal and are not yet widely supported by browser vendors and are unknown whether they will be widely adopted. They are notable though for showing the extent to which the platform has been extended. Other APIs, such as the Web Audio API, have most parts widely supported but also have features (i.e., AudioWorklets) that are not yet supported by all browser vendors.

Since Wyse and Subramanian (2013), the "pain points" described regarding glitching and alternatives to extensibility of the audio engine via Script-ProcessorNode (SPN) have mostly been addressed by the introduction of AudioWorklets to the Web Audio API as well as WebAssembly.

## 10.3   Design approaches to the browser platform

Developing ubimus applications for the browser requires understanding the possibilities of the platform and whether they support the requirements of your application. Answering questions such as:

- What I/O (display, keyboard, touchscreen, sensors, audio, MIDI, network) does your program require?

*Table 10.1* Overview of web technologies

| Infrastructure | |
|---|---|
| Web Workers | Runs code in separate thread and JS context and uses message-based communications |
| WebSockets | Two-way client/server interactive network connections over TCP |
| XMLHTTPRequest | Callback-based API for fetching and posting arbitrary data asynchronously |
| Fetch | Promise-based API for asynchronous network requests |
| Web Storage | Small-scale key/value storage for string data with option for long-term persistence |
| IndexedDB | Large-scale, long-term data storage for structured data, including files/blobs |
| WebAssembly | Runtime for Wasm bytecode, which can be compiled from C, C++, Rust, and other languages |
| Progressive Web App | Technology to install web apps to host system |
| **Media** | |
| HTML5 Audio and Video | Media playback support for various audio and video formats |
| WebRTC | Peer-to-peer communications system for audio, video, and data |
| Media Capture and Streams | MediaStream API for working with streaming audio and video data, used by various other APIs |
| Web Audio | Extensible node-based audio API that communicates with audio hardware |
| Web MIDI | Communications with MIDI devices |
| Canvas and WebGL | 2D and 3D graphics APIs |
| SVG | Scalable Vector Graphics, an XML-based, retained-mode graphics API that supports scripting and animation |
| WebUSB | Communication with USB devices |
| Serial | Communication with devices over serial ports |
| WebVR and WebXR Device | Support for Virtual and Extended Reality hardware |

- Is the browser the only platform you wish to support or do you plan to develop for other platforms?
- How do you plan to deploy your application to users?
- Do you wish to use existing non-browser (i.e., non-JavaScript) computer music libraries and systems as part of your application?
- Do you need single-sample signal processing?
- Do you need an event scheduler?
- What are your computing performance requirements?
- Do you need to run your program offline?

will determine how you will approach developing your application and what set of technologies (e.g., browser APIs, programming tools, libraries) you will need.

The following will focus on three primary concerns for ubimus and the browser: ways to distribute your application, how to implement the sound and music computing needs for your program, and degree of dependency on the platform. Of these concerns, the approaches mentioned for sound and music computing – to use the provided API, extend if possible, and introduce WebAssembly – are applicable to other application domains (e.g., graphics, user input, networking).

### 10.3.1 Distribution and installation

As shown previously in Figure 10.1, the browser is not only a native application that can host web applications, but also a technology that can be a component within the context of a custom native application. The fluid nature and recontextualisation of the browser permit software developers to approach their own application design in multiple ways that affects how their work is distributed to and installed upon their end users' devices.

#### Network-delivered online applications

The primary method for delivering web applications is to deploy the program to the user over the network (i.e., via the HTTP protocol). Users open up a browser program and request a web application via URL from a server that delivers the application files to the browser. Whenever a user loads the application, they will either retrieve the application files from the server or load cached copies from previous executions of the web program.

Assuming the end user has a web browser installed on their system, this form of distribution may be considered a zero-install solution as the browser contains everything necessary to execute the application. The user does not have to install any additional software into the host operating system to run the web program.

The benefits of traditional web applications delivered over the network include easy promotion of and access to the application via URL; developer-controlled and always up-to-date application versions; and zero-install usage in highly controlled computing environments (e.g., computing labs at universities). However, drawbacks include unknown browser versions (a user may use a browser that does not support all of your requirements) and browser host platform (i.e., mobile or desktop browser); access issues depending upon internet limitations (e.g., some countries may ban access to certain domains); requirements to be online; and inability to use the application offline. Of these drawbacks, the largest to address is either implementing and testing for cross-browser support or specifying limits to the application to operate only with specific browser families/hosts (e.g., "designed for Chromium-based browsers on platforms that have multi-touch screens and gyroscopic sensor input").

## Progressive web applications

In addition to zero-install online web applications, developers can enable their web applications for offline usage and appearance as a native application by making their program a Progressive Web App (PWA) (Biørn-Hansen et al., 2017). With PWAs, browsers that support the standard can "install" the web application and needed resources into a local cache and have the program appear in the desktop or mobile system just like any other native application. The PWA will typically have a launcher shortcut installed with a user-definable icon that can start the program when double-clicked (or pressed if on mobile). The application will start in a window or full screen in the same way as any other native program and for all intents and purposes appears to the end user like any other native application. Once installed, PWAs will most often be designed to support offline usage.

PWAs are a fine solution for providing applications that can run both online and offline. The amount of work to enhance an existing web application to be a PWA is generally minimal: the addition of a manifest file describing the web application, the addition of an application icon, and some additional code at runtime to register a service worker that will intercept network loads to determine whether to load files from a local cache or from the internet.

However, there are also drawbacks to this solution. A PWA will not execute any differently than when they are loaded directly within a browser so there are no performance benefits nor any additional APIs or features to expect or use. Also, while installing applications from a browser provides a strong benefit, PWAs are often not as visible to end users as native applications which may be installed through the host system's package repository or app store. Users may or may not be aware of PWAs like they would be through normal channels, nor may they be comfortable with installing your PWA application, despite it being a secure, sandboxed application.

At this time, PWAs are supported on some platforms (primarily desktop systems and Android mobile devices) but not all (most notably, iOS). They are also not supported by all browsers. Consequently, the promise of PWAs for delivery and installation should be considered an additional option for an existing network-delivered program rather than a primary path for distribution to the user.

## Wrapped-browser applications

Beyond PWAs are wrapped-browser applications. Using technologies like Electron[1] or NW.js,[2] developers can create native applications that embed a web browser into their program. The wrapped application requires the user to download and install the program as they would for normal native applications. Compared to PWAs, wrapped applications provide the same APIs as found in the browser as well as additional APIs that permit further integration with the host operating system. For example, a developer working with Electron could write Node.js code employing its foreign-function interface to directly use native libraries.

Wrapped-browser applications allow developers to create native desktop and mobile applications using Web technologies. The drawbacks to such a solution are that the program code may become highly dependent upon the host operating system, limiting its usage across platforms and increasing the complexity and difficulty for building and running the program over time. However, developers can control how much non-standard APIs to use and, since their programs are encapsulated in a native application, may distribute their work in app stores, which may increase visibility and usage.

### 10.3.2   Sound and music computing with the Web Audio API

The Web Audio API provides a system for generating and processing audio signals and communicating with audio hardware. Users create a graph of audio processing by instantiating, configuring, and connecting various AudioNodes provided by the system. Users write their application code using Web Audio's JavaScript API which in turn delegates audio processing either to natively-compiled processing units or to JavaScript code provided by the user. Figure 10.2 illustrates the relationship of application code to the Web Audio API.

Once a graph is connected, signals flow through the system. Users can set parameter values for nodes discretely or use automation with a node's

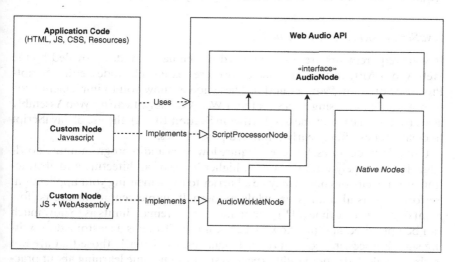

*Figure 10.2* Application code and web audio node API.

AudioParams to change values over time. Signals may also be routed from one AudioNode to another node's AudioParams.

Users may alter the graph at runtime by creating sub-graphs of AudioNodes and attaching them to the overall graph. This covers use cases for real-time responses to user interaction, such as in the case of game audio and musical instruments, but it does not cover sequenced musical events. Typically, an event scheduler would be used to process events that execute actions at a given time, such as dynamically allocating instrument voices. Scheduling systems to work with Web Audio have been developed with solutions that operate outside of the processing graph (Wilson, 2013) and within it (see Section 10.4.1).

### Native nodes

In a browser application using only native nodes, users program their applications using JavaScript, use the Web Audio API directly, and use only the AudioNodes classified as native. Native nodes are backed by natively-compiled code and run in the high-priority audio thread. If these nodes provided by Web Audio sufficiently meet the requirements for your application, this approach has the benefit of the best performance that the browser can offer.

However, while performant and efficient, a number of drawbacks exist to this approach. The Web Audio API contains a limited number of types of native nodes that may or may not cover the signal processing requirements for your application. Also, as noted by Lazzarini et al. (2015), different browsers implement parts of the Web Audio API specification differently, thus making the audible results potentially different between browsers. Finally, since Web Audio uses block-based processing, single-sample algorithms, as well as those requiring feedback, are problematic using only native nodes.

### JavaScript-backed extensible nodes

If your requirements are not supported by the native nodes provided by the Web Audio API, you can use one of two user-extensible nodes, either Script-Processor or AudioWorklet nodes. These nodes allow you to implement your own AudioNodes using JavaScript and WebAssembly. Leaving WebAssembly aside (that scenario is discussed further in Section 10.3.2), the use of JavaScript to create nodes offers nearly unlimited possibilities.

Using JS nodes does, however, require low-level audio programming knowledge. If you largely want to work at higher levels of architecture and abstraction, writing custom nodes may be a barrier to implementing your application. Performance is also an issue: while modern JS implementations are performant due to just-in-time (JIT) compilation, there remain limits as to how much can be optimised and just how fast JS can run. If one is accustomed to writing signal processing code in other languages, particularly those that are not garbage-collected, one should expect to spend some time learning about practices for writing optimal JS code for memory and performance. Fortunately, good practices for Web Audio are largely documented (Adenot, 2019) and one can write code similarly to how one does for non-browser ecosystems.

Each of the extensible node types has its own unique drawbacks. ScriptProcessor nodes are executed on the main thread which means that their performance is affected by any other processing done on that thread. For example, showing an alert dialogue box will block the main thread and can block audio processing. One can minimise the amount of processing done on the main thread by offloading work to a web worker but at the expense of added latency and jitter. ScriptProcessor nodes have also been marked as deprecated, to be replaced with AudioWorklets, but it remains a necessary option for backwards compatibility for older applications as well as to support browsers which do not yet implement AudioWorklets.[3]

AudioWorklets are a more performant option to ScriptProcessor nodes. As a worklet (a lightweight and highly specific kind of web worker), they run in a dedicated high-priority thread. AudioWorklets have two parts: an AudioWorkletProcessor written in JavaScript (which may also use Wasm) that performs audio processing and lives in a separate scope, and an AudioWorkletNode which is the proxy counterpart of AudioWorkletProcessor that takes care of connections to and from other AudioNodes. AudioWorkletNode is also written in JS, is exposed in the main global scope, and functions like a regular AudioNode.

The AudioWorklet design is similar to plugin models found in desktop-based audio ecosystems but requires special attention when dealing with state and communications. Communications with the worklet thread requires message passing (via the MessagePort system) and use of Transferable objects. Communication may be bi-directional with the application posting messages to the worklet as well as the worklet posting messages back to the application. Shared state using SharedArrayBuffers is also an option. Using SharedArrayBuffers requires the use of typed array views and atomic memory access but provides a performant solution for communicating large amounts of data between the application and the worklet.

Despite these drawbacks, JS-extensible AudioNodes open up the possibilities for custom signal processing including single-sample operations. This allows Web Audio to cover many use cases with JavaScript alone. However, when used together with WebAssembly, further options emerge for both processing performance and introduction of cross-platform systems and libraries into the browser platform.

## WebAssembly and extensible nodes

WebAssembly is a binary instruction format for a stack-based virtual machine, designed as a portable target for compilation of high-level languages like C, C++ or Rust. It appeared after the asm.js proof-of-concept, developed by Mozilla engineers, demonstrated that close-to-native performance could be achieved in the web platform by transpiling C and C++ code (thanks to the Emscripten compiler (Zakai, 2011)) into a highly optimizable subset of JavaScript.

Emscripten is a toolchain for compiling C and C++ to WebAssembly and includes emulated low-level APIs (e.g., parts of POSIX, file systems, SDL, etc.). This allows established code bases (libraries or even complete native projects like audio or game engines) to be ported to the web. The introduction and adoption of WebAssembly runtimes in late 2017 by the four major browser engines has enabled the introduction of compiled code into the browser ecosystem.

The introduction of WebAssembly into the browser platform has opened up a number of possibilities to help address issues of pure JS-based solutions for Web Audio. The typical usage pattern for WebAssembly involves the writing of code in a non-browser language (i.e., C, C++, Rust), ahead-of-time compilation of the code into Wasm bytecode library, then loading and usage of the library from JS. Wasm code is executed by the WebAssembly runtime which can be more performant than JIT-optimised JS and approach native speeds (Haas et al., 2017).

Two general usage patterns for employing WebAssembly are to optimise "hot paths" in code as well as to permit coding in non-browser languages. For hot paths, developers typically begin using JS, find that a solution is not performant enough for their requirements, profile their application, then identify branches of code that are often used and taking large amounts of CPU. Once identified, these branches of code become candidates for replacement with WebAssembly. In the case of ubimus applications, a common situation might be that DSP code in a JS node is correct but too slow to use. In this situation, one might replace the DSP code in JS with a call to a Wasm implementation.

While using non-browser languages to generate Wasm binaries introduces technical requirements to a program, it also provides tremendous opportunities to introduce well-known libraries and systems into the browser ecosystem. The WebAssembly runtime provides many of the same platform-independent APIs one expects on POSIX-based systems, which largely covers many of the audio-processing needs for ubimus applications. We will discuss a cross-platform approach to ubimus applications further in Section 10.3.3.

From the perspective of ubimus, WebAssembly provides a unique path for cross-platform development. Because C, C++, Rust, and other languages can be compiled into WebAssembly, libraries and systems which have traditionally been compiled and executed on native platforms can now be reused in the context of the browser. This allows ubimus developers to work directly with the lower-level APIs provided by the browser as well as employ well-known and tested systems as a higher-level framework for developing their music applications.

As we will see in Section 10.4.2, technologies such as Csound and FAUST have been ported to the browser platform via WebAssembly, providing users with the ability to create ubimus applications using these well-known tools.

### 10.3.3   Platform independence

A primary concern for ubimus applications is their availability on multiple kinds of hardware platforms and operating systems. Traditionally, when creating applications for one platform, developers design their application using the services available by the native operating system that are exposed through the set of APIs for that system. To create applications that work on multiple platforms, developers modify their codebases to accommodate differences in different operating systems and APIs. For ubimus applications, one has to determine all of the operating systems and hardware configurations one wishes to support and work out how to accommodate all of the differences.

To simplify matters, developers often use cross-platform libraries or systems to aid development. This additional layer between the application code and the underlying system APIs lets developers program against the cross-platform API and rely on it being available and handle correctly the differences in platforms. For example, rather than have multiple audio interfaces implementations in their code (e.g., CoreAudio on MacOs, WASAPI on Windows, and ALSA on Linux), developers might instead write their audio interface code only once using PortAudio (Bencina and Burk, 2001) and benefit from PortAudio's cross-platform implementation.

In the case of the browser platform, one still must look at their application requirements and target platforms for deployment. However, because the browser is a meta-platform that itself runs on multiple operating systems, one can target the set of APIs available in the browser and rely on the platform itself being cross-platform to achieve deployment and availability for one's requirements. Developers must still account for differences between browser implementations, but if one uses only W3C standards-based APIs, the differences are generally easy to work with either directly or by using cross-browser libraries.

Although the browser platform is cross-platform in nature, there are still scenarios where developers may wish to develop ubimus applications that run both in the browser as well as directly on a native operating system. With the advent of WebAssembly, developers have options to design their applications to run in browsers using traditionally native libraries and systems.

When approaching the browser as a platform, ubimus developers should factor in both their application requirements as well as their own skillset to come to a decision on how to approach implementing their program. If the browser's APIs are sufficient, the availability of browsers covers the desired platforms, and one is comfortable programming in JavaScript, developing for just the browser may be enough. If one wishes to make available their applications on native platforms, or one is more familiar using native libraries or systems, one might consider using cross-platform libraries and systems that support the browser to help facilitate covering all of their required target systems and optimise for their skillset.

## 10.4   Case studies

In this section, we discuss different case studies for browser-based and cross-platform libraries, systems, and applications. We will discuss these categorised by those which target the browser as their primary platform and those for which the browser is but one of many supported platforms.

### 10.4.1   *Browser-based systems*

*Tone.js*

Tone.js (Mann, 2015) is a JavaScript library that provides "a framework for creating interactive music in the browser. It provides advanced scheduling capabilities, synths and effects, and intuitive musical abstractions built on top of the Web Audio API" (Mann, 2019). It has a number of layers to its design such that a user may work just with Tone.js's pre-built instruments, effects, and scheduler – without much knowledge of the Web Audio API–or they may use lower-level layers together with the Web Audio API for further customisation.

In terms of design, Tone.js only uses native-backed AudioNodes and does not use either the ScriptProcessingNode or AudioWorkletNode. Higher-level audio components in Tone.js, such as its PluckSynth and JCReverb, are created by assembling Web Audio-provided nodes together. Tone.js's scheduler system operates by default using a callback that is ticked either by a Web Worker or a setTimeout callback.

Tone.js primarily serves use cases for the development of realtime interactive music systems. Tone provides abstractions Tone.Signal and Tone.AudioNode as well as various implementations of those abstractions for lower-level signal processing primitives. These mostly map to Web Audio's abstractions of AudioParam and AudioNode. Tone.js interoperates well with the Web Audio API and those familiar with Web Audio should feel at home working with Tone.js due to the similar named node methods. Use cases involving offline rendering are supported by Tone.js.

Tone.js serves both as a higher-level API for music making in the browser as well as an example of how the Web Audio API, particularly the native node system, can be used to develop higher-level systems. It does, however, have limitations due to only using native nodes such that signal processing algorithms involving single-sample or short delay-time (less than block size) feedback are not supported. Overall, Tone.js serves many musical use cases, functions well as a layer to build upon in a larger end-user application, and provides the flexibility to work more closely to the underlying Web Audio API.

*Gibber*

Gibber (Roberts and Kuchera-Morin, 2012) is a "creative coding environment for audiovisual performance and composition" (Roberts, 2019a) developed by

Charlie Roberts. Users live code in the Gibber frontend using JavaScript and the Gibber API to perform music and visuals in realtime. While not a typical application that falls under the banner of ubimus, due to its higher-end processing requirements and desktop-based focus, it does provide a model for understanding approaches to the browser platform that is relevant to ubimus developers.

Gibber is a web application that operates within the browser. It uses a layered design consisting of the main Gibber web application and a number of custom libraries for audio, video, networking, and more that ultimately builds upon brower-provided APIs. The system is written completely in JavaScript.

Regarding the audio system, Gibber is built upon Gibberish.js (Roberts et al., 2013), a "fast, JavaScript DSP library that creates JIT-optimised audio callbacks using code generation techniques" (Roberts, 2019b). Gibberish takes a very different approach to Web Audio than Tone.js: rather than build upon Web Audio's native nodes for signal processing, Gibberish takes the opposite approach and does all DSP within custom JavaScript code. Gibberish uses a single-sample processing model, opening up the kinds of signal processing usable within the browser compared to native nodes, and the system as a whole is driven by a single ScriptProcessor node that connects Gibberish's processing to Web Audio.[4] A sample-accurate event system is also implemented within Gibberish.

Gibber, with all of its requirements for multimedia processing, shows that the browser platform is certainly capable of supporting interactive, rich media applications. The signal processing approach, though computationally more demanding than native node systems, shows that optimised JS can be used for realtime performance (at least with desktop-class systems) and that the browser platform is extensible enough to support custom DSP code.

### 10.4.2   Cross-platform systems

*Csound*

Csound (Lazzarini et al., 2016) is a sound and music computing system that runs on a variety of platforms including desktop, mobile, embedded, and browser. Csound contains a domain-specific language compiler, a real-time audio engine, a MUSIC-N style architecture of schedulable processing units (instruments), unit generators (opcodes), signals, and events (notes).

Early explorations (Lazzarini, Costello, Yi, et al., 2014, Lazzarini, Costello, Yi, and ffitch, 2014, 2015) into using Csound on the browser platform involved asm.js as well as Portable Native Client (PNaCl) (Donovan et al., 2010). The asm.js build was created using the Emscripten compiler as well as JS code that tied into Web Audio using ScriptProcessor nodes. The PNaCl build was generated with the PNaCl SDK and used the provided Pepper API to have access to the underlying audio system.

As both asm.js and PNaCl were phased out and later replaced with WebAssembly, Web Audio Csound (Yi et al., 2018) also replaced previous attempts at using Csound on the browser platform. This build compiles the libcsound C source code with Emscripten into WebAssembly as well as provides a JavaScript API for developers to use. The API manages operating Csound through WebAssembly and setting up interoperation with the Web Audio API through a single wrapper AudioNode (either SPN or AudioWorklet).

Developing web applications with Csound requires knowledge of both JS for application code as well as Csound's language for sound and music code. Requiring two languages does increase the technical skills necessary for creating an application. However, using a domain-specific language does have benefits. Since Csound supports many platforms, the code written in Csound's language is portable and may be reused within numerous other computing contexts (e.g., in a custom desktop application, in a composed Csound work, in a VST plugin). Conversely, because Csound has been around since 1986, a wealth of pre-existing Csound work is available to study and draw upon for one's own projects. Finally, since Csound operates in multiple contexts and platforms, collaborative development workflows are possible such that a web programmer who does not know Csound could collaborate with a Csound user who does not know web programming.

The design of Web Audio Csound supports two main use cases: developing Csound-based applications where the user primarily works with Csound's API, and developing Web Audio-based applications where Csound plays a role as a custom AudioNode. Web Audio Csound's JS API is comparable to those provided in Csound's iOS and Android SDKs, desktop C API, and other language bindings. With the JS API, developers work with Csound much like they would on other platforms and the platform details are hidden. The API also exposes the AudioNode that wraps Csound engine execution, allowing the developer to use the API much like a factory for custom AudioNodes where signal processing is backed by Csound code. The two use cases provide multiple paths to integrating Csound into a web application.

An example of a Csound-based ubimus web application is csound-live-code.[5] The project is based around a Csound user-code library (livecode.orc) that provides functions for live code performance with Csound. On desktop systems, a Csound CSD project file (livecode.csd) that uses livecode.orc is provided to use the system with desktop-based live coding setups. The project also provides a web interface that provides a code editor for Csound code, embeds the Web Audio Csound system, and pre-loads the livecode.orc library. The web application is delivered to users via the browser, is always up-to-date with the latest changes to the library, and requires no installation of additional software to use. It is also both cross-browser (i.e., Chrome, Firefox, Safari, Edge) as well as cross-platform (desktop, mobile). Finally, the web application is a PWA and users may install the application to their desktop or phone for

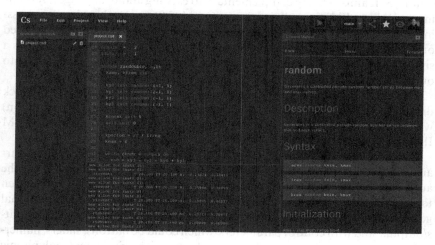

*Figure 10.3* Csound Web-IDE.

offline use when using browsers that support PWA installation (e.g., Chrome on desktop and Android).

The csound-live-code project demonstrates the benefits of using a cross-platform technology like Csound. By Csound supporting the browser platform, csound-live-code is able to provide a ubiquitous music-making application that runs both on low-end devices (e.g., Chromebooks, mobile devices) as well as high-end desktop systems. Because Csound supports other platforms, the underlying livecode.orc code can be reused in other non-browser contexts. Csound provides the foundation for making ubimus applications that can enjoy all of the possibilities provided by the browser platform while also providing opportunities to extend one's applications to other native platforms.

Another example is the Csound Web-IDE (Yi et al., 2019). The Web-IDE,[6] shown in Figure 10.3, is an open-source,[7] browser-based integrated development environment (IDE) for sound and music computing using Csound. The web application offers users the ability to edit and run standard, multi-file Csound projects in the same way they would do on the desktop, mobile, and embedded platforms. The system is also a social-coding platform (Dabbish et al., 2012) that enables sharing of personal work and discovery of others' works. Enabled by modern web technologies, use cases for the Web-IDE include computer music education, music composition, community-building around common music practices, live-coding performance, and development of realtime interactive systems.

## FAUST

FAUST (Orlarey et al., 2004) is a functional, synchronous, domain specific programming language designed for real-time audio signal processing and synthesis. It aims at being complementary to existing audio languages by offering a viable and efficient alternative to C and C++ to develop signal processing libraries, audio plug-ins, or standalone applications. The language is based on a simple and well-defined formal semantics. A FAUST program denotes a signal processor, a mathematical function that transforms input signals into output signals.

The FAUST compiler is organised in successive stages, from the DSP block diagram to signals, and finally to the FIR (FAUST Imperative Representation) which can then translated into several target languages (C, C++, JAVA, LLVM IR, WebAssembly).

As a specification language, the FAUST code only describes the DSP part and an abstract version of the control interface. It says nothing about the audio drivers or the GUI toolkit to be used. Architecture files are written to describe how to connect the DSP code to the external world. Additional generic code is added to connect the DSP computation itself with audio inputs/outputs, and with control parameters, which could be buttons, sliders, numerical entries etc. Architectures files can also possibly implement polyphonic support for MIDI controllable instruments, by automatically dealing with dynamic voices allocation, and decoding and mapping of incoming MIDI events.

A complete ecosystem has been developed over the years. Standalone applications (using for instance CoreAudio and QT on OSX, JACK and GTK on Linux etc.) as well as plugins (VST, LV2, Max/MSP etc.), programs for mobile (iOS and Android) or executable for embedded platforms (Bela[8] and ESP32 cards[9] etc.) can be produced. A lot of them can be easily produced using a remote compilation service running on the cloud (Michon and Orlarey, 2012).

For the Web platform, a Wasm backend has been integrated to generate the binary WebAssembly format. When embedded in the FAUST compiler compiled for the Web as a library using Emscripten, it allows to dynamically compile FAUST DSP programs in WebAssembly modules. Additional JavaScript glue code is added to wrap the WebAssembly modules in fully functional Web Audio nodes (Letz et al., 2018).

Two implementations creating FAUST-based ScriptProcessor or AudioWorklet nodes have been developed. For each one, a polyphonic MIDI controllable version has been done (using the Web MIDI API), with a JavaScript architecture that automatically duplicates the FAUST DSP program written for one instrument voice, and manage dynamic voices allocation (Figures 10.4 and 10.5).

Two main use-cases have been explored:

- Producing self-contained FAUST DSP generated Web Audio nodes that only contain the needed Wasm module. Two scripts named faust2webaudiowasm (generating an HTML page with a generic GUI) and faust2wasm (generating JavaScript and the Wasm module to be loaded and

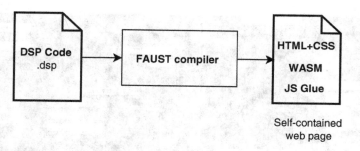

Self-contained
web page

*Figure 10.4* Producing static self-contained pages.

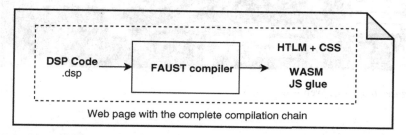

*Figure 10.5* Embedding the dynamic compilation chain.

controlled with additional JavaScript code), can be used. This is a convenient way to create and publish DSP instruments and effects as web pages
• Embedding the complete compilation chain allows for more ambitious projects

The FAUST IDE[10] is a complete Web editor allowing to edit, dynamically compile, and run DSP programs (see Figure 10.6). It can use either Script-Processor or AudioWorklet nodes depending on what the browser supports. Monophonic and polyphonic MIDI controllable instruments can be defined. Audio files can be used to test DSP effects. The DSP block diagram, as well as output signals in time and frequency domain can be visualised using scopes in a separate frame. The remote compilation service running on the cloud can be accessed to finally generate native versions of the program.

The FAUST Playground[11] (Denoux et al., 2015) is a pedagogical platform aimed to give pupils access to graphical programming. A library of DSP instruments and effects is available and can be used to describe graphs of audio nodes.[12] Additional DSP program can be dropped in the platform and compiled. Control parameters can be associated to accelerometer sensors. Then the remote compilation service can be accessed to finally generate native versions of the program, like instruments to be used on the Android or iOS platforms (Figure 10.7).

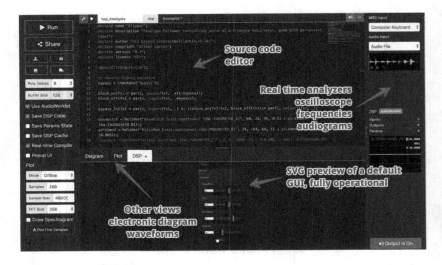

*Figure 10.6* Faust Web IDE.

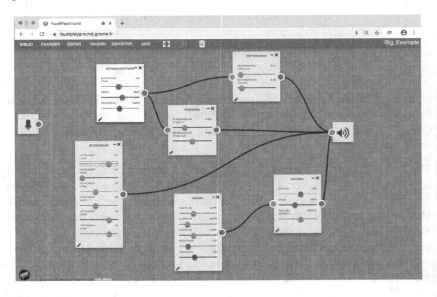

*Figure 10.7* Faust playground.

The FAUST ecosystem now goes from embedded platforms up to the web. Having the FAUST compiler as a web service allows to easily develop tools for designing and testing DSP programs. Thanks to WebAssembly, audio code can now execute at speed approaching native performances. Cross-platform development from native up to the web has become fully achievable.

## 10.5   Conclusions

Given the diversity of hardware, operating systems, programming languages, and APIs that present themselves as options when creating Ubiquitous Music applications, many questions arise when choosing what set of technologies to use to create one's work. The choices to be made depend not only upon the technical requirements necessary to implement the creative vision but also the human elements: what is known, what needs to be learned, and how much time is available to develop the project. The issues of knowledge and time grow as ubimus projects extend into the Internet of Musical Things (Turchet et al., 2018), where the sets of technologies required to operate musical things and applications, along with their connectivity through services, can quickly overwhelm the project's creators. Together with the ever-changing landscape of software and hardware, the "challenge related to the sustainability of its technological infra-structure" (Keller and Lazzarini, 2017) that arises for ubimus applications becomes an additional concern to factor into decision making when choosing what technological stack to use for one's work.

In light of these technical and human requirements and concerns, the browser as a platform offers much for the ubimus application developer to consider when creating their programs. The platform supports many of the same services (e.g., graphics, sound, hardware, networking) as found on desktop systems and does so in a portable context that runs on many different hardware platforms and operating systems. Developers may use various strategies to deploy their programs to their end users on a wide variety of devices via online loading over the network, progressive installation as a desktop program, or traditional installation as a wrapped-browser native application. Standardised browser APIs, together with native libraries and systems compiled into WebAssembly, provide a foundation for building programs that can execute with near-native performance. Finally, the possibility of using well-known systems from other platforms within the browser allows development within the context of an *ubimus ecosystem* (Lazzarini et al., 2014), providing a means to use existing domain expertise and solutions within the browser and further reuse of developed work on other platforms.

## Notes

1 https://electronjs.org.
2 https://nwjs.io.
3 At the time of this writing, only Chrome and Chromium-based browsers support AudioWorklets. Implementation work is underway in other browsers, such as Firefox, but it unknown if or when Webkit-based browsers, such as Safari, will implement this part of the specification.
4 The description of processing refers to the current public release of Gibber; newer versions in the works support AudioWorklets.
5 https://github.com/kunstmusik/csound-live-code.
6 https://ide.csound.com.
7 https://github.com/csound/web-ide.
8 https://bela.io.

9 http://www.wikiwand.com/en/ESP32.
10 https://faustide.grame.fr/.
11 https://faustplayground.grame.fr/.
12 Here using the regular WebAudio API to connect the nodes.

## Bibliography

Adenot, P. (2019).   Web Audio API performance and debugging notes. https://padenot.github.io/web-audio-perf/. Accessed: 2019-11-15.

Bencina, R. and P. Burk (2001). PortAudio – an open source cross platform audio API. In *Proceedings of the International Computer Music Conference*. Havana, Cuba.

Biørn-Hansen, A., T. A. Majchrzak, and T.-M. Grønli (2017). Progressive web apps: The possible web-native unifier for mobile development. In *Proceedings of the 13th International Conference on Web Information Systems and Technologies (WEBIST 2017)*, pp. 344–351. Porto, Portugal.

Dabbish, L., C. Stuart, J. Tsay, and J. Herbsleb (2012). Social coding in GitHub: Transparency and collaboration in an open software repository. In *Proceedings of the ACM 2012 conference on Computer Supported Cooperative Work - CSCW '12*, Seattle, Washington, USA, pp. 1277. ACM Press.

Denoux, S., Y. Orlarey, S. Letz, and D. Fober (2015, January). Composing a web of audio applications. In *1st Web Audio Conference*, Paris, France. IRCAM, Mozilla Foundation.

Donovan, A., R. Muth, B. Chen, and D. Sehr (2010). PNaCl: Portable Native Client Executables. *Google White Paper*.

Haas, A., A. Rossberg, D. L. Schuff, B. L. Titzer, M. Holman, D. Gohman, L. Wagner, A. Zakai, and J. Bastien (2017). Bringing the Web up to Speed with WebAssembly. In *ACM SIGPLAN Notices*, Volume 52, pp. 185–200. ACM.

Keller, D. and V. Lazzarini (2017). Ecologically grounded creative practices in ubiquitous music. *Organised Sound 22*(1), 61–72.

Lazzarini, V., E. Costello, S. Yi, et al. (2014). Development tools for ubiquitous music on the world wide web. In *Ubiquitous Music*, pp. 111–128. Berlin: Springer.

Lazzarini, V., E. Costello, S. Yi, and J. ffitch (2014). Csound on the Web. In *Linux Audio Conference*, Karlsruhe, Germany, pp. 77–84.

Lazzarini, V., E. Costello, S. Yi, and J. ffitch (2015). Extending csound to the web. In *1st Web Audio Conference*, IRCAM, Paris.

Lazzarini, V., D. Keller, M. Pimenta, and J. Timoney (2014). Ubiquitous music ecosystems: Faust programs in csound. In *Ubiquitous Music*, pp. 129–150. Springer.

Lazzarini, V., S. Yi, J. ffitch, J. Heintz, Ø. Brandtsegg, and I. McCurdy (2016). *Csound: A sound and music computing system*. Berlin: Springer.

Lazzarini, V., S. Yi, and J. Timoney (2015). Web audio: Some critical considerations.

Letz, S., Y. Orlarey, and D. Fober (2018). FAUST domain specific audio DSP language compiled to WebAssembly. In *Companion Proceedings of the The Web Conference 2018*, WWW '18, Republic and Canton of Geneva, Switzerland, pp. 701–709. International World Wide Web Conferences Steering Committee.

Mann, Y. (2015). Interactive music with Tone.js. In *Proceedings of the 1st annual Web Audio Conference*. Citeseer.

Mann, Y. (2019). https://tonejs.github.io. Accessed: 2019-11-15.

Michon, R. and Y. Orlarey (2012). The Faust online compiler: A web-based IDE for the Faust programming language. In *Linux Audio Conference 2012*, Stanford, United States.

Network, M. D. Worklet.

Orlarey, Y., D. Fober, and S. Letz (2004). *Syntactical and semantical aspects of FAUST.* Soft Computing, 8(9):623–632, Berlin: Springer Verlag.

Roberts, C. (2019a). Gibber welcome text. https://gibber.cc. Accessed: 2019-11-15.

Roberts, C. (2019b). Gibberish. https://github.com/gibber-cc/gibberish. Accessed: 2019-11-15.

Roberts, C. and J. Kuchera-Morin (2012). Gibber: Live coding audio in the browser. In *ICMC* 2012, pp 63–67. Ljubliana, Slovenia.

Roberts, C., G. Wakefield, and M. Wright (2013). The web browser as synthesizer and interface. In *NIME*, pp. 313–318.

Turchet, L., C. Fischione, G. Essl, D. Keller, and M. Barthet (2018). Internet of musical things: Vision and challenges. *IEEE Access 6*, 61994–62017.

Wilson, C. (2013). A Tale of Two Clocks - Scheduling Web Audio with Precision. https://www.html5rocks.com/en/tutorials/audio/scheduling/. Accessed 2019-11-15.

Wyse, L. and S. Subramanian (2013). The viability of the web browser as a computer music platform. *Computer Music Journal 37*(4), 10–23.

Yi, S., V. Lazzarini, and E. Costello (2018). WebAssembly audioworklet csound. In *4th Web Audio Conference*, TU Berlin, Berlin.

Yi, S., H. Sigurðsson, and E. Costello (2019). Csound Web-IDE. In *Proceedings of the International Web Audio Conference 2019*, pp. 92–97. Trondheim, Norway.

Zakai, A. (2011). Emscripten: An LLVM-to-JavaScript Compiler. In *Proceedings of the ACM International Conference Companion on Object Oriented Programming Systems Languages and Applications Companion*, OOPSLA '11, New York, NY, pp. 301–312. ACM.

# 11 Adaptive and crossadaptive strategies for composition and performance

*Øyvind Brandtsegg*

The term *adaptive* in general means that the parameters controlling a process automatically adjusts to some environmental condition. More specific to audio processing, adaptive means that the audio processing parameters move in accordance with some characteristics of the audio signal. If the features or characteristics controlling the process comes from the same audio signal as the one that is being processed, we could call it auto-adaptive (although we usually just call it adaptive in this case). Adaptive effects have been described by Verfaille et al. (2006) and others since the early 2000s. A recent comprehensive survey including automatic mixing can be found in Reiss and Brandtsegg (2018). When the controlling features originate from another signal, however, it is a *crossadaptive* process, the term determining clearly that some of the characteristics of one sound have crossed over, influencing some change in another sound. Due to the generality of parametric processing, any feature (that can be represented numerically) can be used to control any processing parameter.

The use of audio feature analysis as the source of parametric control can be seen as a form of signal interaction, and this has seen widespread use in several contexts. A simple form of signal interaction is *ring modulation*, where two audio signals are multiplied with each other, creating sidebands. This can be heard for instance in Stockhausen's *Mixtur* (1964), and also in the guitar solo of Black Sabbath's *Paranoid* (1970). Another form of signal interaction is the *channel vocoder*, where the measured energy in different frequency bands of one sound is used to control the amplitude of the same frequency bands on another sound. Thus, the sonic gestural variation of the first sound is imposed on the timbral characteristic of the second. We can hear examples if the vocoder in Wendy Carlos' music for *A Clockwork Orange* (1971), and on Laurie Anderson's *O Superman* (1981). A similar effect (although implemented differently) can be attained from the *talk box*, where one sound is fed through a plastic tube into the mouth cavity of a performer, using this as a dynamically shapeable resonator. The resulting signal is then picked up by a conventional microphone near the performer's mouth, similar to a vocal microphone. This effect was used early by Joe Walsh and later popularised by Peter Frampton. Yet another adaptive effect can be seen in the *auto wah*, where an envelope follower is used to control the cutoff frequency of a resonant bandpass filter.

This allows the sound level to control the position of a spectral peak, creating an animated and funky quack-quack sound.

The auto wah was used extensively by Stevie Wonder on the clavinet on songs like *Superstition* and *Higher Ground* from the early 1970s. Perhaps the simplest adaptive effect is the *compressor*, for dynamic control of an audio signal. Here, the measured signal input level is used to control the signal output level in a nonlinear fashion. If the input signal exceeds a certain threshold, the output signal is attenuated according to some proportion of the input signal level amplitude exceeding the threshold. Today, dynamic compression is used in one form or another on almost all commercial recording productions. It can be used gently, to even out dynamic peaks, and it can be used creatively to shape the transients and the overall envelope of sounds. This brings us back to the topic of *crossadaptive effects*, since the *sidechain compressor* is the most widely used application of crossadaptivity in audio. Here, the signal level of one sound is used to modify the amplitude of another sound. A common use in commercial music is to let the amplitude envelope of the bass drum attenuate the output level of a synth pad (or even the whole mix of other instruments). This creates a pumping effect ubiquitous in electronic dance music, with an early example heard on Eric Prydz *Call On Me* (2004). In a less obtrusive way, sidechain compression is also widely used to gently clean up a mix, for example, to allow the vocals more clarity by dynamically attenuating other instruments.

## 11.1   Crossadaptive processing for live use

The sidechain compressor shows the use of crossadaptive processing where the relationship between sounds is a core aspect of how the sounds are being modulated. Seeing that musical interaction is made up by such relationships between sounds, we wanted to expand the notion of crossadaptivity and allow its use in the most general manner. The aim was to allow any audio feature to be be used as the modulator for any parameter controlling any audio effect. The boldness of such a generalisation could be objected, but let us assume that *any* in the sentence above can be translated to *as many as practically possible, and expanding as needed*. With such a processing technique, numerous applications for audio processing opens up, both for problem-fixing and for creative treatment. This can be applied both in composition, in audio mixing and post production, but perhaps most dynamically as a tool to be used during the actual performance of music. In any musical interplay, the actions of one musician set some premises for what the other musicians can productively do, and this privilege extends to all participating members of an ensemble. This is also used intentionally, for example, in acoustic chamber ensembles, where nuances of collective intonation are used to let a lead melody shine in a pronounced manner. Extending this such that any action on the behalf of one musician can have distinctive modulation effects on any aspect of another musician's sound, can allow new modes of interplay. This any-to-any mapping of relations allows productive and problem-fixing applications, but also unnatural, counterintuitive and straight up silly kinds of modulation mappings. Figuring out *what mappings make sense* for making music together is a long process, and our endeavours so far are just a start. In struggling with the somewhat unfamiliar potential of the technique, we have kept in mind that some signal interactions from known history also could seem arbitrary at the time of conception. For example the auto wah could be seen as silly, even comical in its quack-quack timbral gesture until utilised in an expressive manner by ingenious performers. After the fact, it would be seen as a classic mark of a musical genre.

In enabling new relationships between performers, the general crossadaptive techniques have the potential for disruptive intervention as well as for collaborative sound design. A particular characteristic of this system is that it is non-intrusive: No special sensor technology is needed, no extra interfaces for physical interaction and no modifications to existing (acoustic or otherwise) instruments. Only the sound is used, both to communicate and to modulate. Thus, it can be used on any instrument, relying on the timbral control and sound shaping that the musician has refined over years of practice. These nuances can then be given additional roles as control signals.

## 11.2   System and signal flow

To give an understanding of how these techniques can be applied musically and performative, it can be relevant to also describe the enabling technology. In our project, we wanted to be able to analyse the features of several instruments separately, and also be able to combine these freely, to make control signals for modulation of effects processing parameters. To facilitate the inclusion of these techniques in a variety of audio production workflows, we wanted to make it available inside the framework of a standard Digital Audio Workstation (DAW). We could have opted for building a custom audio mixing system, or a Max patch for processing our audio, but we thought it very important that a sound designer could explore the new control methods while still using audio processors they already know well. This way we also enable crossadaptive control of the huge range of available off-the-shelf commercial audio production tools already out there.

There are some challenges with embedding these control methods inside a standard DAW. Some of these are also covered in early writings about crossadaptive interactions in performance (Brandtsegg, 2015), but we will do a quick recap here, with recent additions and extensions. One basic problem of doing this inside a standard DAW is that it requires some form of communication between different tracks in the DAW mixer. In an effort of optimisation, the analysis of an instrument should only need to happen once, so this could reasonably be done on an input track for that instrument. Still, the routing and processing of each instrument should be flexible, and thus, potentially be done on other tracks. Similarly, the option of flexibly routing and combining analysis signals from several different instruments requires that these control signals be communicated freely across tracks. Digital Audio Workstations (DAWs) commonly allow sending audio between tracks, but there is no common method to send control signals. This is one thing we needed to enable. An example of a crossadaptive setup in a DAW mixer, with instrument inputs, analysers, control bus and effects tracks is shown in Figure 11.1.

There currently exists a number of good choices for a DAW, each with their strong sides. Ideally, the crossadaptive workflow should support as many of the DAWs as possible. The plugin structure and signal routing in our design allow for this kind of support. Still, each DAW is designed and built differently, each with its own specific quirks. To support all (or most) of them would require a substantial effort, akin to a commercial plugin production. We have some experience in this from the Hadron particle synthesiser project (Brandtsegg et al., 2019), so as to know the amount of resources needed. For the crossadaptive project, we have opted to put more resources into the practical application of the techniques, spending more time on playing music with it than on the software support side. For this reason we have also opted for one single DAW as the main supported platform, with an open attitude to supporting other DAWs opportunistically. We have chosen Reaper (Cockos Inc., 2019) as our priority DAW. It is free to try and has a low-cost license. It has cross platform support, with a high degree of configurability and flexibility. The flexible signal routing (multichannel tracks, with channel selection on send/receive) is very practical for inter-channel communication. In our experience Reaper is

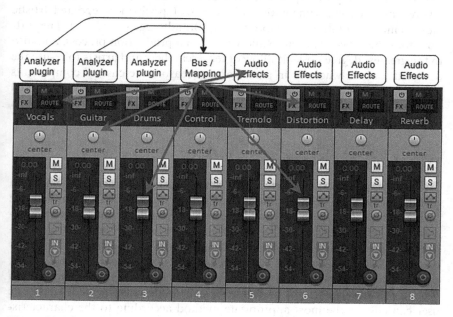

*Figure 11.1* Crossadaptive control signals in a DAW mixer. The signals indicated with arrows are communicated via Open Sound Control.

very stable, and one can run plugins in separate processes should that be necessary. This can be useful when developing new plugins, since a plugin crash will then just crash the process, and not take down the whole DAW. The per-track performance monitoring helps optimise the new plugins for performance, and the per-plugin latency compensation (PDC) allows flexibility in the configuration of latency versus synchronisation. Finally, we have seen excellent support from Cockos whenever we have had questions about implementation, or issues that needed their attention.

The audio processing in our plugins is implemented with Csound (Lazzarini et al., 2016), an open-source cross-platform sound and music computing system. Csound has roots in the digital audio software *Music* by Max Mathews working at Bell Labs in 1957, and its incarnation under the name of Csound by Barry Vercoe working at MIT in 1985. The long history of Csound is a testament to its compatibility across versions, and the backwards compatibility policy in Csound development suggests it can be expected to be reasonably future-compatible. The long history also accumulates to an immense library of opcodes for audio processing, and the language is easily interfaced to other technologies, with an API for most common programming languages. Pertinent to our application is also the ability to wrap Csound code as VST plugins with the tool Cabbage (Walsh, 2019). Development of software for artistic processes, like with these crossadaptive plugins, is a moving target (Trifonova et al., 2008). One does not know the specification until active experimentation has been done on prototypes. The cycle of producing updated design criteria involves practical experimentation, dialogue with performers, updated artistic ideas, reimplementation and more testing (Brandtsegg et al., 2015). The software tools have been chosen to allow for such a production process, and also to the greatest degree possible allow other researchers and artists to re-use the designed tools in whole or in part. For this reason, the custom components we have developed are released as open-source code, and we have attempted to make them reasonably modular. The next section describes these tools in some more detail.

## 11.3   Analyzer and Mediator

The *Analyzer* uses a collection of feature extraction methods based on research within the field of music information retrieval (MIR), for example (Peeters et al., 2011). We have modified these methods to optimise the representations of timbral features to make them more intuitively related to performative and expressive dimensions. Among the analysed features we find *rms amplitude, transient detection, envelope crest, spectral centroid, spectral spread, spectral skewness, spectral kurtosis, spectral flatness, spectral crest* and *spectral flux*. There are also several pitch tracking methods implemented, where the user can choose the most appropriate method according to the characteristics of the audio material being analysed. We have used *mel frequency cepstral analysis* to produce a measure of formant strength which can correspond to *performative energy*, as tension or *pressed-ness* of a sound. Analyses of rhythmic density and complexity are also available. A screenshot of the analyser can be seen in Figure 11.2.

To allow flexible routing and mixing of analysis signals from several sources, we have implemented a separate mapping plugin called the *Mediator*, Figure 11.3. This plugin receives analysis signals from several analyser instances, allowing separate filtering, scaling and shaping as well as adding (mixing), subtracting (absolute differences), or conditional gating of modulator signals. There is also an Open Sound Control (OSC)[1] *learn* function, allowing a simple *touch and map* functionality to assign the modulator output to any control in the DAW. In the Reaper DAW, this line of remote automation of DAW parameters can be set up under Preferences – Control/OSC/Web, as seen in Figure 11.4. The figure shows a custom OSC pattern config named *Crossadaptive*, but the customisation only relates to expanding the allowed number of tracks, sends and effect parameters for automation. With relatively modest setups (8 tracks, 4 sends, 16 effects parameters per device) one

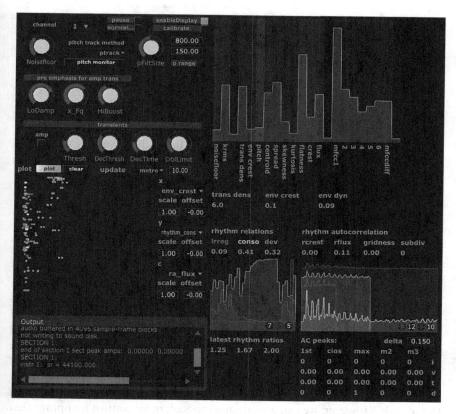

*Figure 11.2* Analyzer: feature extraction from audio signals.

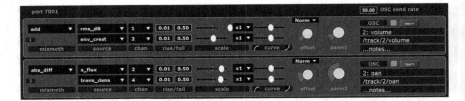

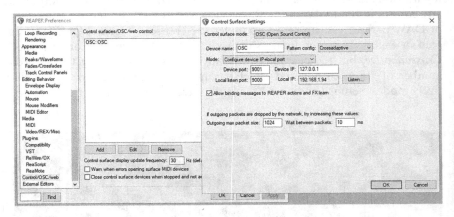

*Figure 11.3* Mediator: Mix and map feature analyses from several sources.

*Figure 11.4* OSC control surface setup in reaper.

can start by using the default pattern config. The modified pattern config can also be found in the github repository with the source code for the plugins (Brandtsegg, 2019).

## 11.4   Perceptual transparence of mappings

Adaptive processes can be designed in a way that intuitively makes sense, almost in a physical manner. Like for example as seen in sidechain compression techniques, where the amplitude of one signal *ducks* the signal level of another signal. An experiential approach to the resulting process could be that our perception allows only *this amount* of sound, and when another sound is interjected, the first sound must yield. Another analogy to the physical world could be a basin of water, when we drop in a stone, some of the water will be pushed out to make room for the stone, flowing back in when the stone is removed. Now, with sidechain compression as described above, it is almost a physical analogy, and thus perceptually easy to accept. We can also easily understand it as an intuitive musical experience of the connection between the sounds. However, we can also design crossadaptive control mappings that have no physical analogy or metaphor, some that are much more opaque and hidden from musical perception, and even some that would appear counter-intuitive. The full repertoire of mappings includes both the intuitive and the counterintuitive, with some less perceptually obvious (more abstract, hidden) areas in the middle ground. All of these types of modulator mappings can be useful for different purposes. Broadly speaking, the intuitive mappings can be seen as aids for more effective production or performance, the counterintuitive mappings as a means to create obvious tension on some level. The more abstract mappings have a variety of applications. Perhaps, because the functions of the abstract mappings are less clear, there are more unknowns to be found there. For artistic reasons, the area with the higher amount of unknowns could be a fruitful ground for exploration.

## 11.5 Perceptual transparence of analysis

In order to make the mappings intuitive, the feature extraction also needs to be perceptually transparent. Naively, one could expect an audio analysis process to extract descriptions of different qualities of a sound, and that these qualities would correlate with timbral nuances that we can hear. Many audio analysis methods from the musical information retrieval (MIR) repertoire will extract statistical features that describe the signal well in a mathematical sense, but these features are not always so easily perceived as proportional timbral or musical expressive variations. The mathematical description of a signal can be very useful for many purposes in classification, machine learning and other forms of information retrieval. However, for the purposes of intentional control, we must rely on analyses that correlates strongly to dimensions of musical expression and (as follows naturally) human perception. That is, the analysed feature must be of a type so we can tell a performer (or ourselves as a performer) to *do more* of a certain type of action to make the specific analysis output increase. Preferably also to have it react in a linear manner in the relation between expressive action and analysed value output. Some analysis methods are easy in this respect, and work without any further modification, like amplitude, pitch and a few others. Others are more problematic. For example, qualities we would musically describe as brightness, articulation, intonation etc. We take a closer look at this in Section 11.6. The field of MIR includes a range of substantial research efforts for higher-level description of music signals. Many of the descriptors from this field would make interesting candidates as methods for extraction of expressive modulator signals for our purposes. However, in most cases, the higher level descriptors also requires longer analysis windows, and thus they are not so immediately suited for frame-by-frame streaming analysis with low latency. Our requirement of low latency is related to how fast an action from a performer can have an effect on the timbral outcome in live performance.

As a general rule, digital musical instruments should aim for a latency less than 10 ms, but continuous gestural interaction with an instrument may allow for a somewhat higher latency (20–30 ms) before being detected by the performer (McPherson et al., 2016). In our case, the triggered actions are seldom of a rhythmic transient nature, so we can allow a latency comparable to those tolerated for continuous gestural interaction. For crossadaptive continuous parameter automation, we find a latency of 20–30 ms has worked reasonably well. High-level descriptors usually need significantly longer windows than this. Examples of such descriptors from MIR are danceability and other features based on detrended fluctuation analysis, typically involving a latency of 300 ms to several seconds (Streich and Herrera, 2005). Even though these types of analysis can be immensely useful for musical purposes, we have not yet seen a way to communicate to the performer *when the analysis is ready and will be effectuated*. That is, with the differing time scales for analysis, how will the performer intuitively know how her actions affects the control signals. One could argue that this too is merely a question of rehearsal and familiarisation, but the time lag involved creates obstacles partly because any action could take tens of seconds to be effectuated. Also any mistake made would have consequences for how the system responds to later action. The time lag and time bleed of mistakes could make the rehearsal process exceedingly frustrating. Such longer-window features could be interesting candidates for future investigations, but for the moment we have focused on analysis methods with a faster response.

## 11.6   Accommodation of analysis techniques

In order to allow a closer relation between perception and analysis, we have in some cases modified feature extraction methods from the MIR literature to make them work better for our purposes. The aim was to make the analysis behave in a linear fashion as relating to perception of musical expression. In some cases this would involve making nonlinear mappings and filters in order to make the output more linear. In general, one could say that an ad hoc approach has been allowed in the process of designing these filters, with empirical adjustment. Other users, researchers and musicians that go down this route would do wisely to look into how these analysis signals behave and see if an adjustment is needed with regards to personal preference on how musical expression can be represented linearly. The signals are also normalised with regards to the expected range, and this also could be done differently with regards to the musical situation and personal preference.

An example of a type of analysis that requires such adjustment is the timbral brightness. Brightness is a perceptual quality that we off-handedly might concur that we know how to constitute, but it can have slightly different meanings on different sounds. Intuitively one might claim that we do know what sonic qualities make a sound bright. Indeed some such qualities are easy to describe, for example the amount of high-frequency content, but they do not always contribute to timbral brightness to the same degree. A certain amount of context dependence occurs in how we perceive brightness. The *spectral centroid* is one measure usually associated with perceived brightness. It represents the location of the centre of gravity in the spectrum (Peeters et al., 2011), i.e. where in the spectrum we can find most of the signal energy. This can indeed give an indication of brightness since the analysed measure will rise to a higher value when there are relatively more high frequencies present in the sound. For the centroid analysis, we also see that it is independent of signal amplitude. This might be useful for a mathematical description, but it will make the analysed centroid rise to a maximum as the signal level drops towards the noise floor. This is simply because such low amplitude sounds will disappear into background noise, and the noise has a flat spectral envelope and as such the centre of gravity will be relatively high. The centroid for sounds used in music will usually vary in the approximate range of 300 Hz to 3 kHz, with shorter excursions upwards for transients and downwards for sinusoid low-frequency sounds. With white noise, the centroid will approach half the Nyquist frequency, and this is what happens in the analysis of sounds near the noise floor. For this reason, it was deemed necessary to use a custom filtering of the spectral centroid when the amplitude of the signal is low. We wanted to keep the independence between amplitude and centroid at audio levels where the sound can be easily perceived. Thus, using an empirical approach, we made an algorithm that increasingly restricts variation of the centroid as the signal level approaches the noise floor. This is done by using two noise floor levels, one representing the actual noise floor and one a few $dB^2$ above it representing signal levels approaching the noise floor. The centroid is then subjected to a sample-and-hold at the upper noise floor, and the difference between this held level and the current analysis is scaled according to the signal level in relation to the noise floor, and finally added to the sampled level. This will diminish the amount of allowed variation in the centroid as it approaches the noise floor, but still allow the pure centroid analysis to pass unmodified if the signal is above the second noise floor level (Figure 11.5).

Similar to the modification of the spectral centroid, we have applied the same nonlinear filtering to the spectral spread, skewness and kurtosis (even though these are less used in our experiments thus far), as well as spectral crest, flux and flatness. The latter three are all used as a measure of noise content for our purposes. The spectral crest is usually low for sounds that we perceive as noisy, while the flux is high. The flatness is also greater for more noisy sounds. We have found that each of these three can be used with differing levels of success for different instrumental sounds, and that experimentation is needed in each case to determine which one will work best for any given instrument and playing register. The playing style of a musician and the effect parameter the modulator is mapped to can also affect the choice of which feature extractor to use. As an example, spectral flux have been useful for guitar and bass, but it breaks down in the lower register. This is because the low fundamental incurs frame-to-frame spectral variations that are picked up by the spectral flux analysis.

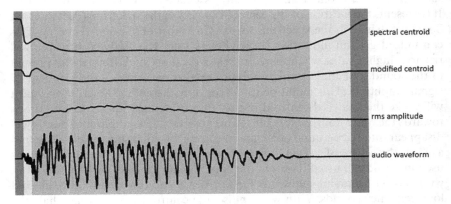

*Figure 11.5* Modified centroid, progressively restrict variation of the centroid analysis as the signal level drops below the upper noise floor (lightest gray area of figure) towards the lower noise floor. Below the lower noise floor, the centroid is effectively stationary.

A musically expressive parameter that we deemed interesting to investigate was the pressed-ness of the tone. Assuming that a heightened performative energy, associated with moments of strong expressive intent, could also lead to a more pressed instrumental timbre. For example, as seen with nonlinear distortion on both acoustic and electric instruments, and with the tension of vocal cords when singing louder. The musical energy is not always related to loudness, as one can aim to produce the same effects at lower amplitudes, so we wanted to find an analysis method that could extract this kind of timbral pressed-ness. Looking into mel frequency cepstral analysis, we found that we could see peaks in different positions in the cepstrum whenever the tone was more pressed. We were testing on vocals for the development phase of this feature, so perhaps also *nasality* could be an appropriate term. More generally, one could also attribute these variations to formant strength. We saw that peaks would occur at one or more of the first few cepstral bands, moving to different positions relating to the vowel produced by singing. We then took the absolute difference between the first 6 Mel frequency cepstral coefficients (MFCC) bands, and let this produce an output we called *mfcc-diff*, that we have found quite useful in detecting this timbral pressed-ness.

Another significant expressive feature is the articulation of musical phrases, for example when playing staccato or legato. This is something that performers and listeners of music relate to intuitively. The envelope crest can be used to give a basic measure of this kind of articulation. The crest represents the ratio of the maximum to the average value. As such, staccato articulation produces a high envelope crest value. Then again, this measure is not entirely intuitive for a performer when playing more legato, since the crest will rise abruptly for example at the end of a long sustained note (if it has a short decay). The envelope crest could be further refined to function better as a staccato/legato indicator.

Similarly, we have seen some challenges related to the analysis of rhythmic features. Even though the field of rhythm analysis has been broadly researched, it seems a fairly common assumption that one should first find the basic meter and tempo and then do a finer analysis based on that. Many of our improvised performances do not relate to a meter, and the tempo fluctuates significantly. For this reason, we have been looking for more neutral means of analysing rhythm. The *transient density* provides a measure of general rhythmic activity. We measure this as the number of transients per second. As a measure of rhythmic complexity, we also look at the relative ratios between successive transients. If we can find low integer ratios (1:2, 2:3, 3:4), then the rhythm patterns can be classified as relatively simple. This represents the internal complexity of the rhythm patterns, independent of tempo and meter. Due to the similarity with harmonic ratios in pitch, where low integer ratios represent consonant intervals, we can call this *rhythmic consonance*. A problem with this approach is that expressive deviations in rhythmic phrasing can lead to complex ratios, even though one allows relatively wide regions of quantisation towards the closest integer ratio. The connectionist approach of Desain and Honing (1989) could be implemented to improve the quantisation methods. We have also explored basic rhythmic autocorrelation and spectral analysis of the temporal envelope but the rhythmic analysis has significant potential for further development. The beat spectrum methods of Foote and Uchihashi (2001) have not been implemented in our current analyser but is a natural candidate for further refinement of our rhythm analysis.

## 11.7 Normalisation of analysis outputs

To be able to freely mix and match different analysis signals, it was deemed necessary to normalise them all to the same range. For pitch, for example, we have the highest expected pitch set for the pitch tracker, and we can divide by this number to create a normalised pitch. However, there is also a lowest expected pitch, and we produce an alternate normalisation taking this into account so that the normalised output can span the whole range from 0.0 to 1.0. This can be practical so that the lower range of the destination parameter can be modulated in the full expected range. The formula for normalisation of pitch is thus:

$$p_{norm} = \frac{f - f_{min}}{f_{max} - f_{min}} \tag{11.1}$$

where $p$ represents pitch, $f$ represent tracked frequency and the min and max representing the expected range of frequencies output from the pitch tracker.

The spectral centroid and related spectral moments are simply scaled with relation to the sample rate, accommodating normalisation that will keep the value in the full 0-1 range for most practical situations. The actual values used are, for a sampling rate $f_s$,

$$\text{centroid}_{norm} = \frac{\text{centroid}}{0.15 f_s} \tag{11.2}$$

$$\text{spread}_{norm} = \frac{\text{spread}}{0.15 f_s} \tag{11.3}$$

$$\text{skewness}_{norm} = \frac{\text{skewness}}{0.0005 f_s} \tag{11.4}$$

$$\text{kurtosis}_{norm} = \frac{\text{kurtosis}}{0.006 f_s} \tag{11.5}$$

Spectral flatness, crest and flux, as well as the mel frequency cepstral coefficients are simply scaled with a static factor, using

$$\text{flatness}_{norm} = \text{flatness} * 3 \tag{11.6}$$

$$\text{crest}_{norm} = \frac{\text{crest}}{250} \tag{11.7}$$

$$\text{flux}_{norm} = \text{flux} * 4 \tag{11.8}$$

$$\text{mfcc}_{norm} = \frac{\text{mfcc}}{200} \tag{11.9}$$

The measure mfcc-diff, representing timbral pressed-ness is then calculated on the basis of these normalised cepstral coefficients (the first 6 of them), and then subjected to median and lowpass filtering,

The analyser also provides an auto-normalising function. When enabled, this runs for a while on realtime data, finds the local maximum and minimum values for each analysis vector and use these to calculate automatic normalisation factors for each vector. However practical this is, it sacrifices repeatability from session to session, since the auto-normaliser would have to be run again on new data each time the system is used in a different context/location/mic-placement/etc.

## 11.8   Intuitive relation to feature extraction

With the adaption and normalisation of analysis vectors in place, we have spent a significant effort in exploring the different analyses and how they relate to perceptually relevant features. In practice, the familiarisation phase and the work on adaption and filtering were interleaved, adjusting the filtering as a result of realising how an analysis feature could actually be used. The goal with the familiarisation phase was to enable an intuitive understanding of the relationship between input sounds and the analysis output. To some extent, recorded sounds were used, but mostly live input sound from the microphone was used. Since singing is readily available for most humans, a vocal input was used in this process. This might mean that the accommodation of the analysis signals is slightly overfitted for vocals as compared to other instruments. Practical use in ensemble sessions has minimised this shortcoming somewhat. The aim of this phase was to tune the system so that it would respond to musically expressive changes, something that you could ask a performer to do *more of this, and less of that*. Also, an intuitive understanding on the system designers' part was necessary to communicate these timbral nuances to performers, and to adjust the description to different contexts, performers and instruments.

## 11.9 Selection of effects as modulation targets

In order to make the adaptive or crossadaptive control methods work in a musically effective manner, the selection of *what is controlled* is also of great relevance. Some audio processing methods produce results that have a close gestural correlation between changes in parameter values and the audio output of the effect. Other processing methods have parameter controls that still produce very audible changes in output, but perhaps are better suited for a more static *set and forget* approach. The musical meaning of timbral changes attained by effects processing obviously also relates to the context and genre in which it is being applied. The pumping effect of side-chain compression is welcome in electronic dance music (EDM) but would be disturbing for most listeners if encountered in a classical orchestral recording. Due to these contextual considerations, we can not infer any hard and fast rules. In the following, we still take the liberty to discuss some basic properties of a selection of effects and how they potentially can be used for expressive modulation purposes.

### 11.9.1 Reverb

Artificial reverberation is a very audible effect, and algorithmic reverbs also have some parameters that can be gesturally effective in timbral modulation. One such parameter is the reverb *decay time*, or simply the *reverb time*. A reverb effect can give the perception of *playing a sound in a space*, and as such, the reverb decay time is perceptually related to the size of the room being simulated. For some listeners, it might seem utterly wrong to change the perceived room size during a musical performance. This is something that would never occur in the physical world, and as such might be deemed *not intuitive*, or *not a useful expressive parameter*. The size of the room and the positioning and balancing between dry and reverberated sound would be carefully adjusted by a mixing engineer in a more traditional mixing situation. Then again, if we allow ourselves to think of the reverb effect not as a simulation of physical reality, but rather as a timbral design tool that allows us to make immediate changes to a sound's perceived size and shape, then we can use it as an expressive device. When referring to this, we are inferring *some physical appearance*, but in this case it is treated much more freely as a virtual physics with no obligation to follow the conventions of the actual physical room where the sound is played (or assumed to have been played). Adjusting the reverb decay time allows a great degree of influence over the musical preconditions for the instrumentalist to whom the effect is being applied. Quick changes between long and short reverb causes a gestural articulation that can have a high degree of influence over the performance.

### 11.9.2   Delay

Since the use of delay is ubiquitous in digital signal processing, we here refer more specifically to the audio effect of creating a repeating pattern of delays. Typical parameters would be the delay time and the number of repetitions (or the amount of feedback). A delay effect is clearly audible on a solo instrument, but the extra copies of the signal might get muddled in the larger sound picture of a polyphonic ensemble. In many situations of a traditional mix, this merging of delays into the overall weave of the audio image is considered aesthetically pleasing. However, as a gesturally effective modulation, the delays will need to have a prominent position in the mix to be heard. If this is done, the resulting effect can also be overpowering and unbalanced. Some care thus needs to be taken to make use of this effect. Using multi-tap delays with no feedback can be clearer than using single taps with feedback to produce several copies. The delay time is a significant parameter to be modulated with this type of effect. However, modulation of delay time usually induces a corresponding pitch shift. Shortening the delay time induce a pitch up, and vice versa when lengthening the delay time. With frequently-ocurring modulation, the constant pitch shifting can oftentimes be considered disturbing. Pitch is such a basic building block of music, that strong pitch modulations can create a too prominent effect. So, what if we use a delay effect that does not induce a pitch shift? This can be done relatively easy by crossfading new delay time segments, or alternatively, by implementing the delay in the frequency domain (Section 11.9.4).

One could expect this kind of free time modulation to be a very effective tool for modulating aspects of a live performance. After all, *sound and time* are closely intertwined. Time is the fabric on which sound is painted. However, in our experience, delay time modulations (without pitch modulation) does not stand out as expressive timbral changes, unless the musical input material is very sparse, and has clear transients. If a high amount of feedback (or a high number of taps in a multitap) is used, the temporal patterns created by the delay are easily perceived, and in this case, a change in delay time can be rhythmically effective. Then again, the change between different static temporal patterns is not very flexible musically. We have still been able to use delay effects quite flexibly, but it requires a careful musical design. A close interaction is needed between the performer affecting the modulation and the performer being modulated. When the modulated performer starts to second-guess future actions of the modulating performer, engaging situations of interplay can occur.

### 11.9.3 Filters

The term filter is used in the DSP literature to describe any process that changes the signal. In our context here, we use *filter* to describe an audio processing method that attenuates a selected frequency range, for example low pass, high pass and so on. Common to all filters that attenuates parts of the frequency range is that the resulting effect is easily masked if any part of the unprocessed sounds can be heard. With acoustic instruments, this is usually the case, at least it is unavoidable for the performer. In combinations with other effects that greatly adds harmonics, sidebands or noise, filters can still be a useful gestural modulation. Also, high amounts of resonance in the filter will add to the audibility of modulating the filter parameters.

### 11.9.4 Spectral processing

Spectral processing techniques give us some distinct possibilities. It is such a vast resource of timbral transformation that one could object to the use of a single category to denominate it as an effect type. We can still associate the use of spectral processing with certain effects like time smearing, freezing, spectral delays, pitch and frequency shift, morphing etc. Some of these can be implemented with other techniques, with similar musical effects. For example, where we can create time modification and freezing with spectral techniques, we can also do the same with granular processing. The potential for parametric control and dynamic transformation of the effects is different with each type of implementation. This means that it is not just the desired effect, but also its range of dynamic transformations that affects the selection of implementation. We will look into some effect types that can be implemented with spectral techniques later in this chapter.

### 11.9.5 Granular processing

Granular effects, like spectral processing, encompass a vast array of sound modulation possibilities. Granular processing, in general, can exhibit a prominent *graininess* in the transformation that can be effective in making the effect processing heard as a distinct gesture. The graininess of a time stretch, for example, can be turned into a complete disintegration of the sound by relatively simple parametric modulations. The timbral dimension from continuous to chopped-up sound is easily perceived. Similar effects can also be achieved with tremolos and amplitude gates controlled by low-frequency oscillators. Time displacement of separate grains can be a very effective sound design tool, slowing down or speeding up parts of the sound, or letting it disintegrate into particle clouds. Regarding time displacement, some of the same considerations as we discussed for the delay in Section 11.9.2 applies, as the gesturally expressive effect can easily be masked by simultaneous activity in other instruments. The characteristic grainy sound one might achieve with this technique may actually be of help in making a timbral context where time displacement is more easily heard as an expressive gesture since the presence of these artefacts can act as a signifier that modulations potentially can occur.

### 11.9.6   Freeze

A freeze effect in audio can be considered an extreme slowing of time, and can be implemented with granular techniques or in the frequency domain. It is easily perceived since it is a quite artificial effect. Gesturally, it can be used very effectively to create step-wise stop-motion phrasing. With longer hold times it can be used to highlight and sustain selected parts of the sound. In this respect it can be put in the family of spectral smearing, smoothing and blurring, which can also be done on separate frequency bands, keeping the general articulation of the sound intact. The selection of frequencies to freeze might be controlled from a secondary signal in a crossadaptive manner, as well as the freeze trigger itself.

### 11.9.7   Pitch and frequency shift

Pitch shifting is very clearly audible. In many cases, one could consider it too prominent to be used in a crossadaptive setting. Pitch is generally used with great care in formulating musical statements, and having an external modulating source for this feature of the sound can be disturbing. Then again, if we want to explore deep interventions in the interactions between performers, it could be used. Frequency shifting can be used to a similar dramatic effect, but with less of a disturbing influence on the melodies performed. Ring modulation is also very prominent, and although it creates frequency-shifted side bands, the general effect is often more of a metallic modulation enriching the original sound. Single sideband modulation, as an extension to ring modulation, can also be used for frequency shifting. The separate control over the upper and lower sidebands give significantly increased flexibility for its use as a dynamic and expressive gesture. With adaptive control (i.e. pitchtracking the modulated sound and controlling the modulation frequency ratios), one can also use these types of modulation for rich distortion-type effects (Lazzarini et al., 2008).

### 11.9.8   Balancing tools

Volume control can be utilised effectively as a crossadaptive modulation source, but there are the same problems as we see in, for instance, filter effects, regarding the dry sound masking the processed output. The audience can be isolated from the source, which opens up more processing options, but the musician playing the instrument can not so easily be isolated. Then the inter-action between musician and processing is not optimal, because the modulated player is not fully enveloped by the effects of modulation. Dynamic shaping of sound volume can still be effective, especially when the amplified signal is used for other treatments so that the volume control is more of a blending of different timbral variations. Similarly, automating send levels to different auxiliary treatments is highly effective, and puts no constraints on the selection of effects. Switching between two or more effects that have distinct percep-tual influence on the source sound can create dramatic shifts, while switch-ing between similar effects can be used to create an expressive and continuous modulation. In the same class as volume and send levels, we can also group panning effects, since the process involves adjusting the amount of sound going to different outputs. Spatial positioning can be a very effective device for crossadaptive modulation, but as with pitch shifting, some care must be taken to do it musically. Very fast panning can also approach tremolo or ring modulation type effects, and a gradual shift between perceived effect types can be very effective as a transformative tool.

## 11.10 Effects with direct signal interaction and cross-synthesis

There is a range of effects that provides direct signal interaction without work-ing with feature extraction and automation of process parameters. These use the audio signal from two sources, directly modulating each other. Ring modu-lation is one such effect. In the examples above, we assumed the use of an inter-nal modulator oscillator, but it could just as easily have been used by multiply-ing two independent signals. When ring modulating two live audio sources, the result if often an extremely rich sonic texture with prominent inharmonic sidebands. However, if the two signals are relatively simple (few overtones), and are played with fundamental pitches in simple harmonic relationships, then the output can be more controlled. In this case, the audio processing is extremely simple, but the performer interaction is complex. The pitch relation between the two musicians then determines the harmonicity of their individual instrument timbres.

Another such effect that directly relates to two input audio signals is the vocoder, where the amplitude of separate frequency bands in the modulat-ing sound is used to control the output amplitude in the same bands on the processed sound. Usually, when this is used as an audio effect, the modu-lating audio source is not heard, and that creates some of the magic of the effect as the image of the modulating source can only be heard as imprints on the modulated sound. When both signals are heard acoustically, the effect is rather less pronounced. Spectral processing can also be used to directly impose the spectrum of one sound on another, with similar implications as the vocoder. A variation on the vocoder scheme is to use adaptive resonators tuned by the modulating source. This can create spectral highlighting with ringing resonances from the modulator being excited by transients in the modulated signal. Finally, we can use convolution to impose both spectral and temporal characteristics of one sound onto another.

### 11.10.1   Convolution

The process of convolution can create dramatic changes in timbre, but traditionally can not be subjected to parametric modulation or dynamic updates, and as such is not an ideal target effect for dynamic modulation. The effect is still highly effective as part of an effect chain where send levels are modulated. For example, the gradual switching of send levels between a dry distorted effect and a big reverberant convolution effect. Also, the implications of convolution being that one sound is *played through another* lends a rich opportunity for crossadaptive interaction to occur. For this to be achievable in live interaction, we need to be able to update the impulse response dynamically.

### 11.10.2   Live convolution

Convolution, as mentioned above, has traditionally been somewhat limited as a modulated effect since at least one of the signals must be known in advance. Dynamically updating the impulse response (IR) has not been possible, without resorting to crossfading of parallel processes. The invention of a dynamic update method was done recently (Brandtsegg et al., 2018), as part of the crossadaptive project. This allows live sampling of the filter coefficients, updating the IR without interrupting the process and without creating unwanted artefacts. When the IR is rewritten from start to end, at the same rate as the filter is being consumed by the input signal, then the convolution of two live signals is feasible. The filter update can be automated with an LFO, triggered by audio feature threshold functions, or controlled manually. In most of our experiments, we have found it effective to control the update manually, so that one of the musicians has voluntary control over the content of the filter. Roles may be assigned such that one is *playing through the filter* and another musician is recording the filter coefficients (the IR). A physical switch or pedal is devised to control the recording. Then it is also a question of *who controls the update of the filter*. The person playing through the filter could control it, selecting bits of what the other person plays as the preferred filter. In other cases, the musician recording the content of the filter will control the update. This can be very effective, as she can then contribute musical content that is hidden from the filter (not recorded), and selectively contribute transient/sparse or continuous/-sustained material to distinctive effect. When continuous (of a very sustained character) audio material is recorded as the IR, it will create an ambient texture with little temporal influence from the other musician other than the energy level of the input. With sparse and transient material in the IR, the convolution process acts somewhat like a delay tap pattern. This situation is somewhat similar to *just playing with an effect* for the other performer. In between these extremes, a world of intertwined sonic manipulations can be found.

## 11.11  Performative habits

In all human performance, one can assume that there exists a repertoire of actions that are more readily available to the performer, due to training and habituation. This is a necessary precondition for creating a language of expression: there must be some expressions that are recognisable, both for performer and listener. The creation of such a vocabulary relies partly on aesthetic considerations, on tradition and convention and on physical affordances and limitations. The movements and phrases of the vocabulary are constituted as muscle memory, and as such also part of an embodied cognition. This allows the performer to react quickly with intuitive responses to external stimuli. As much as these habits are necessary to form a language, they can also inhibit further expansion into unknown territory, since habits usually are hard to break.

Radical interventions into the interplay between performers can aid in breaking such habits. This can allow the opportunity for new variants of these performative languages, new colours in musical expression and new modes of interaction. The crossadaptive performance strategies are intended as one way of creating such interventions. The idea is to create some new *attractors* and *inhibitors*. The attractors enables new devices of expression, like allowing the rhythmic density of your phrasing to control the filter frequency on another performer's sound. If it is indeed a musically attractive feature, it can act to draw the performer into new areas of exploration. If the performer in question has an inclination to using rhythmic density and accelerandos as an important part of the phrasing vocabulary, then it can be integrated quickly and intuitively. The inhibitors, on the other hand, provide roadblocks, making it harder to do what one usually does. In the example of rhythmic density controlling a filter frequency, it might inhibit the performer from playing fast passages if she wants to avoid filtering the other player. More in-depth considerations on the affordances and the instrumentality of crossadaptive performance can be found in Baalman et al. (2018). In some ways, these mechanisms already exist in all kinds of performative interplay, attractors and inhibitors, expressions and habituations of the performative language. The new element in crossadaptive performance is the ability to create new parameters linkages and to do so based in a non-intrusive manner. The sound produced by the instrument is the means with which the performer controls her environment, and the nuanced control of this sound been developed over years of practice. The technology here is just an enabler. The real action happens in the live interaction between humans.

## 11.12  The role of the interaction scene designer

There is a creative component in selecting which timbral modulations to apply to instruments, and selecting the processing parameters to be controlled with the adaptive and crossadaptive methods. There is virtually no limits to what can be controlled. Then, how to decide what makes musical sense? The person doing the scene design of the crossadaptive interaction will inevitably affect what the performers in this situation will be able to do. Which affordances are given, and which restrictions? What would make the musicians comfortable, and what would they find engaging to control? Creating engagement could rely on using something that is well known to the performer in a slightly new way. Also, what could upset them in a way that would encourage performing outside of the normal comfort zone boundaries? The selection of effects can be just as important as the tuning of the control parameters, since the effects define how the instruments will sound, and thus create the *voice* (also instrumentally) of the performer. The configuration of crossadaptive mappings, i.e. *what actions will have which outcomes*, affects the performers' freedom of movement so to speak. The expressive parameters that are mapped crossadaptively will then have to be used with particular care from the performer's side. All the while, we can also design it so that some vital expressive dimensions are kept free, so the performer can utilise these without having to care about modulating others in the ensemble. The overall complexity of the mapping is also an important factor. Should the musicians be tied down such that everything has direct influence over something else, or should we simply create a free situation with just some added affordances? Also, the perceptual transparence for the performers must be taken into account. What can they readily perceive, and how much are they able and willing to take into consideration the automated changes to the environment in which they perform?

## 11.13   Different types of sessions

The previous paragraph contained more questions than answers, and we would be reluctant to provide any predetermined outcomes. Rather, we have tried to do practical experiments in a variety of situations to allow some indications and variations to emerge. The reader is encouraged to test this out in their own musical practices, applying it in different ways than we hitherto have done. Since this project was done in the context of a university with a musical performance education, we have had the privilege of working with a large body of students. We have done sessions with jazz performance students, music technology students, other researchers and professional performers. In addition to the varying constellations provided by these settings, we have also used some ensembles that could work on these challenges more regularly, developing a vocabulary and a deeper understanding of the problems involved. The details of these approaches are treated more in depth in a separate paper (Brandtsegg et al., 2018). Documentation of sessions are available online,[3] and a selection of artistic outputs are refined and collected on a commercial release.[4]

## 11.14   Conclusions and future work

The crossadaptive processes and methods discussed in this chapter open up a wide range of options for interaction in music performance, particularly in settings that include elements of improvisation. From a ubimus perspective, the ideas built into the crossadaptive platform present new interfaces to musicians, which are based on the sound matter itself. This has a significant set of implications for system design, as it potentially creates a whole new set of affordances. Within a crossadaptive setup, the role of interaction scene designer becomes crucial to mediate the connections between musical structure, instrument and performer. As noted earlier in this chapter, there are a number of open questions related to user experience, control, predictability and playability (from the performers' and composers' points of view), which require further theoretical and empirical treatment. Another aspect that is relevant to ubimus is that of system scalability and how crossadaptive performance scenarios can be deployed with varying levels of technological resources. Possible means of enabling a scalable architecture through the browser platform (Chapter 10) could be investigated.

With the relatively new approach of using crossadaptive methods in live performance, a lot remains to be explored. The project so far has merely scratched the surface, making the methods available and exploring but a few interaction scenarios. One could expect that the techniques can be used both for more radical applications and also for more conventional problem solving. As can be seen in commercial audio production,[5] adaptive and crossadaptive methods have a wide range of applications. Many of these fall into the problem-solving category, and one can readily envision crossadaptive methods being used non-intrusively in live performance with the aim of simply clarifying what is already there. For extensions to the more radical applications, we leave this to the imagination of the reader, and we wait enthusiastically to hear what you come up with.

Still, there are some applications that we know we *would have liked to* explore but have not yet been able to. Within these we find *relative mappings*, where the relationship between expressive features of different performers might be used as a combined signal. Say, for example, that if one performer plays loud and another soft, then the absolute difference between them would be high. If both play soft or both play loud, nothing would happen in the modulation, only the amount of difference between them would apply modulation (possibly to a third instrument). The software made in this project allows mapping of such absolute differences in any parameter, so the framework for initiating such explorations is ready.

So far, only absolute values for analysed features have been used, but it would be interesting to see how derivatives of different orders could tease out more dimensions of expression. Music, after all, is about changes, and the derivatives of the feature vectors would capture just that. Likewise, using dynamic mappings, in such a way that the crossadaptive mappings themselves could be modulated, thus creating a meta-modulation layer. One could also envision the use of artificial intelligence for several functions: Letting the system learn a performer's normal actions, and responding to the amount of explorations into the unknown; Letting the system figure out which mappings would provide the most effective sonic transformations (see Jordal (2017)); Letting the system assemble and configure the DSP applied in the effects processors, etc). Recent methods of machine learning in the analysis of gestural data can also be applied in this context, with a reasonable expectation of low latency response (Caramiaux et al., 2015). In this chapter, we have shown a glimpse into a system of crossadaptive processing for live use, the research and artistic exploration leading up to and following up on its implementation, some reflections on uses and use cases and the artistic outputs generated.

## Notes

1 OSC is a control protocol used in a number of musical applications (Wright and Freed, 1997), see Chapter 3.
2 We usually would set this secondary threshold around 8 dB above the noise floor.
3 http://crossadaptive.hf.ntnu.no/.
4 The double album *Poke It With a Stick / Joining The Bots* on Crónica.
5 As seen in unmasking EQs like the Neutron: https://www.izotope.com/en/learn/products/neutron/unmasking-your-mix-with-neutron.html and others.

## Bibliography

Baalman, M., S. Emmerson, and Ø. Brandtsegg (2018). Instrumentality, perception and listening in crossadaptive performance. In *Proceedings of the 2018 Conference on Live Interfaces*. Porto, Portugal.

Brandtsegg, S. Saue, S. Waerstad, T. Johansen, and A. Skeie (2019). Hadron particle synthesiser. http://partikkelaudio.com.

Brandtsegg, Ø. (2015). A toolkit for experimentation with signal interaction. In *Proceedings of the 18th International Conference on Digital Audio Effects (DAFx-15)*, pp. 42–48. Trondheim, Norway.

Brandtsegg, Ø. (2019). Featexmod. https://github.com/Oeyvind/featexmod.

Brandtsegg, Ø., T. Engum, and B. I. Wærstad (2018, June). Working methods and instrument design for cross-adaptive sessions. In *Proceedings of the International Conference on New Interfaces for Musical Expression*, Blacksburg, Virginia, USA, pp. 1–6. Virginia Tech.

Brandtsegg, Ø., S. Saue, and V. Lazzarini (2018). Live convolution with time-varying filters. *Applied Sciences 8*(1), 1–29.

Brandtsegg, Ø., C. H. Waadeland, T. Åse, A. Bergsland, T. Engum, B. I. Waerstad, and S. Saue (2015). T-emp communication and interplay in an electronically based ensemble - technological results. https://www.researchcatalogue.net/view/48123/53023/0/0. Wærstad.

Caramiaux, B., N. Montecchio, A. Tanaka, and F. Bevilacqua (2015). Adaptive gesture recognition with variation estimation for interactive systems. *ACM Transactions on Interactive Intelligent Systems (TiiS) 4*(4), 18.

Cockos Inc. (2019). Reaper. http://reaper.fm.

Desain, P. and H. Honing (1989, 09). The quantization of musical time: A connectionist approach. *Computer Music Journal 13*, 56–66.

Foote, J. and S. Uchihashi (2001). The beat spectrum: A new approach to rhythm analysis. In *IEEE International Conference on Multimedia and Expo, 2001. ICME 2001*, pp. 881–884. Tokyo, Japan.

Jordal, I. (2017). Evolving artificial neural networks for cross-adaptive audio effects. Master's thesis, Norwegian University of Science and Technology, Trondheim, Norway.

Lazzarini, V., J. Timoney, and T. Lysaght (2008). Asymmetric-spectra methods for adaptive fm synthesis. In *Proceedings of the 11th International Conference on Digital Audio Effects (DAFx-08)*. Espoo, Finland.

Lazzarini, V., S. Yi, J. ffitch, J. Heintz, Ø. Brandtsegg, and I. McCurdy (2016). *Csound: A Sound and Music Computing System*. Berlin: Springer.

McPherson, A., R. Jack, and G. Moro (2016). Action-sound latency: Are our tools fast enough? In *Proceedings of the International Conference on New Interfaces for Musical Expression*, Volume 16 of *2220-4806*, Brisbane, Australia, pp. 20–25. Queensland Conservatorium Griffith University.

Peeters, G., B. L. Giordano, P. Susini, N. Misdariis, and S. McAdams (2011). The timbre toolbox: Extracting acoustic descriptors from musical signals. *Journal of The Acoustical Society of America 130*, 2902–2916.

Reiss, J. D. and Ø. Brandtsegg (2018). Applications of cross-adaptive audio effects: Automatic mixing, live performance and everything in between. *Frontiers in Digital Humanities 5*, 17.

Streich, S. and P. Herrera (2005). Detrended fluctuation analysis of music signals: Danceability estimation and further semantic characterization. In *Proceedings of the AES 118th Convention*. Barcelona, Spain.

Trifonova, A., M. L. Jaccheri, and K. Bergaust (2008, 08). Software engineering issues in interactive installation art. *International Journal of Arts and Technology 1*, 43–65.

Trifonova, A., M. L. Jaccheri, and Ø. Brandtsegg (2008). Software engineering in an artistic project: Improsculpt case study. In *Proceedings of the Third International Conference on Digital Interactive Media in Entertainment and Arts, DIMEA 2008*, Athens, Greece, pp. 1–8.

Verfaille, V., U. Zolzer, and D. Arfib (2006). Adaptive digital audio effects (a-dafx): A new class of sound transformations. *IEEE Transactions on Audio, Speech, and Language Processing 14*(5), 1817–1831.

Walsh, R. (2019). Cabbage audio. https://cabbageaudio.com/.

Wright, M. and A. Freed (1997). Open sound control: A new protocol for communicating with sound synthesizers. In *Proceedings of the ICMC*, Thessaloniki, Greece, pp. 101–104.

# 12 The analogue computer as a musical instrument

*Victor Lazzarini and Joseph Timoney*

The steady resurgence of analogue technology in electronic musical instruments has been a feature of the first two decades of the 21st century. As discussed in Chapter 3, the emergence of digital devices, alongside the rise of the microprocessor, focused much of the attention in instrument design in the latter decades of the last century. Much of it was due to the greater reliability of digital computing hardware, allied to the advances in manufacturing technology which targeted the mass production of such devices. Another important factor was programmability, which meant that generic processing hardware could be deployed in different functions and applications simply by writing different software. However, as digital technology became ubiquitous, users (musicians, sound designers, multimedia artists, and hobbyists) started to look back at the analogue instruments of the previous generation, admiring the different sonic possibilities that were somehow lost in the development of digital audio technologies. This also spurred attempts at a recreation of such sonorities in software form, giving rise to the *virtual analogue* field of research (Pakarinen et al., 2011). An interest in recreating these in proper hardware form also emerged, spurring a new industry of analogue modular synthesisers, which is grounded on the Do-it-Yourself (DIY) practice and ethos.

From another perspective, since the early experiments by Mathews in 1957 (Lazzarini, 2013), we have also had general-purpose computers as musical instruments (Mathews, 1963). The devices used for this application, for the most of the history until recently, are what we generally class as the *digital stored-program computer*.[1] In this chapter, we propose to look at a different type of computer and its potential to sound and music design, within the context of ubimus and the resurgence of analogue audio processing. In particular, we would like to trace in detail the relationship between the general-purpose analogue computer and the music instrument technology of voltage control. As we will see, within the context of such devices, both the elements involved in computation, the modelling, and the problem design are approached from a different perspective to that in digital computing. We can therefore categorise these as belonging to a different class of methods, which we call *analogue computing*.

The principles that constitute analogue computing can be seen from two perspectives that are somewhat independent of each other. On one hand, the hardware that implements it allows for the solution of problems containing continuous variables, whereas digital circuitry implies a discretisation of these (even in models that assume underlying continuous quantities). In the case of music, the possibility of time and amplitude-continuous computation is significant, considering the amount of work that has been dedicated to solving discretisation issues in areas such as virtual analogue models (Pakarinen et al., 2011).

From a different perspective, analogue computing approaches problems in a way that largely dispenses the algorithmic approach of digital computer programming in favour of hardware reconfiguration, setting up the computation not so much as a sequence of steps, but as an interconnection of components (Ulmann, 2013). This also implies that the hardware model set up in this way is an *analogue* of the problem at hand. Additionally, while analogue computers may be able to compute problems related to the steady state of a system, they are more frequently used to providing solutions relating to transient behaviour (Navarro, 1962). Such problems are significant to sound and music applications, where the dynamic properties of a system are fundamental.

Analogue computing has had a long history, which began with mechanical devices that were used as aids to the calculation of specific problems (navigation, gunnery, accounting, etc.), and became a major scientific field of research with the advent of practical electronic devices. These could be combined more flexibly to realise various types of modelling. From a music perspective, these developments influenced the technology of voltage control (VC), and the modular aspect of electronic analogue computers appears to be significant in providing the principles underpinning early modular synthesisers (Moog, 1967). As we will argue in this chapter, the re-emergence of such instruments makes analogue computing relevant to the ubimus ecosystem.

This text is organised as follows. We will start by exploring the principles of analogue computation with electronic computers. This will be complemented by an introduction to modular voltage-controlled synthesisers, discussing these from the perspective of analogue computing. Then we will examine the possibilities of general-purpose electronic computers as musical instruments, followed by an examination of the current state of the art in the area. We will conclude by discussing the new perspectives for ubimus research and practice in the context of analogue computing.

## 12.1  Analogue computing

Analogue computers, as discussed in the introduction to this paper, operate under different principles to their digital stored-program counterparts. Generally, they are set up to provide solutions to a problem that is laid out in terms of a mathematical equation or set of equations, providing an answer to these, given a certain input. In this case, the type of problems that are applied to them can be of different characteristics, provided that they can be described in an algebraic form. Programming the computer is then a matter of setting an analogue to the original problem (Ulmann, 2013) by means of various computing elements. Therefore, the capabilities of a given analogue computer are determined by the types of computing blocks it can offer, and how they can be connected in a program.

### 12.1.1   Components

The typical analogue computer is composed of various types of computing elements that often operate as *black boxes*, providing an output given a set of inputs and conditions, within a certain level of tolerance. The inputs and outputs of such boxes are electric signals whose voltages play the part of the variables that are manipulated in a program. Programs will then be made up of patching connections between these different blocks, setting up the initial conditions that configure the problem and then running the computer, from which the answer or answers can be read by appropriate output devices.

While the components of an analogue computer can be quite varied in nature, there are some key blocks that are present universally in these devices, to provide basic computing operations.

### *Arithmetics*

We can divide the arithmetic operations into three fundamental categories, that are addressed by specific types of electronic circuits: (a) multiplication by a scalar; (b) addition/sum; (c) multiplication of signals. In the case of (a) and (b), a fundamental component is the *operational amplifier* (Ragazzini et al., 1948). This component allows a gain to be applied to the signal and facilitates both multiplication and addition to be implemented. Of course, if only attenuation is required, then a signal can be passively modified by a variable resistance (Figure 12.1), but in all other cases, the op amp is required.

Gain scaling is implemented simply by setting the multiplier constant $k$ in the op amp, which is the ratio of the resistances $R_f/R_i$ that are employed in the circuit (Figure 12.2)

$$V_{out}(t) = -kV_{in}(t) \tag{12.1}$$

Note that the op amp will normally have the effect of inverting the sign of the voltages applied to its input, due to the fact that only its inverting input is used.

Summing two voltages also require an op amp (Figure 12.3), and the input signals are scaled by the ratios of the individual input resistances and the

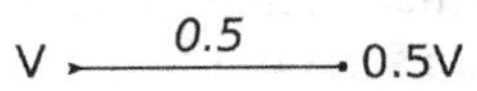

V ———0.5———→ 0.5V

*Figure 12.1* Attenuation example.

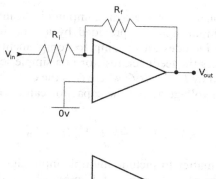

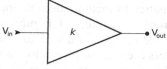

*Figure 12.2* Op amp circuit schematics and gain scaling symbol.

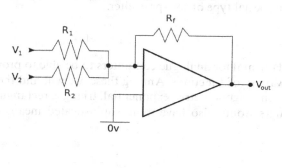

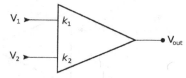

*Figure 12.3* Summing amp circuit with two inputs and symbol.

feedback path resistance, $k = R_f/R_n$. Note that adding units such as these can be set up for more than two inputs.

$$V_{out}(t) = -\sum_{0}^{n} k_n V_n(t) \qquad (12.2)$$

Multiplication of two signals is generally taken as a separate category as it requires more complex circuitry. In this case, the output is equivalent to the instantaneous value of the multiplication of its inputs, scaled by a constant.

*Integration*

Another key component of an analogue computer is the integrator. The means of integrating an input signal is provided by a capacitor, and the circuit (Figure 12.4 ) also includes an op amp to complement it. As we can see, the capacitor replaces the feedback resistor in a simple scalar multiplier. The output is also scaled by $k = 1/R_iC$ where $C$ is the capacitance in the op amp feedback path. The voltage across the capacitor can also be set as an initial condition $V_0$.

$$V_{out}(t) = -k \int_0^t V_{in}(t) + V_0 \qquad (12.3)$$

It is also a simple matter to include multiple input signals to an integrator, using a combination of the circuits of Figures 12.2 and 12.3 . In this case, the different inputs are scaled and added together before the integration is performed. Integrators are used in programs where differential equations are required. In musical applications, these occur in the implementation of filters, as discussed in Sections 12.2.1 and 12.3.2. In fact, an integrator on its own can be classed as a special type of low-pass filter.

*Functions*

It is also fundamental for analogue computers to be able to provide means of generating a variety of functions. Among these, we will find the usual single-variable functions trigonometric, exponential, triangle, rectangular, ramp, etc. Some computers would also have more sophisticated means of generating

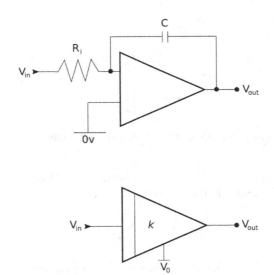

*Figure 12.4* Integrator circuit and symbol.

user-defined functions (Ulmann, 2013). It is worth noting that function generators are a general class of modules that also include the multiplication, summa-
tion, and integration blocks described above (Navarro, 1962).

*Other modules*

Various other modules exist in various analogue computing devices (Ulmann,
2013). Logic blocks such as comparators allow voltages to be compared for
binary decisions (such as opening and closing signal connections) and step-
function implementations. Limiters are special-purpose comparators that can
keep signals within a given range. Time delays provide a means of shifting the
phase of functions and can be implemented in discrete capacitor circuits called
bucket brigade devices (Sangster and Teer, 1969) Output of analogue compu-
tations involve some means of measuring the voltage of a program, which can
be done by various means such as strip-chart and *xy* recorders, oscilloscopes,
voltmeters, and similar components. A sound and music computing relevant
output block would consist of an audio pre-amplifier that allows line-level
connections to a mixer and power amplifier. This is of course, the main output
component of a voltage-controlled synthesiser.

## 12.2   Modular synthesisers

Modular electronic sound synthesis, especially the variety involving voltage
control technologies, has been a cornerstone of electronic music since the post-
war era (Wells, 1981). In examining the devices that have been and are currently
used for this purpose, we can see very clear parallels with the technology of
analogue computers. In fact, modular analogue synthesisers (Figure 12.5) have
been identified as special-purpose computers (Ulmann, 2013). In this platform, modules play an important part as the components of programs. In the

*Figure 12.5* A modular synthesiser.

case of the typical modular design, such programs are made up of patch-cord connections between them, as illustrated in Figure 12.5.

### 12.2.1   Modules

Voltage-controlled synthesiser modules are generally built at a higher level of operation if compared to analogue computing blocks. This means that access to fundamental aspects of computation is less common. For example, function generators in the form of oscillators realise compound operations, which in the case of an analogue computer would be provided in smaller building blocks of a time function generator, plus multipliers and adders. However, some basic elements are given: ring modulators implement two-input multiplication, mixers are summing modules, and offset/scaling modules can provide addition and multiplication of signals and scalars.

The following are the basic modules of a synthesiser: voltage-controlled filters (VCFs), oscillators (VCOs), and amplifiers (VCAs).

#### Voltage-controlled oscillators

A VCO is a special type of function generator that produces a period signal of a given shape having a frequency that is dependent on an input voltage. The common standard is that a 1V change is equivalent to an interval of 1 octave (2:1). There are other standards, such as the so-called Hz/V, which define a given voltage reference (e.g. middle C to 1V) and then a straightforward translation of voltage ratios into interval ratios. The two systems of course are not compatible without logarithmic/exponential conversion.

Typical controls on a VCO are frequency offset and range (footage), which allow oscillators to be finely tuned independent of any input voltage. The kind of output function is also generally selectable from various basic shapes (e.g. sawtooth, square, triangle, sine, etc.). A waveshaping control is often included allowing, typically, the change of square waves into narrow pulses (also known as pulse-width adjustment). Many oscillators offer this as a voltage-controlled parameter. An example of a standard VCO is shown in Figure 12.6, which includes range and tune controls to offset the input voltages; two frequency CV inputs, the second with a scaling control; pulse-width control, plus two CV inputs for this parameter. It can output four different functions at the same time (sawtooth, triangle, square/pulse, and sine). Finally it includes a means to synchronise the frequency of the output to an input audio master clock signal (e.g. the output of another oscillator).

#### Voltage-controlled filters

A VCF implements differential equations, also known as filter equations, and therefore are equivalent to a bespoke packaging of analogue computing elements that include integrators, active and passing scaling, mixing, and possibly special types of function generators in the case of filters that include

*Figure 12.6* Typical VCO: Doepfer A110 (Doepfer, 2019b).

some sort of non-linear amplification. Active filter elements are set to be voltage controlled, which is done in an indirect way by translating the typical parameters of filter frequency, bandwidth, or resonance into the correct scaling element values in the filter equation.

VCFs can take various forms, normally categorised according to their amplitude response (low-pass, high-pass, band-pass, etc.). Their applications tend to be related to their effect on the audible spectrum, but depending on the characteristics of their filter equations, they can also be used for other purposes. Low-pass filters for instance are examples of special types of integrators and they can be applied in the smoothing of voltage signals, for instance when any step changes in these are seen as undesirable. A typical application is to provide continuous frequency glides for oscillator voltage control. An example of a typical lowpass VCF is shown in Figure 12.7, which includes cutoff and resonance frequency voltage controls.

### Voltage-controlled amplifiers

VCAs are effectively an application of an active scaling computing element in modular synthesis. They allow the scaling of input signals according to an input voltage. These can be designed so that they work well for the scaling of audio signals (e.g. the output of oscillators or filters), or for the scaling of control signals (e.g. control voltages), but they may be dedicated to one or the other type. The difference between these is that audio signals occupy a higher frequency range (e.g. > 20 Hz for audio-range signals), whereas control voltages are generally in the low-frequency spectrum and include a significant

*Figure 12.7* Typical VCF: Doepfer A120 (Doepfer, 2019c).

0 Hz component. This is sometimes discussed in terms of AC-coupling and DC-coupling, meaning that in the former a lo-cut filter is applied at the input, eliminating any very low-frequency and DC components, whereas amplifiers for control voltages do not include such filtering.

VCAs may also appear in the form of mixers, where more than one input may be present. As we have seen with summing elements in analogue computers, mixers will also include active components to control the scaling of input signals. VCAs can respond linearly or exponentially to the CV input. Generally speaking, in V/oct systems it is better to use linear VCAs for control voltages as there is a linear relationship between CV and frequency. Exponential response is better suited to audio signals, as our hearing mechanism has a nearly logarithmic response to amplitude or intensity. Figure 12.8 shows a typical VCA, which allows two signals to be summed, with different CVs applied to their amplitude.

*Other modules*

In general, modular synthesisers provide a rich set of components, many of which can be seen as different types of function generators, for example:

- Piecewise functions: generating either linear or exponential (or a combination of these) segments, determined by time breakpoints. These are normally called envelope generators. Typically, they are provided with a set number of piecewise sections: three (attack-sustain-release) and four (attack, decay, sustain, release) are very common configurations.
- Random voltage sources: these can be used as audio signals (broadband noise sources) or as random value generators for CV purposes. Often they

*Figure 12.8* Typical linear VCA: Doepfer A130 (Doepfer, 2019d).

are coupled with a sample-and-hold circuit, which holds voltages for a given time duration, to allow for band-limited noise or held CV values.

• Step sequencers: these are user-defined function generators with a number of discrete voltage steps. Continuous functions can be achieved by connecting the output CV to an integrator (a low-pass filter as discussed above).

Additionally, as we noted at the start, we will find arithmetic modules (scaling, offsetting) and a specialised component that allows two signals to be properly multiplied together within a tolerable error range (the ring modulator). There are a significant number of variations on the above examples, as well as on the basic modules (specialised types of oscillators, filters, etc.).

### 12.2.2   Programmability

We should note, at the outset, that the wide set of modules available for the synthesiser systems represents not only a very specialised form of analogue computing, but also constitutes an example of high-level black-box components, from a programmability point of view. It is possible to observe from the descriptions given above, that each module, be it a VCO, a VCF, or other types, wraps a complete analogue program in a single package. Voltage inputs and outputs are preset to certain configurations, and there is little possibility for re-routing or re-configuring the circuits, in other words, re-programming the functions.

Therefore, it is important to consider this very fundamental distinction between general-purpose analogue computing and the specialised, domain-specific, nature of modular synthesisers. There is no access to the fundamental building blocks of computation, which on one hand, simplifies the programming tasks, but on the other, presents limitations, which may be significant depending on the applications intended. Programming modular synthesisers is effectively based on patching high-level functional blocks. If a different module is required, it needs to be sought in a pre-packaged form and is not easily user-defined (without the recourse to circuit design and building skills).

It is possible to trace an analogy to the domain-specific languages for music programming in digital computers. These typically offer a high-level approach based on black-boxes (called unit generators) (Lazzarini, 2013), and programming often is reduced to connecting these together in a similar way to modular synthesiser patching (in fact, in some graphic music programming systems, programs are often referred to as *patches*). However, the most common of examples of music programming languages also offer the option of re-defining, or designing from first principles, the unit generators employed. This lower-level of programming is completely absent from the typical analogue module. It is clear that digital computing in this case offers a clear advantage from the perspective of programmability. Even in the case where an implementation language (such as C/C++) is used for unit generator development, we still have a much less obtuse workflow than what is needed to design and implement a module circuit. As we will propose later, this may be addressed by the new generation of analogue computing hardware that is becoming available to researchers and practitioners of ubimus.

## 12.3   Analogue programming examples

In order to expand the discussion of analogue computing for sound and music, it is interesting to consider some examples to illustrate simple operations. While we would put these problems from a general-purpose computing perspective, we would also like to consider them with respect to typical sound synthesis applications.

### 12.3.1   Linear functions

The simplest example of the application of analogue computation is to set up the solution to a linear problem, such as

$$f(t) = ax(t) + b \tag{12.4}$$

which may be applied, for instance, to glide the pitch of a tone from one frequency to another. The program for this is shown in Figure 12.9, smoothly sliding by a user-defined interval. In this case, each increment of 1V in the input starting from a voltage $V_0$, will provide a jump of $k$ semitones, when used as a 1V/oct exponential frequency signal.

This, of course, can easily be set up in a modular synthesiser by the use of an amplifier and an offset, which are blocks that are readily available. At this

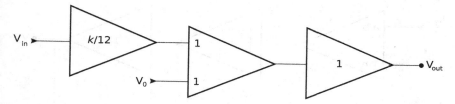

*Figure 12.9* Linear equation program.

*Figure 12.10* Linear function module: Doepfer A183-2 (Doepfer, 2019a).

level of simplicity, the synthesiser can match the analogue computer almost on a one-to-one component basis. An example of a module implementing a similar arrangement, in a pre-packaged form, is shown in Figure 12.10, where a voltage input can be scaled and offset based on a linear equation such as Eq. 12.4.

### 12.3.2 Differential equations

A more common application of analogue computers has to do with the solution of differential equations. Consider the following example,

$$y(t) = ax(t) - b\frac{dy(t)}{dt} \tag{12.5}$$

which is a simple first-order differential equation. This can be translated into an analogue computer program as shown in Figure 12.11. The significance of this is that such a differential equation also implements a simple infinite impulse response low-pass filter. With this approach, could implement filters

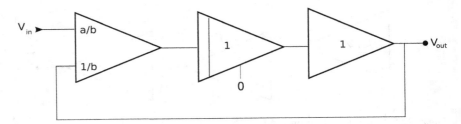

*Figure 12.11* Difference equation program.

of different designs, more complex of course, but using the common blocks of an analogue computer.

Hutchins (Hutchins, 2013) pointed out that the fundamental voltage-controlled building block used here (Figure 12.11), the integrator, is applicable to the well-known state variable filter (SVF) design. He noted that the fact that the SVF is formed from elemental blocks of two integrators and a summer in a loop has been known from analogue computer programs, where it was used in physical simulations of second-order responses by producing voltages corresponding to the magnitudes of the *state variables* of the system.

This first-principles approach is contrasted now with the filter modules implementing different topologies, with various particular characteristics, that are found in voltage-controlled synthesisers. The significant difference is that these are fixed to a given design, and do not allow access or manipulation of its circuit connections. This demonstrates an example where there is no one-to-one match between an analogue computer and a synthesiser.

### 12.3.3   *Analogue computers as musical instruments*

Given the examples discussed above, it might be surprising to see that not a lot has been made in terms of utilising general-purpose analogue computers in musical applications. The composer Hans Kulk appears to be a solitary figure working in this field (Kulk, 2012). This may be attributed to various factors: cost, as in the heyday of analogue computers, it was very expensive to access these; complexity, programming analogue computers required significant technical expertise, which was not mitigated by music-directed approaches, as for instance provided by music programming languages in the case of digital computers.

The existence of the modular synthesiser, in fact, can be seen as the analogue counterpart to the digital computer music programming environments. However, as noted above, they were not developed to provide lower-level access to computation, which, as we showed, is the case in digital computer programming (see, for instance, the Csound (Lazzarini et al., 2016) language as a typical example). Finally, also we should consider that the obsolescence of the general-purpose analogue computer, in parallel with the ubiquitousness of the digital computer, also played a part in the process. However, some new prospects in the analogue computing domain may allow us to reappraise these devices as possible vehicles for music making. The main consideration is that there is no fundamental impediment to this; on the contrary, there seems to be fertile ground for work in this respect.

## 12.4 New technologies for analogue computing

While analogue computers may appear to some to have passed their heyday and be generally obsolete today, that does not seem to be the case if we look at some cutting-edge research in the field. The direction of travel seems to involve the development of very large scale integration (VLSI) components that implement a collection of computing elements. These can then be made available for programming in flexible ways and used as dedicated processors within a larger host system (Cowan et al., 2006). The technology of Field Programmable Analogue Arrays (Lee and Gulak, 1991, 1992, 1995) has also opened some interesting possibilities in the particular case of analogue signal processing.

It is within this context that a number of prospects for musical signal processing may arise. The interest in re-creating analogue environments using digital simulations that sparked virtual analogue model research may have exhausted its potential for further refinements, and work that is actually directed to the *real* thing is an attractive proposition. Music production is one of the few areas of technology where analogue signal generation and processing techniques continue to be used, and in fact, have enjoyed a significant resurgence.

### 12.4.1 *Field-programmable analogue arrays*

Recent developments in analogue signal processing technology included the development of application-specific integrated circuits (ASICs), used in the implementation of synthesiser modules such as filters and oscillators. However, as the name implies, ASICs target specific purposes and re-designing them is very expensive. What would be more suitable is to have an analogue equivalent of the digital field programmable gate array (FPGA). Fortunately, the concept of field programmable analogue arrays (FPAAs) was introduced with the promise that it facilitated analogue components to be connected together in an arbitrary fashion, allowing for rapid testing and measurement of many different circuit designs.

A similar but less sophisticated technology is the PSoC (programmable system-on-chip) by Cypress Semiconductor. These chips include a CPU core and mixed-signal arrays of configurable integrated analogue and digital peripherals. The FPAA was introduced in 1991 by Lee and Gulak (Lee and Gulak, 1991). The idea was further enhanced by the same authors in 1992 (Lee and Gulak, 1992) and 1995 (Lee and Gulak, 1995) where op-amps, capacitors, and resistors could be connected to form a biquad filter, for example. In 1995, a similar idea, the electronically-programmable analogue circuit (EPAC) was presented in (Pierzchala et al., 1995).

Within the FPAA explored in (Nease et al., 2014) it was organised into three functional blocks: (1) the computational analogue block (CAB), which is a physical grouping of analogue circuits that act as computational elements, (2) the switch matrix (SM), which defines the interconnection of CAB components, and (3) the programmer which allows each device to be turned completely on, turned completely off, or operated somewhere in-between. This flexibility means that switch elements can be used for computation as well as routing. This is especially beneficial in audio applications since transistors set to a constant bias are often necessary.

Only in recent years have FPAAs become powerful enough to be considered for facilitating complex analogue sound synthesis, in the implementation of common modules. Two papers investigated whether FPAAs were capable of creating entire synthesis systems. One paper illustrated how the lowpass VCF developed and popularised by Robert Moog (Moog, 1969) could be implemented using an FPAA (Nease et al., 2014). For this implementation it was found that the FPAA could support 12 VCFs, assuming perfect utilisation of all the available resources by the CAB, but it may also be possible to include another 8–10 filters under alternative constraints. A second paper looked at the FPAA configuration for a VCO and VCA, and two common control modules, the low-frequency oscillators and the envelope generator, which would allow for the development of a complete synthesiser (Nease et al., 2018). The paper identified a number of challenges, which included whether the VCO implementation would be controllable over a wide pitch range and remain stable with temperature changes. In general, FPAAs appear to be one of the most promising analogue technologies for sound and music computing.

### 12.4.2   *Programmability revisited*

Programming a modular synthesiser with patch-cords is a significant undertaking, and the traditional analogue computers presented much bigger challenges in that respect. Clearly, if we are to be able to implement signal-processing operations from first principles, the question of programmability takes is a key concern. In modern VLSI-based systems such as the one described in (Cowan et al., 2006) and in the case of FPAAs, some means of setting up connections between components is provided (and storing/retrieving these), which can be at various levels.

We could trace a parallel with digital computers, where the code may be represented by an assembly-type language for a given hardware, or in a high-level language such as C. In an analogue computer, we could manually translate equations (such as for instance eq. 12.5) into the actual hardware connections (e.g. Figure 12.11 ), or potentially use an algebraic compiler to synthesise the necessary circuits (such as the one discussed in (Achour et al., 2016)). We can hypothesise that such a high-level language could be developed targeting the requirements of analogue signal processing for music computing applications.

A very recent development is represented by a new hardware project developed by zrna research, described as a *software-defined analogue* processor (Miller, 2019). It provides an application programming interface (API) for the Python language, which allows the programming of a number of pre-defined modules, including gain scaling, filters, oscillators, fundamental arithmetics and functions (such as integration, multiplication, division, square root, etc), delay lines, and input/output elements. The hardware platform is based on an FPAA and an ARM processor, and as such may be classified as a hybrid system (although it is not clear to what extent analogue and digital processing may be intermixed in applications). The zrna platform as described in its documentation promises to bridge the high and low-level of programming as described in this paper.

### 12.4.3 Hybrid digital-analogue systems

Another emerging characteristic of modern analogue computing appears to be the development of hybrid digital-analogue systems. One such arrangement is described in (Guo et al., 2016), where a combination of digital and analogue circuits are used to construct a programmable device. This type of arrangement is mirrored in modern polyphonic analogue synthesisers, where audio signals are kept in the analogue domain, and control signals originate from digital representations and are transformed into voltage control via a number of digital-to-analogue converters. This allows some level of interconnectivity via so-called modulation matrices that mimic the modular approach, albeit on a smaller scale.

## 12.5 Analogue computing in ubimus

Within the perspective of ubimus, technologies such as the ones discussed here can open up new possibilities for approaches that aim to reproduce early electronic music practices. From the perspective of programmability, which is one of the cornerstones of ubimus practices (Keller et al., 2014), the aim is to provide musicians of all levels, as well as researchers, flexible tools that would allow them to manipulate sound with analogue means. The technology is not prescriptive in terms of what its applications are, and that open-endedness can be translated into components of digital-analogue devices for use in, for instance, the Internet of Musical Things (IoMusT) (Keller and Lazzarini, 2017, Lazzarini et al., 2015, Turchet et al., 2018) applications in professional and everyday-music settings.

### 12.5.1   Access to analogue audio

As we have noted in the introduction, access to analogue audio synthesis and processing has become something highly desirable for many musicians, sound designers and multimedia artists. Means of enabling these have already been a topic of discussion in ubimus research. In Zawacki and Johann (2014), the authors introduced a remote method of accessing analogue instruments for sound recording, which would provide possibilities for composers attempting to employ sounds with these desirable qualities in their own fixed-media electronic works. They describe analogue audio as having irreplaceable characteristics linked to particular musical aesthetics, which are hard to reproduce with strictly digital hardware. They also discuss the fact that cost is a factor in the access to such devices.

It is true that in recent years, we have seen a change in the direction of the wider availability of analogue hardware, which has contributed to lessening the cost constraints for users. However, we should still note that access to analogue audio hardware continues to come with strings attached, in the sense that there is not the same level of flexibility and generality observed in the software approach, through the means of a modern music programming system as described in Lazzarini (2013). As it stands, there is generally a choice between the use of specialised devices or the generality of programming, although as we are advocating in this text, this is probably in the process of changing with projects such as the one developed by Miller (2019).

### 12.5.2   The DIY perspective

It appears to be clear that the route to providing a generally programmable and accessible analogue computing platform passes through the experience of DIY instrument-building. The best candidate for this seems to be a combination of existing and well-know DIY programming platforms discussed in Chapter 3, such as for instance the Arduino (Arduino, 2019) and Raspberry PI (Upton, 2015) boards, combined with some sort of analogue or hybrid hardware. As we noted above, the zrna research analogue device also appears to provide support for the implementation of some of the ideas raised in this text. Alongside its Python API, it has means for easy integration with other DIY hardware.

We can envisage that some of the instruments described by Nikoladze in Chapter 4 would very much benefit from the possibilities provided by analogue hardware. It is interesting to note that some of his Beat Machines were actually employing mechanical means of sound generation. The use of continuous signals of the kinds produced by analogue hardware (VC or audio) could enhance the potential for this electromechanical approach, without the need for the use of digital to analogue conversion. Likewise, measurements of analogue parameters (touch position on a ribbon controller, temperature, light intensity, etc.) could also be used directly in sound synthesis and processing, with no mediation of an analogue-to-digital conversion. The advantages of working completely in the analogue domain are an increased precision, on one hand, and the opportunities for different types of direct control and modulation of sound synthesis and processing.

### 12.5.3   *A ubimus research platform*

Another aim for the implementation of an analogue, or hybrid, computing platform is to enable work on a series of ubimus research questions. These would cover the various areas which are touched by this book. Such a platform would be an interesting environment to cover topics such as

- programming interfaces for analogue audio processing: as we have been emphasising in this text, programmability is an essential aspect of ubimus, both in terms of research, but also in music-making practice. An open question, for example, is whether the MUSIC-N paradigm (Lazzarini, 2013) is well suited to analogue computing. Another important consideration is to what extent a music programming system can be extended to include analogue components, and how transparent this should be. Of course, from the perspective of ubiquitous computing, we would ideally want all computing elements to disappear in the background, as users transit seamlessly between different modes of music-making. However, there is something distinct about the audio quality of analogue devices that seems to be important for some users, therefore their specific presence within a system may need to be highlighted.
- interactive systems: equally, the affordances of a system that includes a full analogue control path raise a wide-ranging set of questions. For instance, the fact that there are no digital-to-analogue or analogue-to-digital conversions in the hardware may or may not be of great significance, depending on the specific ubimus applications. We could also ask if there are innovative user interfaces that can take advantage of analogue computing, and what are the possibilities provided by the different way of thinking induced by this approach.
- musical signal processing: much of the research in musical signal processing has been devoted to digital audio. The art of analogue design has received much less attention in the literature and it appears to be a niche area, with only a few dedicated researchers. This is probably due to the practical difficulties in pursuing new lines of investigation, if compared to the environment of digital audio. As we discussed in this chapter, it is much easier to prototype and implement new ideas in software form than to implement these strictly in an analogue piece of hardware. Furthermore, as the research environment is skewed towards digital solutions, the exchange

of new ideas in analogue audio is much slower. Possibly with the coming onstream of these new forms of analogue computing, we might see more activity in these forms of musical signal processing research.

- composition and performance: all of the research topics discussed above line up and inter-thread with a surge in new possibilities for composition and performance. Again here we find a number of open questions related to these new means of sound making and of interaction. We can also consider whether they might provide a creative look at the technologies of the past, since electronic music of course has a rich background that is founded on analogue audio.
- everyday creativity and educational applications: the DIY dimension that is linked to analogue computing has a significant potential for these areas of ubimus. It brings together ideas from the maker movement and the creative applications of computing that can be applied in the study of everyday musical creativity (Chapter 2), on one hand, and in the development of educational approaches to teach the several subjects touched by ubimus (from art to science, see Chapter 7 for some possible application contexts). For example, the computational thinking ideas and the mathematics-music relationships discussed in Chapter 8 can be implemented through the use of analogue computing, within the context of a creative maker lab.

In general, we can say that analogue computing is yet another component of the ecologies of ubimus. The examples of its research applications discussed here, although comprehensive, are not exhaustive.

## 12.6　Conclusions

In this chapter, we have demonstrated the usefulness of an analogue computing approach to electronic and computer music research. It provided a general introduction to the area, alongside tracing a parallel to modular voltage-controlled synthesisers. Examples were given that had direct relevance to analogue audio signal processing, demonstrating some immediate applications in research and music production.

A survey of the state-of-the-art in analogue computing provided us with some first candidates as technologies that might be ready for use. In fact, in one case some interesting results had already been presented. Challenges remain, however, given that the target outputs of analogue computing for music applications have some key constraints of quality, including low signal-to-noise ratios and pitch/voltage stability. Assessing this should play an important part in any future research.

Another aspect which we have emphasised was to do with programmability. We see that key developments in the area are necessarily linked to the potential of music programming systems. Having analogue computing-dedicated music tools, similar to what exists for standard digital computers, will play an important part in making the technology available to a wider range of users (musicians, artists). This possibly points out to another fertile field of computer music research.

## Note

1 This (correct) terminology has by now fallen in disuse, due to the ubiquitous nature of digital computing.

This chapter is a revised and expanded version of Lazzarini and Timoney (2019).

## Bibliography

Achour, S., R. Sarpeshkar, and M. Rinard (2016). Configuration synthesis for programmable analog devices with Arco. In *Proceedings of PLDI 16*, Santa Barbara, CA, pp. 177–193.

Arduino (2019). Arduino - home. http://www.arduino.cc/.

Cowan, G., R. Melville, and Y. Tsividis (2006). A VLSI analog computer / digital computer accelerator. *Journal of Solid-State Circuits 41*(1), 42–53.

Doepfer, D. (2019a). A-183-2 offset-generator/attenuator/polarizer. http://www. doepfer.de/a1832.htm.

Doepfer, D. (2019b). A110 standard oscillator manual. http://www.doepfer.de/a100_ man/a110_man.pdf.

Doepfer, D. (2019c). A120 lowpass filter manual. http://www.doepfer.de/a100_man/ a120_man.pdf.

Doepfer, D. (2019d). A130 linear vca manual. http://www.doepfer.de/a100_man/a130_ man.pdf.

Guo, N., Y. Huang, T. Mai, S. Patil, C. Cao, M. Seok, S. Sethumadhavan, and Y. Tsividis (2016). Energy-efficient hybrid analog/digital approximate computation in continuous time. *Journal of Solid-State Circuits 51*(7), 1514–1524.

Hutchins, B. (2013). Revisiting some vcf ideas – and a few new ideas. *Electronotes 23*(215), 1–23.

Keller, D. and V. Lazzarini (2017). Ecologically grounded creative practices in ubiquitous music. *Organised Sound 22*(1), 61–72.

Keller, D., V. Lazzarini, and M. Pimenta (2014). *Ubiquitous Music*. Berlin: Springer.

Kulk, H. (2012). Proposal for extending analog modular electronic music synthesizers with function modules from the analog computation repertoire. In *Symposium Think Analogue! Humboldt University*, Berlin.

Lazzarini, V. (2013). The development of computer music programming systems. *Journal of New Music Research 42*, 97–110.

Lazzarini, V., J. ffitch, S. Yi, J. Heintz, Ø. Brandtsegg, and I. McCurdy (2016). *Csound: A Sound and Music Computing System*. Berlin: Springer Verlag.

Lazzarini, V. and J. Timoney (2019). The analogue computer as a voltage-controlled synthesiser. In *Proceedings of 14th International Symposium on CMMR*, Marseille, pp. 663–674.

Lazzarini, V., J. Timoney, and S. Byrne (2015). Embedded sound synthesis. In *Proceedings of the Linux Audio Conference 2015*, Johannes Gutenberg University, Mainz, Germany, pp. to appear.

Lee, E. K. F. and P. G. Gulak (1991). A cmos field-programmable analog array. *IEEE Journal of Solid-State Circuits 26*(12), 1860–1867.

Lee, E. K. F. and P. G. Gulak (1992). Field programmable analogue array based on mosfet transconductors. *Electronics Letters 28*(1), 28–29.

Lee, E. K. F. and P. G. Gulak (1995). A transconductor-based field-programmable analog array. In *Proceedings ISSCC '95 - International Solid-State Circuits Conference*, pp. 198–199. San Francisco, CA.

Mathews, M. (1963). The digital computer as a musical instrument. *Science 183*(3592), 553–557.

Miller, N. (2019). Zrna research. https://zrna.org/.

Moog, R. (1967). Voltage controlled electronic music modules. *AES Preprint 346*, 1–19.

Moog, R. (1969). Electronic high-pass and low-pass filters employing the base to emitter diode resistance of bipolar transistors. US Patent 3475623A.

Navarro, S. (1962). *Analog Computer Fundamentals*. Belmont, CA: Wadsworth Publ. Co.

Nease, S. H., A. D. Lanterman, and J. O. Hasler (2014). A transistor ladder voltage-controlled filter implemented on a field programmable analog array. *Journal of Audio Engineering Society 62*(9), 611–618.

Nease, S. H., A. D. Lanterman, and J. O. Hasler (2018). Applications of current-starved inverters to music synthesis on field programmable analog arrays. *Journal of Audio Engineering Society 66*(1/2), 71–79.

Pakarinen, J., V. Valimaki, F. Fontana, V. Lazzarini, and J. Abel (2011). Recent advances in real-time musical effects, synthesis, and virtual analog models. *Eurasip Journal on Advances in Signal Processing 2011:940784*, 1–15.

Pierzchala, E., M. A. Perkowski, P. Van Halen, and R. Schaumann (1995). Current-mode amplifier/integrator for a field-programmable analog array. In *Proceedings ISSCC '95 - International Solid-State Circuits Conference*, pp. 196–197. San Francisco, CA.

Ragazzini, J., R. Randall, and F. Russell (1948). Analysis of problems in dynamics by electronic circuits. *Proceedings of the IRE 35*, 444–452.

Sangster, F. and K. Teer (1969). Bucket-brigade electronics - new possibilities for delay, time-axis conversion, and scanning. *IEEE Journal of Solid State Circuits 4*(3), 131–136.

Turchet, L., C. Fischione, G. Essl, D. D. Keller, and M. Barthet. (2018). Internet of musical things: Vision and challenges. *IEEE Access 6*, 61994–62017.

Ulmann, B. (2013). *Analog Computing*. Munich: Oldenbourg.

Upton, E. (2015). Raspberry pi. http://www.raspberrypi.org.

Wells, T. (1981). *The Technique of Electronic Music*. New York, NY: Schirmer Books.

Zawacki, L. and M. Johann (2014). Analogue audio recording using remote servers. In D. Keller, V. Lazzarini, and M. Pimenta (Eds.), *Ubiquitous Music*, pp. 83–107. Berlin: Springer.

# Index

Ableton Live, 74
acousmatic music, 28, 96, 99, 148
acoustic ecology, 96
adaptive, 196
    definition of, 190
    effects, 190, 191
algorithm, 215
analogue audio, 230
analogue computing, 12, 135, 144, 215
    arithmetics, 216
    components, 216
    definition of, 214
    functions, 218
    general-purpose computer, 224
    hybrid system, 229
    integrators, 218
    modular synthesiser, 219
    modules, 219
    new technologies, 227
    programming, 224–226
analogue device, 59
analysis, 194
    envelope crest, 194
    rms amplitude, 194
    transient detection, 194
Anderson, L., 190
Arduino, 60–62, 74, 119, 230
ASIC, 56, 227
Atmel, 61
attractors, 209
Audacity, 100
auto wah, 190

auto-reflection, 111
automagic, 99

balance, 206
Baroque, 137
Barron, Louis and Bebe, 54
basic education, 13, 109, 112, 114, 124
BASIC Stamp, 60
BeagleBone Black, 62
beats, 141
Bela, 64
Beuys. J., 40
biosensing, 6, 9
Bitraf, 6, 72, 73, 76, 78, 79
Black Sabbath, 190
Boulez, P., 9
browser, 11, 42
Browser Platform, 170

Cabbage, 194
Cage, J., 54
canon, 142
cantus firmus, 139
CAp-UFRGS, 109, 112
Carlos, W., 190
centroid, 199
cepstrum, 194, 200
channel vocoder, 53, 190, 207
chord, 133
CODES, 118
cognitive-ecological approach, 109, 125
collaborative technologies, 111

collective knowledge construction, 110
Columbia-Princeton EMC, 54
compressor, 191
computability, 131
computational thinking, 14, 129
    and music, 135
    definitions, 130
    support tools, 146
condition, 132
convolution, 142, 208
counterpoint, 139
    algorithm, 139
    example, 140
CPU, 59, 63
Creating Music (software), 101, 102
creativity, 7, 110, 124, 125
    activities, 109, 125
    cognitive-ecological practices, 110, 111
    everyday musical, 23, 115, 124
    frameworks, 150
    general and artistic, 29
    musical, 103, 109, 110
    studies, 27
    teleological approach, 111
    types, 103
critical thinking, 129
crossadaptive
    definition of, 190
    effects, 191, 192, 203–208
    plugins, 193
Csound, 63, 64, 131, 133, 181, 194, 227
Csound Web-IDE, 183
csound-live-code, 182
cymbal, 74

danceability, 198
database, 83, 84, 89, 90
DAW, 41, 42, 64, 74, 192, 193
dehumanisation, 98
delay effect, 204
delays, 142
derivative, 144
detrended fluctuation, 198

dialogical approach, 36–38, 43, 45, 109–111, 124, 125
differentiation, 144
digital device, 59
DIY, 5, 11, 52, 95, 214, 230, 232
documentation, 81–84, 87–89, 91
Doppler, 144
drum kit, 73, 74
DSP, 57
DSP (software), 101, 102, 104
dynamic score, 77

e-textiles, 160
eco-composition, 109, 110, 115, 124
ecological approach, 110–112
ecology, 4
ecosystem, 5, 124
EDM, 58, 203
educational context, 121
EEPROM, 60
Elbphilharmonie, 78
electroacoustic music, 96
electromagnet, 74
electronium, 54
Elektronische Musik, 54
ELK, 64
EMS, 106
epistemic activities, 111
ethnomusicology, 112
event sequencing, 149
everyday musical creativity, 110, 115, 124
    technology, 122, 124

FAUST, 183
Ferneyhough, B., 141, 142
FIAC, 119
filter, 205, 218, 220, 225
FLOSS, 52, 56
Fluxus, 40
FPAA, 227, 228
FPGA, 227
Frampton, P., 190
frequency modulation, 57, 144
frequency shift, 206

function, 134
  μ-recursive, 131, 134
  computable, 131
  goto, 131, 133
Futurism, 53
Fux, J. J., 139

g-ubimus, xv, 4, 109, 111, 118, 125
gamification, 101
Garageband, 100, 102, 104
Garbarek, A., 105
Gaynor, G., 137
Gertduino, 62
Gibber, 180
globalisation, 104
Google, 98
Gradus ad Parnassum, 139
granular processing, 205

habituation, 209
Hadron particle synthesiser, 193
Hafler, D., 54
Hendrix, J., 55
hi-hat, 74

IC, 56–58
ICT, 14
IFRS, 118
IFTTT, 131, 132
impulse response, 143, 208
Incredibox, 100, 102
inhibitors, 209
installation, 89–91
Intel edison, 63
Intel Galileo, 62, 63
interaction, 80, 83, 85
  design, 8, 112
interdisciplinarity, 113
intuition, 203
IoMusT, 11, 64, 66, 112, 149, 154,
  161, 164, 230
IoT, 95, 160
IRDA, 62

k'ni, 79
Kinect, 90

knowledge
  acquisition, 111
  heterogeneity, 25, 33, 37, 38, 43,
    45
  transfer, 26, 27, 40, 145
Kolberg, K., 98

LCM, 118
Lego, 142
linear, 136
Linux, 56, 61, 64
little-c music, 4, 7, 9, 10, 15, 16, 23, 27,
  30, 38, 44, 46, 110
  activities, 25, 26
  knowledge heterogeneity, 38
  semantics, 40
  stakeholders, 37
live convolution, 208
logarithmic, 136
loop, 132
luthiery, 8

Maciunas, G., 40
Maker Faire, 58
maker movement, 6, 57, 58, 65, 72
mapping, 210
Max, 77, 97
mel scale, 194, 200
metadata, 83
metalanguage, 135
metaphor, 135
microcontroller, 52, 53, 57–61, 66, 67,
  74, 77
MIDI, 55, 57, 60, 131, 136
MidiBox, 57, 60
MIR, 197, 198
mixDroid, 119
mobile devices, 157–159
modular synthesiser, 215, 219
  modules, 222
  programming, 223
  VCA, 221
  VCF, 220
  VCO, 220
Moog, R., 55

multi-sensory, 163
   data, 90, 91
   display, 88
   information, 89
   installations, 88–90
   performance, 80
multimedia, 80–83, 88, 89, 91
Music for Magnetic Tape, 54
MUSIC N, 97, 231
musical haptic wearables,
   159, 160
musical interval, 136
musical knowledge, 114, 120, 122
   formal, 121
musical things, 154, 157, 163
Musique Concrète, 54

NAP, 119
natural interaction, 149
Nordheim, A., 98
normalisation, 201
NOTAM, 96, 97, 100

Ondes Martenot, 53
organised sounds, 96
OSC, 57, 195

PC, 55
PCB, 56, 58
performance, 80, 82, 83, 85, 87–91
performer, 80, 90
physical computing, 59
physiological computing, 88
PIC, 60
PICAXE, 60
PISA test, 99
pitch
   12-tone equal temperament, 136,
      138
   as a parameter of music, 152
   definition, 135
   interval, 136
   manipulation, 136
   shift, 206
preservation, 81–88, 91

problem solving, 111
process control, 149
Progressive Web Applications, 174
Prophet 5, 55
Prydz, E., 191
PWM, 61
Pythagorean scale, 137
Python, 229

query, 89, 90
   by content, 89, 90

radio, 97
RAM, 59
Raspberry PI, 61, 62, 230
Reaper, 193
recursion, 133, 137, 142
rehumanisation, 98
reverberation, 203
rhythm, 74, 201
   ametric, 141
   metric, 141
ring modulation, 190
ROM, 59
round, 142

scene design, 8, 209
Schaeffer, P., 8
school context, 99, 109, 115
Scott, R., 54
semantic web, 97
Sensus Smart Guitar, 155
sequencer, 54, 73
Sibelius Academy, 97
sidechain, 191, 196
Smart Cajón, 156
smart instruments, 155
Smart Mandolin, 156
SoC, 61–63, 66, 227
social connectivism, 103
social networks, 112
sound mixing, 149
Soundation, 100
soundscape, 115
SoundSphere, 119

spectral analysis
    centroid, 194
    crest, 194
    flatness, 194
    flux, 194, 199
    kurtosis, 194, 199
    skewness, 194, 199
    spread, 194, 199
spectral effects, 205
Stockhausen, K., 136, 190
Stravinsky, I., 142
students
    basic education, 110
    high school, 109, 119
SVF, 226

Tactile Internet, 160, 162, 164
talk box, 190
TB-303, 58
Theremin, 53
time tagging, 9, 38
Tone.js, 180
tonnetz, 137
torus, 138
TR-808, 75
transdisciplinarity, 113
Trautonium, 53
triad, 133
Truax, B., 96
Turing machine, 131

UART, 63
ubicomp, 1, 2
ubimus, 52, 53, 59, 64, 66, 67, 74, 78, 95, 104, 105, 109, 154, 162–164, 211, 214, 215, 224, 229–232
    acceptances, 3
    and IoMusT, 25, 66, 132, 154, 155, 162, 164
    computational thinking, 146, 147
    definition of, 1, 2, 94, 104
    design patterns, 149
    ecological approach, 110, 112
    ecologies, 5–7, 24, 64, 66, 124, 145, 154, 215, 232

everyday settings, 15, 16, 23, 109–111, 114, 115, 122–125
high-end and professional, 8–10, 163
in basic education, 110, 119, 123, 124
in educational contexts, 13–15, 99, 105, 109, 111, 115
interdisciplinary and transdisciplinary approach, 113
little-c, 4, 7, 9, 10, 15, 16, 23, 104
platforms, 63
technologies, 11–13
temporality, 31
Ubimus Workshop, 118
Ubiquitous Music Workshops, xv
UDO, 133
UFAC, 119
UFRGS, 109, 114
Ultima festival, 76
unit generator, 224

Vaggione, H., 148
VCA, 228
VCF, 220, 228
VCO, 220, 221, 228
virtual reality, 80, 91
VLSI, 227, 228

Walsh, J., 190
wearable devices, 159
Web Audio, 175
Web Technologies, 172
WebAssembly, 177
Wiggen, K., 98
Winderen, J., 99
Wiring, 61, 62
Wonder, S., 191
WSN, 160

Xenomai, 64
xObOx, 58

Young, L. M., 40

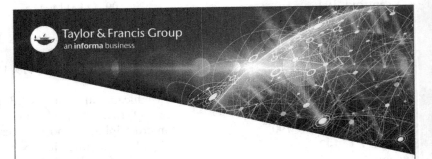

Printed in the United States
By Bookmasters